The French Revolution Sourcebook

The French Revolution Sourcebook

Edited by
John Hardman

A member of the Hodder Headline Group
LONDON

First published in Great Britain in 1981 as *The French Revolution: The Fall of the* Ancien Régime *to the Thermidorian Reaction 1785–1795*
Published as *The French Revolution Sourcebook*
(with revisions and additional material) in 1999
This impression reprinted in 2002 by
Arnold, a member of the Hodder Headline Group,
338 Euston Road, London NW1 3BH

http://www.arnoldpublishers.com

Co-published in the United States of America by
Oxford University Press Inc.,
198 Madison Avenue, New York, NY 10016

British Library Cataloguing in Publication Data
A catalogue record for this book is available from the British Library

Library of Congress Cataloging-in-Publication Data
The French Revolution Sourcebook / edited by John Hardman.
p. cm.
Includes bibliographical references and index.
ISBN 0-340-71982-6 (hardcover). – ISBN 0-340-71983-4 (pbk.)
1. France–Politics and government–1774–1793–Sources.
2. France–Politics and government–1789–1799–Sources.
I. Hardman. John.
DC136.A2F72 1998
944.04–dc21   98-27135
CIP

Production Editor: Julie Delf
Production Controller: Sarah Kett
Cover Design: Andy McColm

ISBN 0 340 71982 6 (hb)
ISBN 0 340 71983 4 (pb)

Typeset by Photoprint, Torquay, Devon

Contents

Preface   xv

Introduction   1

I The Fall of the *Ancien Régime*

1 Doubts   7

  1 *Chancellor Maupeou embraces discourse theory*   10

  2 *Hopes and fears at the end of d'Ormesson's ministry*   10

  3 *Turgot on provincial assemblies: extract from the diary of the abbé de Véri*   12

  4 *The changing social and political composition of the ministry*   13

  5 *Vergennes to Noailles, French ambassador to England, 15 November 1776*   15

  6 *Pessimism: Montmorin to Vergennes, 30 October 1780*   15

  7 *War scare: memoranda read by La Luzerne, secretary of state for the marine, to the* conseil d'état   16

2 The breakdown of relations between crown and Parlement   18

  8 *Calonne's loan of 1785 and the Parlement*   19

  9 *Article on Calonne in Lefevre d'Amécourt's unpublished* Ministres de Louis XVI   20

  10 *Calonne tries to break d'Aligre: extract from a letter from Miromesnil to the king, 5 August 1786*   21

  11 *Miromesnil to the king, 8 December 1786*   22

3 The Assembly of Notables   25

   12 *A survey of the programme of reforms: Calonne's speech
      at the opening of the Assembly of Notables, 22 February
      1787*   28

   13 *Memorandum on the establishment of provincial
      assemblies, presented to the Notables on 23 February
      1787*   30

   14 *Memorandum on the land tax*   31

   15 *Mirabeau to Calonne, Paris, 13 June 1786*   32

   16 *Memorandum from Calonne to the king, late August
      1786, entitled 'Observations on the difference between
      Estates-General and Assemblies of Notables'*   33

   17 *Memorandum from Calonne to the king, November
      1786, entitled 'Objections and replies'*   33

   18 *Memorandum from Calonne to the king, December 1786,
      entitled 'Ideas submitted for the king's decision
      concerning the necessity, timetable, composition and form
      of the Assembly of Notables'*   35

   19 *Miromesnil to the king, 28 December 1786*   36

   20 *Miromesnil to the king, 1 February 1787*   38

   21 *Calonne to the king, undated but c. 26 February 1787* 38

   22 *Extracts from the debates of the second committee of the
      Assembly of Notables, that chaired by the king's second
      brother, the comte d'Artois*   39

   23 *Conversation between the king and Castries, February
      1787*   40

   24 *The* Avertissement   40

   25 *Exchange between Castries and the king, 2 April 1787* 41

   26 *Miromesnil to the king, 4 April 1787*   42

   27 *Miromesnil to the king, 5 April 1787 and Miromesnil's
      dismissal*   43

   28 *Memorandum of Loménie de Brienne, 17 April, together
      with the marginal annotations of Louis XVI*   44

   29 *Further thoughts of Louis XVI: extract from Brienne's
      diary, 21 April*   46

   30 *Entry in Castries' diary for 20 May 1787*   47

   31 *From the section on provincial assemblies in Brienne's
      speech during the last session of the Assembly of
      Notables, 25 May 1787*   47

32 Brienne to Calonne, Versailles, 17 June 1787   48

33 Calonne to d'Angiviller, director-general of the king's
    buildings, late July 1787   48

4 The edicts of 8 May 1788   50

34 Brienne made principal minister: circular letter sent by the
    king to all the ministers on 27 August 1787   53

35 The séance royale of 19 November: Marie-Antoinette to
    her brother Joseph II of Austria, 23 November 1787   53

36 Louis XVI's reply of 17 April 1788 to the Parlement's
    remonstrances of 11 April against the séance royale   54

37 Marie-Antoinette to Joseph II, 24 April 1788   54

38 The Parlement's view of the Fundamental Laws or
    constitution of France: resolution proposed by Duval
    d'Eprémesnil, 3 May 1788   55

39 Biron, colonel of the French guards, to Breteuil, 5 May
    1788   56

40 Breteuil to d'Agoult, captain in the guards, 6 May   56

41 Breteuil to the king, Paris, 6 May, 7.45 a.m.   57

42 Breteuil to d'Agoult, 6 May, 9.30 a.m.   57

43 D'Agoult's report of the arrest of d'Eprémesnil, Paris, 6
    May, 10.30 a.m.   57

44 Breteuil to the king, 6 May, 11.00 a.m.   58

45 Crosne to Breteuil, 7 May   58

46 Crosne to Breteuil, 7 May   58

47 The May Edicts   59

48 Breteuil to de Crosne, 9 and 10 May 1788   60

49 Biron to Breteuil, 26 May 1788   61

50 Judicial reactions to the coup d'état of 8 May   61

51 Marie-Antoinette to Joseph II, 16 July 1788   62

52 The Pope to Louis XVI, 9 September 1788   62

5 Preparations for the Estates   64

53 Lamoignon to Breteuil, 6 July 1788   66

54 Extract from the memoirs of Loménie de Brienne   66

55 Royal declaration registered by the Parlement on 25
    September 1788   67

56 Resolution of the Parlement concerning the preceding
    declaration   68

57 Mirabeau to Montmorin, the foreign secretary, 28
    December 1788   68

58 The memorandum of the princes of the blood   69

59 Barentin's account of the ministerial discussions leading to
    the résultat du conseil   72

60 The résultat du conseil, 27 December 1788   73

6 The cahiers de doléances *and the elections*   75

61 A combined cahier *of the three orders of the* baillage *of*
    Fenestrange   76

62 General cahier *of the three orders convoked at Vesoul*
    (Franche Comté)   78

63 The cahier *of the clergy of Saintes*   79

64 The cahier *of the nobility of Bouzonville*   79

65 The cahier *of the Third Estate of Paris* intra muros   80

66 The cahier *of the Third Estate of Nemours*   81

67 The cahier *of the parish of Vitry-sur-Seine*   82

68 The cahier *of Les Arcs, Provence*   83

69 The cahier *of the inhabitants of Montauroux and Les*
    Adrets   83

70 Extracts from two of Robespierre's election pamphlets   83

71 Robespierre casts a damper: The duc de Guines, governor
    of Artois, to Laurent de Villedeuil, minister for the
    interior, 20 April 1789   84

II THE CONSTITUTIONAL MONARCHY

1 From Estates-General to National Assembly, May–July 1789   87

72 The king to the duc de Liancourt, undated (but 15 March
    1789)   91

73 Louis XVI to Necker, c. 1 May 1789   91

74 A missed opportunity: contact between Bertrand de
    Molleville and the Breton deputies   92

75 The king of the Third Estate: extract from the memoirs of
    the comtesse d'Adhémar   93

76 Robespierre to Buissart, 24 May 1789   94

77 Barentin, keeper of the seals, to the king, 12 June 1789   95

78 Barentin to the king, 17 June   95

79 Barentin to the king, 19 June   96

80 Necker to Louis XVI, 20 June 1789   96

81 The chevalier de Coigny to the bishop of Soissons, 20
    June 1789   97
82 Saint-Priest, minister without portfolio, to the king,
    undated (but 22 June 1789)   98
83 Barentin to the king, 22 June 1789   100
84 The séance royale of 23 June   101
85 Barentin to the king, 24 June 1789   104
86 Barentin to the king, 25 June 1789   104
87 Necker on the troop movements   104
88 The duc de Broglie to the baron de Besenval, lieutenant-
    colonel of the Swiss Guards, Versailles, 1 July 1789,
    12.30 p.m.   105
89 Broglie to Besenval, 5 July 1789   105
90 Fears for the safety of the Bastille: Broglie to Besenval, 5
    July, 3.30 p.m.   106
91 Barentin to the king, 8 July 1789   106
92 Broglie to Besenval, 11 July 1789   107
93 Saint-Priest on the collapse of royal authority in Paris
    after 14 July   107
94 Robespierre to Buissart, 23 July 1789   108

2 The legislative work of the National Assembly, 1789–1791 109
    95 The August Decrees   111
    96 Two extracts from Mirabeau's notes for the court   112
    97 The law of 19 June abolishing nobility   113
    98 The end of the parlements   113
    99 The civil constitution of the clergy, 12 July 1791 115
    100 The Loi Le Chapelier, 14 June 1791   116
    101 The Declaration of the Rights of Man   117
    102 Robespierre to Buissart, undated (dated by the recipient 9
        November 1789)   120
    103 The rights of the 'princes possessionés'   121

3 The response of Louis XVI to the Revolution   122
    104 Louis XVI to Charles IV of Spain, 12 October 1789 125
    105 The king to the baron de Breteuil, 20 November 1790 126
    106 Louis XVI's objectives in the 'flight to Varennes': the
        account of the duc de Choiseul   126
    107 Marie-Antoinette to Mercy-Argenteau, 3 February 1791 127

108 The king's declaration on leaving Paris, 20 June 1791   128

109 Mme. Roland's account of the massacre of the Champ de
     Mars (from a letter to Bancal des Issarts of 18 July 1791)   136

110 From Louis XVI's secret memorandum to his brothers
     concerning his acceptance of the constitution, 25
     September 1791   137

111 Conversation between Louis XVI and Bertrand de
     Molleville concerning the constitution at the time of the
     latter's appointment as minister for the marine, October
     1791   139

112 Louis XVI to Breteuil, 14 December 1791   140

113 War-mongering: from two speeches by Brissot to the
     Legislative Assembly   141

114 Declaration of war on Austria, 20 April 1791   141

115 Marie-Antoinette to Mercy, 26 March 1792   142

116 Marie-Antoinette to Fersen, 5 June 1792   142

117 Marie-Antoinette to Fersen, 11 July 1792   143

118 The Girondins and the king: memorandum dictated by
     Gensonné to the court painter Boze and transmitted to
     the king by his valet de chambre, Thierry   143

119 Further contacts between the Girondins and the court:
     extract from the memoirs of Dejoly, the last keeper of the
     seals of the monarchy   145

120 The king abandons the Tuileries on 10 August: Dejoly's
     account   146

121 An idealized view of the journée of 10 August:
     Robespierre's account in Le Defenseur du peuple   147

III The National Convention

1 Girondins and Montagnards   151

122 Vergniaud's notes for his defence before the Revolutionary
     Tribunal   155

123 Brissot to Mme. Roland (sometime after 10 August 1792)   156

124 Mme. Roland to Bancal des Issarts, 2 September 1792   156

125 Mme. Roland to Bancal, 5 September 1792   157

126 Robespierre's notes for the accusation of Danton, 1794   158

127 Robespierre on faction: from a speech in the Convention,
     28 December 1792   158

128 Garat on Robespierre's view of parties   158

129 *Rousseau on faction: from the chapter 'Whether the general will can err' in* Du contrat social 159

130 *Louvet on the Girondins* 159

131 *Robespierre's first speech to the Convention on the king's trial, 3 December 1792* 160

132 *Robespierre on the food riots of 24 and 25 February 1793: speech in the Jacobins, 25 February* 161

133 *Speech of Robespierre to the Jacobins on 8 May 1793* 161

134 *A stormy debate in the Convention, 25 May 1793* 162

135 *The mechanics of insurrection: a note of the Evêché Committee, 2 June 1793* 162

136 *Undated memorandum of Robespierre, June 1793* 163

137 *General Biron to Cambon on the state of Bordeaux, 31 May* 163

138 *Extracts from Pétion's account of the Federalist rising in Normandy* 164

139 *Robespierre rejects compromise* 167

140 *The punishment of Lyon: Achard,* agent national *of Lyon to Gravier, juror in the Revolutionary Tribunal in Paris, 17 frimaire year II (7 December 1793)* 167

141 *Administering the Terror: Collot d'Herbois to Robespierre, Ville-Affranchie (Lyon), 3 frimaire year II (23 November 1793)* 168

142 *Thibaudeau on the extinction of parliamentary life after the fall of the Girondins* 169

2 The constitution of 1793 and its Enragé critics 172

143 *The constitution of 1793* 173

144 *Hérault de Séchelles and Barère discuss the constitution after dinner, autumn 1793* 177

145 *Speech of Jacques Roux to the Gravilliers section, 19 September 1792* 177

146 *Session of the Cordelier Club, 22 June 1793* 178

147 *The 'manifesto' of the Enragés. Jacques Roux before the Convention, 25 June 1793* 179

148 *Session of the Jacobin Club, 5 August 1793* 182

3 Gouvernement révolutionnaire: *politics, Terror and bureaucracy* 183

149 *From a report by Robert Lindet concerning the* comités de surveillance, *20 September 1794* 184

150 Decree establishing the Committee of Public Safety, 6
     April 1793   185

151 The declaration of gouvernement révolutionnaire
     preceded by extracts from Saint-Just's speech, 19
     vendémiaire year II (10 October 1793)   186

152 The law of 14 frimaire   187

153 Javogues, representative-on-mission in Saône-et-Loire to
     Collot d'Herbois, 16 pluviôse year II (4 February 1794)   189

154 Bo, representative-on-mission in Cantal and Lot, to the
     Committee of Public Safety, 24 pluviôse year II (12
     February 1794)   190

155 The Committee of Public Safety to Roux-Fazillac,
     representative-on-mission in Corrèze and Puy-de-Dôme,
     26 pluviôse year II (14 February 1794)   190

156 Questionnaire sent by the Committee of Public Safety to
     the district authorities, together with the replies of the
     district of Le Mans, January 1794   191

157 The law of suspects, 17 September 1793   194

158 The abbé Morellet applies for a certificat de civisme   195

159 Decree on the maximum général, 29 September 1793   196

160 Two private reflections   198

4 The Hébertists and the Dantonists   199

161 Garat on Danton's plans   201

162 Early tension between the ultras and the citras, from a
     session of the Jacobin Club of 5 August 1793   203

163 Extracts from no. 3 of Camille Desmoulins' Le Vieux
     Cordelier, 15 December 1793   204

164 Extracts from an open letter by Philippeaux on the war
     in the Vendée, 6 nivôse year II (26 December 1793)   206

165 Camille Desmoulins on the Committee of Public Safety
     (from no. 7 of Le Vieux Cordelier, published
     posthumously)   207

166 Police report, 18 nivôse year II (7 January 1794)   208

167 Police report on the session of the Cordelier Club of 26
     ventôse year II (16 March 1794)   210

168 Bouchotte, minister of war, to Robespierre, 4 frimaire
     year II (24 November 1794)   212

5 Robespierre's red summer   213

169 Fragment from Saint-Just's notebook   218

170 *Two sections from Saint-Just's* Fragments sur les
institutions républicaines, *summer 1794*   219

171 *Saint-Just's economics: from his* Fragments sur les
institutions républicaines   219

172 *The ventôse decrees, 3 March 1794*   221

173 *The law of 27 germinal,* sur la police générale   221

174 *Decree of the Committee of Public Safety, 2 floréal (21
April 1794)*   223

175 *Extracts from the memoirs of Barère*   223

176 *Robespierre's lists*   224

177 *Robespierrist appointments: the replacement of the
president of the tribunal and the* agent national *of Saint-
Briez (Moselle): evidence given by one of Herman's
officials during Herman's trial in 1795*   225

178 *Robespierre's values: extract from a speech of 5 February
1794*   225

179 *The mindset of the Robespierrist official: Herman's
circular to the employees of the* commission civil   226

180 *Decree on the Supreme Being, 18 floréal year II (7 May
1794)*   226

181 *Robespierre's directives at the* bureau de police   227

182 *Letter of the Committee of Public Safety to their
colleague Saint-Just, on mission to the Army of the North,
6 prairial year II (25 May 1794)*   228

183 *Payan to Roman-Fonrosa, judge in the Orange
Commission, 20 messidor year II (8 July 1794)*   229

184 *The law of 22 prairial (10 June 1794)*   229

185 *From Robespierre's speech in the debate on the law of 22
prairial*   230

186 *From the debate in the Convention on the law of 22
prairial, 24 prairial (12 June)*   231

187 *The prison 'conspiracies'*   232

188 *Payan to Robespierre, 9 messidor year II (27 June 1794)* 232

189 *The Robespierrists plan to indict Fouché: Achard to
Gravier, 10 thermidor (28 July)*   232

190 *Fouché's counter-conspiracy: two letters written just
before 9 thermidor*   233

191 *Police report on Tallien, Bourdon de l'Oise and Thuriot,
19 messidor year II (7 July 1794)*   233

192 The wooing of the right: report dictated by the
     Commune's police officer Faro to Payan, 5 thermidor
     (23 July)   234

193 Rehearsals for the Barra and Viala festival: Fleuriot-
     Lescot, mayor of Paris, to the clerk to the Commune,
     8 thermidor year II (26 July 1794)   235

194 The conclusion to Robespierre's speech to the
     Convention, 8 thermidor year II (26 July 1794)   235

195 The response of functionaries from the Quinze-Vingts
     section in the faubourg Saint-Antoine, to the Commune's
     appeal for help on 9 thermidor   236

196 At the Commune: the testimony of H. G. Dulac,
     employee of the Committee of Public Safety   236

197 From the chapter 'Of voting' in Rousseau's Du contrat
     social   236

198 An account of the fall of Robespierre by the
     conventionnel Dyzez, 11 thermidor year II (29 July 1794)   237

6 The Thermidorian reaction   239

199 Repeal of the law of 27 germinal, 18 frimaire year III (8
     December 1794)   240

200 The abolition of the word révolutionnaire, decree of 24
     prairial year III (12 June 1795)   241

201 Thermidorian politics: extract from the memoirs of
     Levasseur   241

202 The drafting of the constitution of the year III, from the
     memoirs of Thibaudeau, a member of the constitutional
     commission des onze   245

203 Larévellière-Lépaux on the constitution of the year III   248

204 Larévellière-Lépaux's account of the last weeks of the
     Committee of Public Safety   249

Further reading   254

Index   256

Preface

Almost 20 years have elapsed since the publication of *The French Revolution*, a precursor of this book. These years have seen a greatly increased interest in the political history both of the late *ancien régime* and of the Revolution, the main though not the only focus of that book. However, the brand of political history which has found most favour, discourse theory, is not the kind practised by conventional historians of politics. Discourse theorists, like conventional political historians, reject the explanatory primacy of economics but, unlike them, they are not really interested in main-stream politicians. Rather than examine the documents of the key political players for their content, they parse, as a literary text, the productions of lesser or non-players (often pamphleteers) for their style or their rhetoric. Their aim is to discover their assumptions and the relationship between the writer or often the disembodied text and the public they address, reflect and seek to form.

I have myself always been interested in close textual analysis (compiling a book of documents is related to such an approach); but whereas the discourse theorists are mainly (and for the late *ancien régime* exclusively) interested in people with no conventional political power, I am as exclusively interested in those who do possess it – kings, ministers and their advisers – because such people have a more demonstrable impact. So when Louis XVI's finance minister, Turgot, admitted to a confidant his intention over a period to make the king more democratically accountable (3), that would seem to me to be of greater consequence than a pamphleteer's use of 'patriotism' and 'citizen' in a proto-revolutionary way. But if Chancellor Maupeou himself was worried by the use of such expressions in *parlementaire* remonstrances (1) then perhaps we should sit up and take note. Similarly, if the abbé de Véri, whom Turgot wanted to make minister of the interior was a crypto-republican (3), that also would seem to have serious implications. As we move further into the Revolution, my argument loses some of its validity because political power is more diffused and the practitioners of discourse theory do analyse the language of some of the major politicians, especially Robespierre. Those who are interested in discourse theory will, I hope, find grist to their mill in the enlarged section on Robespierre and his faction, and particularly documents 70, **128** and 178–81. But I hope also that they will exercise their skills on documents emanating from the key politicians of the late *ancien régime*.

There has also been a growing consensus over the last 20 years that the collapse of the *ancien régime* and the outbreak of the Revolution were two separate processes. There was no 'big bang' which destroyed the one and left the other as some mysterious residue. The *ancien régime*, in short, collapsed for reasons peculiar to itself. The decision to include a section on this process in the first edition has therefore been vindicated and an enlarged selection is now presented. But though there is agreement between conventional political historians and discourse theoreticians that there were two separate processes, there is again an important distinction to be made. For it seems to me odd that the second school, whilst stressing the importance of the separate and prior collapse of the *ancien régime*, shows so little interest in how it actually happened. Perhaps it is part of their belief that the archival approach to history is old-fashioned. For with this approach one can show, fairly precisely, how the *ancien régime* government machine broke down. 'Government machine' is only a metaphor – the 'machine' consisted of human beings. Why these lost their faith or their will to persevere is a harder question to answer, but documents 1–7 provide some clues.

In some ways, also, the distinction between political and social and economic history is artificial. For example, the history of the popular movement in the Revolution is more political than social. The *sans-culottes* were political animals. An a-political artisan may not have worn *culottes* (knee breeches) but he was not for that a *sans-culotte* in the technical sense. Only the Enragés (**145–47**) articulated a mainly social and economic programme. And though one may disagree with Soboul's central argument in *Les sans-culottes Parisiens de l'an II*, namely that the Jacobin leadership smashed the popular movement for class reasons and paid the penalty on 9 thermidor, the body of his text shows that they smashed it for reasons of efficient administration and of pure politics. Indeed it was pure politics on both sides – a naked struggle for power clothed in bogus ideology.

Again, one of the central themes of this book, from the beginning to the end of the decade covered, concerns the role the nobility should play in France, or, as Alexander de Lameth put it in November 1789, the question of 'civil and political equality'. But the answer to that question involves social, political and constitutional issues.

In political terms, it is necessary to go back to the last years of the *ancien régime* in order to appreciate the continuity between the policies attempted by the king and those accomplished by the National Assembly – both concerned with creating uniformity out of France's disparate social and geographical composition – and thus the tragedy that these changes did not come about peacefully, as the *cahiers de doléances* (61–69) seemed to promise: this is the central theme of the first two parts of this book and is embodied in the person of Louis XVI, who receives sympathetic treatment. By 1786, also, France may be said no longer to have possessed an agreed constitution. By convoking the Assembly of Notables at the end of that year, Louis XVI implicitly recognized that the political system of the *ancien régime* was defunct and that something would have to be put in its place. The quest for a constitution was pursued throughout our period as a matter of urgency, but became more difficult as each phase of the Revolution added a new division in the country. For political consensus is necessary to the proper working of constitutional government and it was found, or judged, to be impossible to preserve the gains of the Revolution, from attack at home and abroad, under the rule of law. Thus the rule of the National Convention from 1792 to 1795, which forms the third part of this book, became a caricature of the worst features of the *ancien régime*, which could be capricious but was hardly oppressive: the fitful operation of the *lettre de cachet* was generalized as the law of suspects and the inefficient *dirigisme* of the old monarchy became the bureaucratic Terror.

John Hardman
Hartford
1998

Introduction

This volume is concerned with the constitutional and political problems (there were no solutions) of France in the decade 1785–95. This was a decade of revolution but the whole decade was also *révolutionnaire* in the special, technical sense in which that word was used in the period 1793–5. During that period of crisis for the infant republic the constitution was suspended, and with it the certainties which we associate with the expression the 'rule of law'. This provisional form of government was termed *révolutionnaire*. But this state of affairs existed to a greater or lesser extent throughout our period although nominally France was governed, until 1789, under the unwritten constitution or Fundamental Laws of the old monarchy and thereafter under the constitution of 1791.[1] For during the last years of the *ancien régime* (part I of this book) the main parties to the political system, the king and the *parlements* who registered his legislation, differed fundamentally in their interpretation of the constitution, their respective powers under it and the constitutionality of the king's legislative proposals; during the period of the constitutional monarchy, 1789–92 (part II), the constitution was despised by the king who ruled under it and flouted by the National Assembly which had framed it; as if to emphasize its irrelevance, this constitution continued to be the one under which France was nominally governed for three years after the proclamation of the republic, i.e. 1792–5 (part III).

This outcome was far from the designs of the deputies who gathered at Versailles in May 1789 for the first meeting of the Estates-General since 1614.[2] They had assembled to give France a written constitution and end the obscurity and arbitrariness, as they saw it, of the previous system. But the divisions which they created in the country were such that France

1 The date of its completion and acceptance by the king.
2 The Estates-General, consisting of the elected representatives of the three orders of society – clergy, nobles and Third Estate – was the nearest equivalent to the English parliament, with the important difference that, as early as 1356, it had lost the 'power of the purse'.

lacked that consensus necessary for the proper working of constitutional government. For changing the constitution meant more than changing the legal basis for political activity. Thus when the princes of the blood in their memorandum of December 1788 (58) talk of defending the constitution they mean not just the political institutions of the *ancien régime* but also the political ordering of society: for example, the existence of the nobility as a separate order in the Estates-General and the size of its deputation was related to its existence as a separate order in and its influence on society as a whole, of which the Estates-General was the political manifestation. Thus also when Louis XVI writes in 1791 to his *émigré* brothers (110), 'The nation likes the constitution because the word recalls to the lower portion of the people only the independence in which it has lived for the last two years and to the class above [the bourgeoisie] equality. . . .Vanity is satisfied', the constitution is almost synonymous with the Revolution.

In this second, wider constitutional category, the main issue throughout the period was the role of the nobility. The crisis of the *ancien régime* arose out of the king's need to end tax evasion by the nobility and make the clergy pay regular taxation. The nobility, who regarded paying taxes as socially as well as financially disagreeable, were led in their resistance by the *parlements*, whose members were all noble. Uncertain as to the permanent success of this resistance, the nobility then acted according to the old argument 'no taxation without representation' and successfully demanded the calling of the Estates-General. However, that body did not turn out to be the aristocratic instrument intended and, when it became the National Assembly, it not only removed the financial privileges of the nobility but abolished first feudalism (95) and then the nobility itself (97). Finally, at the height of the Terror, Saint-Just introduced legislation which treated nobles automatically as 'suspects' and obliged them to report to the authorities daily (173). This legislation re-conferred social distinction, however grim, on the nobility and was repealed after the fall of Robespierre and Saint-Just (199).

The narrower constitutional objectives were found to be incompatible with the deeper changes in the constitution of society. Many of the nobility took up arms against the Revolution and strove to enlist the support of France's neighbours. The king also, though he had been the first to attack the financial privileges of the nobility, had not intended to undermine, let alone abolish, their social position. This distinction was not understood and the National Assembly was disappointed in his attitude. In its distrust of him, the National Assembly reduced his role, in the constitution of 1791, to that of a figurehead with less power than the king of England. Though he had been ready to be a constitutional monarch (60), the constitution of 1791 assigned him a role which no eighteenth-century monarch could accept and which was, moreover, appropriate to no European country at that time.

Thus the various assemblies, operating within the constraints of resistance at home and abroad, felt that they could not preserve the gains of the Revolution under the rule of law. For example, the constitution of 1793 was never implemented because, as Saint-Just observed, 'people would use it to destroy it' (151). Again, in 1795, free parliamentary elections would probably have resulted in a royalist majority, so the National Convention ruled that the electorate must re-elect two-thirds of the sitting members. The dividing line between constitutional and political acts was very thin; in a period of revolutionary change it was inevitable that political acts should assume constitutional significance and vice versa: for example, when the keeper of the seals, for political reasons, advised the king that he could not dismiss the head of the Parlement without putting him on trial (10), he was creating a dangerous constitutional precedent, whilst the constitution which the Girondin survivors drew up in 1795 (202–3) was in large part a commentary on the factors which they considered had led to their downfall in 1793. There are obvious dangers in the possession by a political body of what Siéyès termed 'the dictatorship of constituent power'.

The constitution-makers of the Revolution are often accused of being too abstract and politically innocent. In fact the reverse is the case: the various constitutions were marred by being too politicized, too specific, too influenced by the circumstances of their birth. In this respect, and in their tampering with the constitutional safeguards they had themselves provided, the revolutionary leaders had failed according to their own lights. For from 1785 to 1795, from Calonne to Cambacérès, they were all lawyers, to whom legal forms mattered; their coins bore the legend 'Le Regne de la Loi', their officials took an oath of fidelity to the law. It was their tragedy that, faced with the lack of consensus in France, the rule of lawyers was unable to bring about the rule of law.

The three parts of the book correspond with three distinct phases of the constitutional and political struggle. Part I, 'The Fall of the *Ancien Régime*', deals with the disintegration of the classical political system of the *ancien régime*: rule by the king and the *parlements* without reference to representative institutions such as the Estates-General (I(2)). The king first unilaterally repudiates this system by seeking endorsement in 1787 from the quasi-representative Assembly of Notables for a revolutionary programme, aimed at ending the social and geographical privileges and variations of France, which the *parlements* would have rejected out of hand (I(3)). In rejecting the reforms, the Notables assume some of the characteristics of the English parliament and several constitutional landmarks are passed limiting the king's power. Prompted by revenge and despair, the Parlement successfully demands the convocation of the Estates-General, whilst the king fails in his attempt to abolish the political role of the Parlement (I(4)). Throughout this period, the king explores the possibilities of an alliance with the Third Estate against the nobility and clergy but meets with little response.

In Part II, we see the Estates-General, transformed into the National Assembly, carry through the very reforms which powerful vested interests had prevented Louis XVI from implementing. Tragically, this is not accomplished with the full consent of the king and this is at the root of the revolutionary conflict. The misunderstanding between the king and the Estates-General, with the king seemingly abandoning his policy of alliance with the Third Estate, is complex and is examined at some length (II(1)), whilst the king's response to the Revolution as a whole – much more nuanced than is commonly supposed – is the subject of (II(3)).

Part III deals with the rule of the National Convention during the first years of the republic. The great legislative monuments of the Revolution were the work of the National Assembly (II(2)), and the National Convention, whose proper function was to draft a republican constitution, was occupied largely with fierce political struggles and with coping with war against most of Europe. There are sections on the Girondins (III(1)), the Dantonists and Hébertists (III(4)), and Robespierre (III(5)), as well as on the most distinctive of the popular political groups, the Enragés (III(2)). There is also a section on the emergency, war-time *gouvernement révolutionnaire* directed by the Convention's Committee of Public Safety (III(3)). The book ends with the last year of the Convention, the period known as the 'Thermidorian reaction', following the fall of Robespierre (III(6)). However, the divisions in the country and the resultant lack of stable constitutional government which characterize our period continued for over a century, and in many respects may be said to continue to this day. For, as La Fayette told the Assembly of Notables in 1787, 'We should not lightly tamper with a constitution under which France has flourished so gloriously for nearly 800 years.'

THE FALL OF THE
ANCIEN RÉGIME

|1|

Doubts

One of the great historical mysteries is why, after lasting so long and surmounting so many apparently identical crises, the *ancien régime* died in the late 1780s. (I say the late 1780s because the regime died so quietly that one is not sure whether its death occurred in 1787, 1788 or 1789.) In I(2) we shall look at the irreparable breakdown in relations between crown and Parlement. If one defines the *ancien régime* as the period when these two institutions ruled France without reference to her representative institution, the Estates-General then, *ex hypothesi,* this breakdown was the end of the regime. But the crisis in the relations between crown and Parlement, apart from its result (the calling of the Estates), was so similar to a string of crises under Louis XV (some of which the crown won, some the Parlement)[1] that its explanatory assistance for the larger issue, the why as well as the how, is limited. So in this first section we try to discover the preoccupations of some of the men in the governmental milieu in the hope that they will provide some inkling of why the regime fell.

Reform was in the air. Many of the measures Calonne presented to the Assembly of Notables in 1787 had been prefigured, notably by Dupont de Nemours and the finance minister d'Ormesson in 1783, as part of the stocktaking which often accompanied the end of a war (in this case that of American independence in which France fought on the colonialists' side against England) (**2a** and **2b**). Even the date – 1787 – had been pencilled in because a key tax expired that year. They envisaged the abolition of tax farming and the taxation of the clergy, hitherto largely exempt. Such reforms were in line with government thinking over nearly half a century. But Dupont's memorandum displays a profound pessimism about what can be accomplished, given the chronic instability of the post of controller-general of finances and the ability of the *parlements* to block reform. He also hints darkly that reform of the major indirect taxes (on salt, alcohol, etc.) 'cannot be modified unless there is a way to consult with the nation'. As a disciple of Turgot (controller-general, 1774–76), Dupont would not have

---

1 On this, see P. R. Campbell, *Power and Politics in Old Regime France, 1720–45* (1996), pp. 314–18.

intended the Estates-General by these words since the Estates were regarded as hopelessly antiquated, being based on a society of orders (clergy, nobility and Third Estate) which in some respects was waning by the 1780s and was to be revived specially for the convocation of the Estates in 1788 (against the advice of Turgot's friend Malesherbes, then minister without portfolio).

Turgot's thinking on these matters is shown in document **3**. There was talk of some devolution of power to provincial assemblies; Necker (finance minister, 1776–81) had set up three pilot ones. Turgot had planned something more ambitious but had wanted to wait until the king (only 19 when he ascended the throne in 1774) was experienced enough to implement a measure 'which would alter the monarchical constitution' with his eyes open. Despite his scruples over timing, Turgot consciously sought to introduce a measure which would lead to the end of the absolute monarchy. In time, the new assemblies, elected on the basis of class not order, would have elected a national assembly and would have eclipsed the *parlements* and ended the absolute monarchy. The abbé de Véri, whom Turgot proposed as minister of the interior, in the same document confesses republicanism (to his diary). The question of Véri's appointment was the immediate issue over which Turgot was dismissed by the king. Was that dismissal such a crass mistake?

Whilst Turgot, Véri and Malesherbes were hoping for a more democratic evolution of the polity, there were others in the government, or soon to enter it, who favoured a more aristocratic outcome. The social composition of the ministry was fast changing. Until mid-century the typical minister had, like Calonne, spent his entire career in the direct service of the crown: as a young man presenting cases in the *conseil d'état* as a *maître des requêtes*, then ruling a province as an *intendant*, finally returning to Versailles as a minister. His loyalties were not divided. Until the 1750s, the court aristocracy had spurned ministerial office as menial work beneath their dignity (**4a**), but thereafter they claimed at least the service ministries as their right (**4b**). The marquis de Castries, naval minister 1780–87, is the prime exemplar of this new thinking. He favoured a decentralized, aristocrat-dominated, constitutional monarchy, with provincial and national estates formed according to the traditional division of society into orders. It is perhaps also significant that on his own estates he was tightening up on the collection of feudal dues.[2] For in his person one sees both a feudal reaction (the king's chief vassals forcing their way back into his council or, in eighteenth-century parlance, 'storming the closet') and a seigneurial one. At the time of his resignation in 1787 he thought, in common with many of his kind, that an aristocrat-dominated Estates-General was in prospect. He told the queen that he wanted the Estates-General but he felt obliged to tell her that they would ruin the king's authority. This ended for him a period of internal conflict between 'my situation as a Frenchman and my particular situation as a minister'. The context of this agonizing was the king's decision to exile the Parlement to Troyes for blocking government measures. With such

2 A. Soboul, *The French Revolution* (1989) introduction by G. Lewis, p. xiii.

divided loyalties, it is not surprising that government policy seemed irresolute.

Similarly, *parlementaires* entered the ministry in increasing numbers: Miromesnil, for instance, had been First President of the Parlement of Rouen which had been so rebellious that Louis XV had abolished it in 1771; Miromesnil had also received a personal rebuke from that monarch. The question arises whether the dissolution of the regime did not begin at the very centre, within the king's own council, with opposition from the *parlements* and other quarters merely reflecting this.

The threat to royal authority posed by *grands seigneurs* (who tended to favour a liberal-aristocratic gloss to the constitution) and *parlementaires* entering the ministry is obvious. Moreover, if one considers that the rights of the nobility and the powers of the *parlements* were precisely the burning issues in government at the time and, further, that the French Revolution started as an aristocratic revolt against royal authority in 1787–8, then – assuming that most men cannot transcend the limitations and loyalties of their class – the defeat of the king, supported only by his controller-general and perhaps another minister, is a foregone conclusion.

There were, of course, still a few loyal servitors of the absolute monarchy in the government, pre-eminent among whom was Vergennes, foreign secretary from 1774 until his death in 1787. But though he did not have doubts, he certainly had fears, prompted by France's performance in the American war. France emerged from that war with increased prestige but at a total cost of 1 billion livres (there were 24 livres to the £). Other wars had cost as much or more, but what was new was the king's decision at the start of his reign not to resort to the usual procedure of forcibly reducing the rate of interest on loans at the end of a war (which they called a 'bankruptcy'). In document **5** Vergennes casts an envious glance across the Channel and links England's ability to raise money for armaments with the operation of public 'opinion, which cannot develop in an absolute monarchy to the extent that it can in a mixed monarchy' such as England's. If the war had continued for another year, France's fleet could easily have been annihilated and her Caribbean sugar islands lost. The repercussions at home would have been incalculable. The correspondence between Vergennes and Montmorin (**6**), the king's favourite and ambassador to France's principal ally, Spain, brings out the heartbreaking worry and the palpable relief when it was all over. This is probably why Vergennes threw himself behind Calonne's audacious reform programme, which would have ended the *ancien régime* by an *increase* in royal authority. Apart from the fragility of the French war machine, foreign (and home) policy was distorted throughout the reign of Louis XVI by the mistaken belief that England was ready to take advantage of any French weakness to seize her colonies. This was Vergennes' principal argument for entering the American war in 1778. Ten years later the government had to take its important decisions of 1788–9 whilst labouring under a similar delusion, namely that England was about to take advantage of France's internal difficulties to fight a naval war against her (**7**). This belief partially explains royal weakness – for example, the king's decision not to flee from Versailles during the October Days must have been influenced by La Luzerne's report of 2 October 1789, i.e. just three days before the Paris women marched on the Palace; but also the king's acceptance of representative government: in document **35** Marie-Antoinette specifically links the calling of the Estates-General with this (imaginary) war threat.

1   Chancellor Maupeou embraces discourse theory

René-Charles-Augustin de Maupeou (1714–92), chancellor from 1768, had replaced the Parlement with a more docile body in 1771. On his accession, Louis XVI restored the old Parlement and exiled Maupeou to his estates in Normandy. In 1786 Maupeou, aware of the impasse between crown and Parlement, sent Louis XVI projects for the administration of justice based on the principles Louis XV enunciated in 1766 in the *séance de flagellation* before the Parlement. Lenoir, as royal librarian, took delivery and gives this summary of one of them.

In one of these memoranda the chancellor presented [*parlementaire* remonstrances] as harbingers of the revolution which supervened later. In it he picked up several expressions employed by the *parlements* in former [pre-Louis XVI] remonstrances which troublemakers sought to resurrect in 1789, such as *liberty, patriotism, the rights of the citizen*; and he reminded [the king] that the former committees composed of *conseillers des enquêtes*[3] advocates had been hotbeds of sedition.

> Bibliothèque municipale d'Orléans,
> Lenoir papers, Ms 1423, section 93

2   Hopes and fears at the end of d'Ormesson's ministry

(a) From Dupont de Nemours' 'Secret memorandum on the financial situation', August 1783, addressed to the controller-general d'Ormesson

Pierre-Samuel Dupont de Nemours was a senior bureaucrat who, like d'Ormesson, had collaborated closely with Turgot. He later played a role in the reshaping of France during the Revolution. Henri François-de-Paule Lefevre d'Ormesson (1751–1807) was controller-general for eight months in 1783.

Chapter I[knowing the size of the problem]

M. Necker's *compte rendu* does not provide an accurate enough basis. It contains several genuine mistakes on the part of the author and even more very deliberate inaccuracies. [Turgot's figures showed that revenue and expenditure were in rough balance in 1776; since then involvement in the American war left the following situation]:

---

3 Generally the youngest and most radical *parlementaires*.

1 The arrears on the various life and perpetual loans or anticipation [of future revenues] by M. Necker and M. Joly de Fleury[4] which should cost 60 to 70 million livres a year to service.

2 The upkeep of a greatly augmented navy which must not be allowed to be run down [as after the previous war] and which should take from 12 to 15 million a year more than before the war.

[The gradualist approach he is about to outline depends on maintaining peace] because if we cannot avoid war, as great resources will be required in a kingdom whose credit is currently exhausted, so we will need to decide on bold measures. [However] . . . a war, always perilous for the finance minister could, provided he is not destroyed by it, become for the nation both the occasion and the driving force of reforms and changes of such utility as to make up for all the misfortunes.

Chapter II: measures to implement in time of peace

AMALGAMATE FARMS AND *RÉGIES*[5]

[The advantage of a *régie* was] that one could modify taxes entrusted to a régie and cut some of them without indemnity.

This is a very important advantage which must be retained to determine the total tax take from the indirect taxes at the end [1786] of the present contract [of the farmers] which is intended to be the last if the administration of M. *le contrôleur-général* lasts as long as the expiry of the contract and if he retains the credit and authority which his hard work, intelligence and virtues merit. . . . [6]

THE CLERGY

It is proved by the old charters and only too well in an excellent memorandum by M. Anson [d'Ormesson's *chef de bureau*] that the clergy has no privileges over and above those of the nobility and so should not be exempt from the *vingtièmes*[7] or *capitation*. [Dupont proposed that instead of paying 15,000,000 every five years as a *don gratuit*, they should pay 9,000,000 a year *vingtième* and 2,000,000 a year *capitation*.]

Their lordships will be consoled by the suppression of some monasteries which can no longer be filled and amalgamating some abbeys with the bishoprics with the result that no one's income will end up being diminished. . . .

4 Jean-François Joly de Fleury (1718–1802), finance minister, 1781–3.
5 Tax farmers made a profit out of tax collection (but paid the state in advance); *régisseurs* were salaried officials.
6 D'Ormesson fell in November 1783, trying to convert the farm into a *régie*.
7 The *vingtième*, a tax of one-twentieth on landed income, was instituted in 1749 – the first *permanent* tax to be paid by nobles as well as commoners. Sometimes two *vingtièmes* were levied or even, as in 1782–6, three.

[Certain reforms cannot even be attempted]:

Economies: They would require more authority than a *contrôleur-général* can perhaps possess. . . .

Major indirect taxes, such as the *gabelle, aides*, tobacco duty: it is thought that these cannot be modified unless there is a way to consult with the nation and come to an understanding with it on replacements. . . .

The *vingtième*: this is a subject of which M. *le contrôleur-général* has a thorough understanding and on which above all the agreement of the *parlements* must be reached. . . .

Archives Nationales (AN), 144 AP
131 dossier 4. 11

(b) A perspective on reform: d'Ormesson to the king, August 1783

Happily the approaching expiry of the last lease of the general farms and of the third *vingtième* which both fall due in 1786 enable us to prepare a new internal order for this fast approaching date, whether we then change or modify the consumption taxes presently farmed out which may be harmful to agriculture and commerce or whether Your Majesty is finally enabled to know the respective wealth of his provinces, which is still unknown, by a better assessment of the two *vingtièmes*, the only tax which is uniform throughout the whole kingdom and consequently the only one which can be used to provide a fair basis of comparison between the various provinces.

AN, 144 AP 131 dossier 4. 4

3 Turgot on provincial assemblies: extract from the diary of the abbé de Véri

Anne-Robert-Jacques Turgot (1727–81) had been controller-general of finances, 1774–76. The context is Necker's introduction of a pilot Provincial Assembly in Berry in 1778 in which Véri was to serve. Turgot begins by explaining why he had not introduced such institutions during his ministry.

It was not just the fear of opposition [at court] that closed my mouth on the question of provincial Estates or assemblies.

Whatever restrictions it might be possible to put on these assemblies to start with, there is no doubt that, being established in each province and able to concert action, they would acquire a degree of force which would surely change the present monarchical constitution. As a citizen I should have been perfectly happy; but acting as the king's minister I scrupled to abuse his confidence to damage the extent of his authority. It is not that I did not plan to do it but I wanted to wait until the king was older, more experienced and mature enough to judge for himself rather than rely on another's judgement. I wanted to give him the time to come, by himself, to an informed opinion about the sacrifice of a portion of his power it was appropriate for him to make in accordance with the justice he owed his people. . . .

Also my scheme [unlike Necker's] did not involve a single assembly in each province – still less was it based on the separation of the three orders of the clergy, the nobility and the Third Estate. I was contemplating a sort of municipal administration, grouping a small number of 20, 30 or at the very most 40 parishes. I would not have admitted of any distinction of rank or orders. . . .

I [Véri] cannot hide from myself that deep down I have a secret wish to render the peoples less dependent on the absolute wishes of the court.

I never go to Versailles without coming away with a feeling of silent indignation at seeing us subjected to the caprices of that horde of valets.[8] Assuredly this impression is not caused by talking to ministers nor by the known intentions and personal conduct of the king but by the arrogant and self-important tone of the others who surround the royal family. Their noble ignorance, their servile dignity and their so-called superiority over the people who are ransomed to support them inspire strong republican sentiments in me. They are even more aroused in the breasts of those who meet with humiliation at the hands of the petty bureaucrats at Versailles; of Parisians who complain of the unjust extensions of the excise duties collected by the farmers general; and of those in the provinces who are constantly harassed by the collectors of stamp duties, taxes on alcohol, salt and the *taille*.

Abbé de Véri, *Journal 1774–80*, ed. J. de Witte (2 vols., 1928), vol. II, p. 147

4   The changing social and political composition of the ministry

(a) The maréchal-duc de Belle-Isle becomes secretary of state for war in 1758

M. de Richelieu assured him that he had not come to pay his respects to the post he occupied but to himself personally . . . and that he had come also in the name of all the peers to thank him for having graciously accepted the office of secretary of state.

---

8 Véri delights in emphasizing the menial origins of the offices at court.

M. de Belle-Isle hesitated a long time before accepting the post of secretary of state; but the precedents of M. le cardinal de Richelieu and later of M. le cardinal Dubois made up his mind for him.

> *Mémoires du duc de Luynes sur la cour de Louis XV, 1735–58*, ed. L. Dussieux and E. Soulié (17 vols., 1860–65), vol. XVI, p. 390

Belle-Isle's colleague, Bernis, adds:

M. de Belle-Isle still persisted in the old error that a duke and peer who was also a marshal of France could not, without losing caste (*déroger*), become a secretary of state – as if it were beneath anyone's dignity to govern a great kingdom.

> *Mémoires et lettres de François-Joachim de Pierre, cardinal de Bernis*, ed. F. Masson (2 vols., 1878), vol. II, p. 61

(b) The maréchal de Castries, minister for the marine, reporting a conversation with the queen on the subject of his successor, 23 June 1787

I said that if there were any possibility of a lawyer [*homme de robe*] succeeding me then I should consider myself obliged to tell the king that his navy would be ruined; that we needed at the head of this department a man who knew how to command, who was used to it and who had the authority to make himself obeyed, and that M. de Bouillé seemed to me to deserve preference over those of his rank whom the king could consider.

> Archives de la Marine, 'Journal du maréchal de Castries', Ms 182/7964 1–2, 1, fo. 374

(c) Calonne on the grands seigneurs *and the ministry, from his* Lettre du marquis de Caraccioli à M. d'Alembert, *published anonymously in 1781*

Ever since places in the ministry have been given to *grands seigneurs* – who are all equally entitled to believe they have the same degree of aptitude to fill them – they all devour these places with their eyes and they have all been seized with ministerial mania.

> Calonne, *Lettre du marquis de Caraccioli à M. d'Alembert*, p. 21

(d) Divided loyalties

When Louis XVI exiled the Parlement to Troyes in August 1787, the maréchal de Castries observed:

I could have wished to have been spared having to choose between my situation as a Frenchman and my particular situation as a minister; not that the two are incompatible but as a citizen I might form an opinion and as a minister have to perform a duty which went against it.

And shortly afterwards, informing the queen of his decision to resign, he added:

As a Frenchman I want the Estates-General, as a minister I am bound to tell you that they might destroy your authority.

'Journal du maréchal de Castries',
fos. 389, 395

(e) Parlementaires and the ministry, extract from the abbé de Véri, Journal, August 1774

I have just read a memorandum by M. de Malesherbes in which he demonstrates that the post of keeper of the seals should not be given either to him or to anyone of his class.

Abbé de Véri, *Journal*, p. 175

5   Vergennes to Noailles, French ambassador to England, 15 November 1776

Charles Gravier, comte de Vergennes (1717–87) was foreign secretary, 1774–87. In 1778 he brought France into the War of American Independence, on the side of the colonists and against England.

There is something admirable, almost gravity-defying in the facility with which the [English] nation or rather its representatives embark on such terrifying [naval] expenditure. Assuredly we have more solid resources than England but are far from being able to call them into play so easily. This is the result of [public] opinion, which cannot develop in an absolute monarchy to the extent that it can in a mixed monarchy.

H. Doniol, *Histoire de la participation de la France à l'établissement des Etats-Unis de l'Amérique* (6 vols., 1886–89), vol. II, p. 18

6   Pessimism: Montmorin to Vergennes, 30 October 1780

Armand-Marc de Saint-Hérem, comte de Montmorin (1746–92) was at this time ambassador to France's ally, Spain. The American war had been waged for two years without results. The allied victory at Yorktown came in 1781. Montmorin succeeded Vergennes as foreign secretary and perished in the September massacres.

I see the lustre of the reign which began so brilliantly becoming equivocal at best. Because let us not fool ourselves, the peace which concludes the present war will certainly have an influence on the whole of the rest of the reign. You have raised our international standing, which was totally destroyed, and it is once again about to slip from your grasp. . . .

Doniol, *Histoire*, vol. III, p. 515

7   War scare: memoranda read by La Luzerne, secretary of state for the marine, to the *conseil d'état*

(a) 14 December 1788

The troop reinforcements which the English have sent both to the Indies and to the Western colonies and the considerable supplies they have accumulated there led us to assume, until the month of October, that war with this naval power was very likely and perhaps indeed very near at hand. Hence Your Majesty has ordered considerable armament and provisioning. Your Majesty even ordered me to keep a sufficient number of sailors assembled in the barracks of the three great ports to arm a squadron should Great Britain commit hostilities off Newfoundland. . . .

Bibliothèque Nationale (BN), nouvelles acquisitions françaises (naf) 9434, fo. 172

(b) 12 August 1789

Since the beginning of the month of May I have repeatedly informed Your Majesty, both in my individual working session with you and in your *conseil d'état*, of the anxiety caused me by the armament of all kinds going on in the English ports. . . .

I have already demonstrated a thousand times that the English will find us weak everywhere. The penury of our finances has prevented Your Majesty from replying by arming ships, the only way of protecting our distant possessions.

Even at Brest there are fears. I have already ordered M. d'Hector to be ready at a moment's notice to arm the batteries which cover the roadstead and the entrance to the port but not to do so yet because it would be impolitic to provoke by these measures an attack which is not perhaps intended.

I lay these facts and these considerations before Your Majesty with the request that he give me his orders. [La Luzerne notes: It was decided that, given our inability to arm, we must confine ourselves to the measures previously agreed.]

BN, naf 9434, fos. 213–14

(c) 2 October 1789

I informed the king that although the English fleet had returned to the ports of Portsmouth and Plymouth, everything was ready for armament, that all the supplies had been laid in, and that abundantly; that a letter from my brother [the ambassador to England] warned me that despite the appearance of the greatest tranquillity, it was intended to keep up the internal troubles of the kingdom and that if calm seemed about to return they would not fail to profit from our lack of financial and other resources. I explained that if Great Britain were to attack our colonies unexpectedly, the most dire consequences were to be feared; that she had 5,400 troops in the Windward Islands to our 4,000; in the East Indies she maintained 80,000 men including European and native troops; that as soon as she prepared to arm we would have to match our efforts to hers but that we would find ourselves short of the salt provisions necessary to put a great fleet to sea whenever it might be needed unless we took the precaution now of procuring provisions from Cork.

I put at an extra 1,500,000 or 1,600,000 francs the amount that would be necessary for the subsistence of nearly all our armed vessels for one campaign.

I added that this extraordinary expenditure would occasion a loss if we did not need to use these salt provisions because the ministry would not be able to sell them for the price it had paid.

The king felt the weight of these reasons but in view of the penury of the finances he decided that only 300,000 francs' worth should be purchased over and above the normal provisions. . . .

BN, naf 9434, fo. 209

|2|

The breakdown of relations between crown and Parlement

The short answer to the question 'why was there a French Revolution?' is 'because the *ancien régime* came to an end'. The defining characteristic of the *ancien régime* was a political system in which the central representative institution, the Estates-General, was in abeyance and legislation was enacted by the king in conjunction with 13 local courts of appeal (*parlements*), the most important of which was the Parlement of Paris. The political role of the *parlements* (which tended to overshadow their primary judicial role) was to 'register' royal edicts. In theory, the king saw registration as law publication rather than as law making – as no more than a formality necessary to give an edict its official character – whereas the *parlementaires* gave themselves a more positive function: they were 'verifying' whether or not the proposed legislation conflicted with the unwritten constitution (Fundamental Laws) and natural justice. In practice, for much of the *ancien régime*, the two positions converged. For example, the king knew that if the *parlements* really thought that a tax was just and necessary people would pay more readily.

However, from about 1750 the system began to show signs of strain – largely because of Louis XV's attempts to tax the nobility of whom the *parlementaires* were the political leaders – and in 1785–6 it broke down, forcing Louis XVI to experiment with the quasi-representative Assembly of Notables (the subject of I(3)). The impasse in relations between crown and Parlement centred on Charles Alexandre de Calonne, controller-general of finances since 1783. As a young man, Calonne had earned the undying hatred of the *parlementaires* when, in 1766, he had drafted the speech in which Louis XV asserted royal authority and chastised the Parlement in the *séance de flagellation*. After a brief honeymoon period, the Parlement attacked Calonne's administration in earnest in 1785: the loan of that year (**8**) and the re-coinage (**9**). In these circumstances most controllers-general would have been forced from office but instead Calonne tried to regain control of the Parlement by having his two most powerful enemies dismissed: the *rapporteur de la cour*[1], Lefevre d'Amécourt, and the head of the

---

1 His function was to present a report on proposed royal legislation and guide its passage through the Parlement.

Parlement, the *premier président* d'Aligre. He succeeded in breaking d'Amécourt (9) but in the case of d'Aligre he was thwarted by his own ministerial colleague, Miromesnil, the keeper of the seals (10). Only after his failure to break d'Aligre (early August 1786) did Calonne communicate to the king his plans for an Assembly of Notables.

8   Calonne's loan of 1785 and the Parlement

This document gives a rare glimpse into the mechanics of the legislative process at the end of the *ancien régime*. The legislation in question is Calonne's loan of 1785. Loans, chiefly in the form of annuities (*rentes*), were essential to royal finances and Calonne raised three loans of some 100 million livres (francs) in 1783, 1784 and 1785. The edicts creating these loans were registered in the Parlement because this reassured creditors. The Parlement could either register an edict immediately or send the king 'remonstrances' or even (as in this document) 'repeated remonstrances'. If (after modifications to the edict and negotiations) the Parlement still refused to register, the king could enforce registration by *lit de justice*.[2] However, the forced registration of a loan would be counter-productive and indeed any reluctance on the part of the Parlement to register the edict would impair the success of the loan.

Thus Calonne is worried and annoyed at the difficulties his loan encounters in the Parlement – he never risks another – and the fact that 'registration was coupled with a resolution calculated to discredit the loan'. He sends the former minister Bertin to quiz d'Amécourt about what went wrong. Bertin's report is very confused – he was an old man – but we have included it, scrappy though it is, because it is the only concrete evidence available for a landmark in the deterioration of relations between crown and Parlement. The report takes the form of six statements by Calonne and d'Amécourt's replies. Calonne was obviously unconvinced, as he had d'Amécourt relieved of his functions (9).

First Fact. First [private] discussion between the controller-general and M. d'Amécourt; registration after remonstrances agreed without difficulty, the whole passing off amicably. [D'Amécourt accepts Calonne's account.]

Second Fact. Discussion in the apartments of the keeper of the seals.[3] [D'Amécourt notes some opposition but] . . . regards it as impetuosity which would easily calm down in private committees and gives the controller-general to understand this by nods and winks. . . .

Third Fact. [Calonne sends d'Amécourt the memorandum he had used in these preliminary discussions.]

---

2 In a *lit de justice* the king appeared in person before the *Parlement* or sent his representative. The *parlementaires* exercised functions delegated to them by the king and, according to the Roman law maxim, 'in the presence of the delegator the powers of the delegate cease'. The *parlementaires* sometimes challenged the legality of the *lit de justice*.
3 This would include the first president and other influential *parlementaires*.

Fourth Fact. [D'Amécourt's] report on the edict [to the Parlement]; criticism of the edict, etc., etc., etc. . . . I [i.e. Bertin] asked him whether he had made use of the memorandum to refute it or otherwise . . . [he replied] that I knew that several members of the Parlement itself were saying that he had made use of . . . this memorandum . . . *to disprove the accuracy of the various items of expenditure* and that he had gone so far as to treat the various declarations in the preamble with affected sarcasm. 'But', he said, 'you, Monsieur, can have no doubt how ridiculous and mendacious such an accusation is. Do you imagine that I would be so foolish as to say such things, even if I believed them to be true, about the measures of a man who has offered to try to make me a *conseiller d'état?*'

Fifth Fact. Second report: the memorandum sent previously to the *chambre des enquêtes.* [Further criticisms; d'Amécourt's reply:] . . . There were many criticisms on all sides about the contents of this memorandum, notably on expenditure and the payment of the debts of the princes[4] . . . As for his opinion, having fruitlessly attempted in committee to suggest immediate registration (together with the other active supporter in the meeting with the keeper of the seals) he proposed repeated remonstrances as being safer and got them adopted.

Sixth Fact. Registration coupled with a resolution at the end calculated to discredit the loan. [D'Amécourt's reply:] . . . Given the evident disposition to beg the king to withdraw his edict, a resolution to this effect having been read, proposed and having received 19 votes, and other attendant circumstances, he thought he had been lucky to spare the king a *lit de justice* over a loan and to have had the edict registered with this bandage, leaving it to the government to remove it if it saw fit.

Public Record Office, PC 1/125.68

9   Article on Calonne in Lefevre d'Amécourt's unpublished *Ministres de Louis XVI*

D'Amécourt's own account of his dismissal. Note Louis XVI's typically brusque, staccato manner, exaggerated when dealing with *parlementaires*, whom he detested.

. . . In the affair of the re-coinage[5] the king was made to reply to his *parlements* that this operation did not concern them.

The king was made to say: 'I want it to be known that I am very satisfied with my controller-general.'

At the same time M. d'Amécourt was stripped of his office of *rapporteur de la cour.*

4 Louis XVI's brothers, the comte de Provence and the comte d'Artois.
5 The gold coins were undervalued and were therefore exported in large numbers. Accordingly Calonne reduced their weight by one-sixteenth, only to be accused of profiteering.

It was at the *lit de justice* of 23 December 1785 that these rigours took place.

King's speech: [The Parlement is criticized for publishing] 'matters which should have remained in the secrecy of the intimate relations which I permit the Parlement to have with me'. [The king accepts the practice of remonstrances] 'but I do not expect it to abuse my goodness to the point of constituting itself at all times and in all places the censor of my administration.

'I am going to destroy an *arrêt* which is as ill-considered as it is disrespectfully drafted. [Here the king himself personally scored out a portion of the *arrêt*.] For the rest I want it to be known that I am satisfied with my controller-general.'

Then the king gave the baron de Breteuil[6] a piece of paper which he had taken from his pocket and told him to order the chief registrar to inscribe all that he had just said on the registers.

His Majesty: 'You will understand that the *arrêt* must be printed as it now stands.'

As the Parlement was withdrawing the king summoned the first president [d'Aligre] and told him: 'I no longer want M. d'Amécourt as *rapporteur* of my affairs. You will suggest another to the keeper of the seals who will report to me.'

We were a long time without a *rapporteur de la cour*. Finally the abbé Taudeau accepted.

BN, naf 22104, fo. 74

10   Calonne tries to break d'Aligre: extract from a letter from Miromesnil to the king, 5 August 1786

In the summer of 1786 Calonne tried to ruin d'Aligre's reputation with the king by dragging up two five-year-old debts owed by d'Aligre to the crown, with the intention of forcing his resignation. Miromesnil, as keeper of the seals, was the minister responsible for the *parlements* and this letter clearly shows the impasse which relations between the crown and the Parlement had reached. The minister informs the king of the 'implacable opposition' of the head of the Parlement towards Calonne, yet advises him (quite erroneously) that 'it is not possible to force a first president to resign without putting him on trial'. What also has to be realized is that d'Aligre probably did want to resign and that Miromesnil is persuading him to stay on because of his own growing antagonism towards the finance minister. Miromesnil, in short, whether wittingly or not, ensured that the existing system could not continue.

6 Louis Charles le Tonnelier, baron de Breteuil, 1730–1807; minister for the *maison du roi* and Paris, 1783–8, *chef de conseil royal des finances*, 12–17 July 1789, appointed the king's plenipotentiary 20 November 1790.

... Your Majesty will easily appreciate the delicacy of my position. There is no point in blinding ourselves to the fact that there is a division between the first president and the controller-general which it would be idle to hope we have much chance of healing. The controller-general would be more amenable to this reconciliation, partly because he is of rather easy-going temperament, though quite liable to flare up. He would soon be reconciled with the first president if he thought that the latter intended to support his administration. But the first president seems to me to be implacably opposed to the controller-general and I doubt whether a perfect reconciliation between them could be effected. The first president's conduct over the business of last December's loan and over the re-coinage has demonstrated only too clearly that he could not be less well disposed towards the controller-general. Moreover the timing and the manner in which the controller-general informed him through M. d'Harvelai [the keeper of the royal treasury] that for five years he had owed the royal treasury 50,000 francs for the office destined for his son and the capital on a life annuity from which he was receiving income – so many causes have all instilled the first president with a resentment which it seems to me impossible to destroy.

The controller-general knows full well how disadvantageous it will be to have at the head of the Parlement a man always disposed to undermine his measures. He passionately desires M. d'Aligre's resignation and I cannot blame him ... [However] it is not possible to force a first president to resign without putting him on trial and whatever M. d'Aligre says I see plainly that at the moment he has no desire to hand in his resignation.

AN, K163 no. 8.14

11   Miromesnil to the king, 8 December 1786

Miromesnil's next letter shows a further deterioration in the relations between crown and Parlement. The intention to send two financial edicts before the Parlement, one increasing the stamp duty, the other alienating the crown lands, leaks out. Moreover the source of the leak is none other than Calonne's colleague, the baron de Breteuil, minister for the *maison du roi* and for Paris. He, together with d'Amécourt, plan a further surprise for the finance minister.

Calonne has borrowed more money on his loans than was vouched for by the Parlement. The registers of the *rentes* are kept in the Hôtel de Ville to which Breteuil has access as minister for Paris. He plans to hand this information to d'Amécourt to use for a denunciation in the Parlement and 'deliver such a blow to the finance minister's credit that he will no longer be able to raise money'. On this occasion, Miromesnil defends Calonne, though in a very back-handed way, and suggests an ingenious and (presumably) successful way of scotching the plot.

However, Miromesnil is later to advise the king that there is no point even sending the proposed legislation before the Parlement. This advice – that urgent financial measures would not even receive a hearing – amounted to an admission that the classical political system of the *ancien régime* had come to an end and that something else would have to be tried.

I have recently been informed of certain matters which it is my duty to lay before Your Majesty but it is important that *you alone* should know of them.

People in the Parlement expect that M. de Calonne will shortly be forced to present you with measures for raising money. The proposed stamp duty and the measure concerning the crown lands have leaked out and there is a plan to seize the first opportunity to make a dramatic denunciation which could destroy public credit and overthrow the minister of finances. M. d'Amécourt is behind this plot which so far has only been confided to two or three people, and the first president himself knows nothing because of the fear that he may let slip some indiscretion or show hostility.

The plan is to denounce in the Parlement the way in which, it is claimed, the last loan of M. Necker, that of M. de Fleury[7] and even those of M. de Calonne have been abused by selling *rentes* to a sum greatly in excess of that stipulated in the edicts; to declare all the sales null on the ground that they contain a kind of stellionate; to make strong representations to you – and thereby deliver such a blow to the finance minister's credit that he will no longer be able to raise money.

I have even been told that at this very moment the baron de Breteuil is having his agents at the Hôtel de Ville take copies of sales of *rentes* in excess of the figure stipulated in the edicts in order to hand them over to M. d'Amécourt. . . .

I did not want to mention this to M. de Calonne; it would have gratuitously envenomed the animosity which exists between him and the baron de Breteuil, thrown your council into discord and caused you embarrassment. But I thought it right to warn you alone and to suggest a simple means of preventing, if possible, proceedings in the Parlement which though doubtless irregular would nonetheless prejudice your affairs, given that the public in its alarm would not be on the side of the ministers and that these proceedings would be coloured by an appearance of justice. I will go further because it would be right never to exceed the figure stipulated in the edicts and always to keep faith with the public. But it is for your administration to safeguard this and act on these principles and I could never respect *parlementaires* who, motivated by ambition, borrow the appearance of equity the better to disguise their passions and to give themselves plausible pretexts for their intrigues. Here is the expedient which occurred to me in order to prevent a scandal.

7 Necker and Joly de Fleury were finance ministers from 1776 to 1781 and from 1781 to 1783 respectively.

It would be best if Your Majesty asked M. de Calonne next Sunday whether the sums stipulated in the loan edicts of M. Necker, M. de Fleury, M. d'Ormesson and of the two loans floated since he has been in office have been exceeded and that Your Majesty should tell him to hand over the lists. Your Majesty should then tell the baron de Breteuil that you want to have these lists checked secretly and ask him whether he can't procure this secret information from his contacts in the office of the Hôtel de Ville, recommending the while the greatest discretion.

The baron de Breteuil, flattered by this confidence and hoping to enlighten Your Majesty himself, will in all probability prevent M. d'Amécourt and his emissaries from acting and that will give you time to avoid any scandal and decide about the plans Your Majesty is occupied in examining at the moment. . . .

AN, K163 no. 8.21

|3|

The Assembly of Notables

In 1786 Calonne, perhaps at the instigation of the foreign secretary, Vergennes (**33**, last paragraph), presented the king with a comprehensive programme of administrative and financial reform with social, political and constitutional implications. This was debated over a six-month period (**5–18**) and appears in its final form in **12**. The aim was to increase royal revenue by ending the tax privileges and tax evasion of the nobility and clergy, which would have increased the yield from the *vingtièmes* by about 50 per cent. The spur for the reforms was necessity: there was an annual deficit of nearly 100 million francs on an income of 600 million, nearly half of which went on servicing the debt. In these circumstances the ending of the third *vingtième*, which brought in about 25 million and was due to expire at the end of 1786, assumed major proportions. There was no question of the Parlement either prolonging the third *vingtième* or endorsing another of the massive loans which had kept the government afloat for the last ten years.

The centrepiece of Calonne's programme was a new land tax which was to replace the two remaining *vingtièmes* and yet, by a fairer and more efficient assessment and collection, produce more than the previous three (**14**). It was to be payable in kind and as a percentage of the crop, and as such would be substantially proof against both tax evasion and inflation. This tax was to be assessed by elected assemblies of taxpayers (**13**) and as their composition was to be based on wealth rather than birth, the nobility could be expected to pay their fair share. The connection between the composition of Provincial Assemblies and the land tax was intimate and all parties realized this.

The programme was enthusiastically adopted by the king but there was no chance of its being accepted by the *parlements* (who by 1786 were ready to block even orthodox government measures). For Calonne's proposals not only· undermined the immunities and prerogatives of the nobility; the Provincial Assemblies would directly rival the authority of the *parlements* (**17**, 'Sixth reply') and might ultimately replace them. Therefore Calonne hit upon the idea of seeking endorsement for his plans, not from the Estates-

General but from a quasi-representative Assembly of Notables,[1] a body which had last met in 1626, before sending them to the *parlements* as a formality to be registered by *lit de justice* in the first instance. The crisis in relations between king and Parlement (I(2)), and in particular Calonne's inability to break d'Aligre (10), explain the decision – at first sight surprising and at the time wholly unexpected, for there was no public demand for the revival of the institution – to convoke the Notables. This is clear from Calonne's memoranda to the king (16 and 17). Document 11 has a certain dramatic irony because it shows the Parlement attempting to block the normal channels of government precisely as, unknown to them, the king is preparing to announce the convocation of an assembly designed to enlarge them.

The first known reference to the Assembly of Notables is contained in a letter to Calonne from the future 'tribune' Mirabeau (15). The king was apprised in August, but despite his enthusiasm insisted on a series of discussions in his presence by a ministerial committee consisting of Miromesnil, Vergennes and Calonne. Miromesnil made fundamental criticisms of the proposals which are contained in letters to the king (19, 26 and 27b), the last two written whilst the Assembly was in session. He stresses the sanctity of regional, personal and corporate privileges, whereas the essence of Calonne's proposals is uniformity in the interests both of justice and efficiency. Miromesnil's position is legitimist – time hallows; Calonne's rationalist – time only '*seems* to hallow' (12) and, essentially, revolutionary. Not daring to advise outright rejection of reforms upon which the king had set his heart, Miromesnil contented himself with undermining them 'throughout the whole session of the Notables'.[2]

The opening of the Assembly was delayed until 22 February 1787. This delay, critical to Calonne's tight schedule (18), was occasioned by the death of Vergennes on 13 February which robbed Calonne of his only ministerial supporter. Moreover the Assembly itself, led by its clerical and *parlementaire* members, immediately attacked Calonne's proposals (21). The clergy stood to lose most from these because they would be included in the general assessment of taxation for the first time. Moreover, the king's offer to facilitate repayment of the clergy's debt was somewhat disingenuous: the whole administrative apparatus of the church existed to service the debt – abolish the debt and the independent organization of the church (a veritable *imperium in imperio*) would wither away unbidden.

Few Notables – for an exception see the speech of Angran d'Allerai (22b) – openly rejected the principle of equal taxation. Instead they attacked the land tax as unconstitutional, stressing that the king could only ask for a specific sum to meet a specific need (speech of Castillon, 22b). As regards provincial assemblies (22a), they rehearsed Montesquieu's argument that the nobility should be powerful in order to defend the people against the

1 The 144 members were chosen by the king but his choice was largely determined by precedent. Thus the first presidents and public prosecutors of all the *parlements* were customarily summoned, as were the mayors of the principal cities and the chief members of the episcopate.

2 The words are the king's, extract from 'Journal de l'abbé de Véri', *Revue de Paris* (November 1953), pp. 84–5.

government. They also exploited the undeniable fact that the assemblies would be dependent on the king's agent in the province, the *intendant* (13 and 28). Naturally they omitted to say that if the assemblies were dominated by the nobility and independent of the *intendant* then their assessment of the land tax would be rigged.

Faced with this opposition, the king and his minister – document 25 would suggest that the initiative was Louis XVI's personally – adopted the audacious course of trying to bring public pressure to bear on the Assembly. They caused a pamphlet, the *Avertissement* (24), outlining the king's beneficent intentions, to be distributed widely throughout the country and read out from all the Paris pulpits on Palm Sunday, 1 April 1787. The *Avertissement* failed to stir the people whilst its half bullying, half ironic tone made Calonne desperate with the Notables who now resolved not only to emasculate his projects but to bring about his fall. In this they were aided by Calonne's own ministerial colleagues – Castries (23 and 25) and Miromesnil (26) expressed themselves to the king in decided language. The identity of views between these ministers and the Notables is striking and inevitable, bearing in mind their backgrounds (11).

Louis XVI put up a desperate resistance to pressure from all sides to dismiss Calonne, even momentarily agreeing, on 5 April, to the latter's request to dismiss Miromesnil (who was replaced by Calonne's nominee Lamoignon)[3] and Breteuil and appoint a united ministry of Calonne's choosing – a landmark in the history of the monarchy brought about by the presence of an Assembly which was assuming the characteristics of an English parliament. However, minutes later, Louis finally succumbed and Calonne followed Miromesnil into the wilderness, Breteuil remaining in the ministry (27b). This was another constitutional landmark because it was the first time for over a hundred years that a king of France had been forced – and forced by a national assembly – to dismiss a minister against his will.

Moreover, the man who had been acting as a 'leader of the opposition' in the Assembly, Loménie de Brienne, archbishop of Toulouse,[4] now started to negotiate his entry into the ministry with the king on the basis of an agreed series of modifications to Calonne's proposals which he hoped the Assembly would endorse (22). Louis makes devastating written criticisms of Brienne's proposals (22 and 23), is able to salvage little of the original plan, and yet is obliged to appoint Brienne to lead the ministry on 1 May. The dismissal by the king of a man in whom he had confidence and the appointment of a man in whom he did not obviously stretched the constitutional conventions of a theoretically absolute monarchy to the limit, and it became necessary not only to make the king say that Calonne had lost his confidence but to make him lose it in fact. This is the main point that emerges from the letters of Brienne to Calonne (32) and Calonne to d'Angiviller (33) which deal with Brienne's attempts to accuse Calonne of financial

---

3 Chrétien de Lamoignon, 1735–89, keeper of the seals, 1787–8.
4 Etienne Charles de Loménie de Brienne, 1727–94, archbishop of Toulouse 1765, *chef du conseil royal des finances* 1 May 1787, *ministre principal* 27 August 1787, archbishop of Sens (better paid than Toulouse) 1788, made cardinal on resignation from the ministry but deprived of his hat by the Pope for accepting the Civil Constitution of the Clergy in 1791.

malpractice. These events naturally wrought a profound change in Louis XVI and from this period his hunting and eating increased and he had periods of depressive apathy. Also Marie-Antoinette, whom Louis had hitherto rigidly excluded from affairs, started to play a greater role in government, both to supplement the king's inactivity and to support Brienne, who was her protégé.

Unfortunately Brienne was unable to persuade the Notables to endorse fully the modified proposals, even though they were largely based on their criticisms. Their equivocal attitude is summed up by Castries in document **30**. Finally the Assembly was closed on 25 May.

The resistance of the Notables was the first phase in the 'revolt of the nobility', who by strengthening their position – at the expense of the king – made it impossible for the Third Estate to dislodge them without the unprecedented force of revolution. Although the Third Estate had not responded to the king's appeal, they remembered it and expected him to fulfil his promises when he was in a position to do so. For his part, the failure of the Assembly of Notables threw the king back on his narrow dialogue with the *parlements*, but with this difference: the king's attempt to circumvent them created in the minds of the *parlementaires* a condition of doubt about their political future that was shortly to lead them to demand the convocation of the Estates-General, even though that body was bound to eclipse them and did in fact abolish them (**98**).

12   A survey of the programme of reforms: Calonne's speech at the opening of the Assembly of Notables, 22 February 1787

The programme underwent modification during a six-month period of gestation, but the final version, together with the memoranda on provincial assemblies and the land tax, is presented first, for ease of comprehension.

Gentlemen, I am all the more honoured at this moment because the measures of which His Majesty has ordered me to present you with a summary have become entirely his own through the extremely close scrutiny His Majesty has brought to bear on each before adopting it.

[After considering the flourishing state of France, Calonne reveals that for centuries there has existed an underlying deficit in the royal finances which stood at 80 million francs a year when he took office in 1783. He rejects more loans, a higher rate of taxation or economies as insufficient, by themselves, to cover this deficit and continues:] What then remains . . . in order to restore the state of the finances?

Abuses

Yes, gentlemen, abuses themselves constitute a source of wealth which the state has a right to exploit . . . They are defended by self-interest, influence, wealth and ancient prejudices which seem to be hallowed by time; but what are all these together compared with the common good and the necessity of the state?

Such are the abuses which oppress the wealth-producing, labouring class: the abuses of pecuniary privilege, exceptions to the general rule, and so many unjust exemptions which can only relieve one section of taxpayers by aggravating the condition of the others. . . .

The projects which the king intends to impart to you . . . are neither doctrinaire nor novelties. They represent a summary of . . . the plans for the public weal long meditated by the most consummate statesmen and often held out in perspective by the government itself. Some have been attempted in part and all seem to have the backing of the nation but hitherto their complete implementation appeared impracticable because of the difficulty of reconciling a host of local customs, claims, privileges and conflicting interests. [This is now possible because the territory of the kingdom has reached its natural frontiers and there is stability at home and abroad.]

To this end, His Majesty has first of all considered the various forms of administration which occur in those provinces without [local] Estates. In order that the distribution of taxation may cease to be unequal and arbitrary, he has decided to confide the task to the landowners themselves and he has derived from the first principles of the monarchy the general plan of a graduated series of deliberative assemblies whereby the expression of the taxpayers' wishes and their observations on everything which concerns them will be transmitted from parish to district assemblies, thence to provincial assemblies and through them to the throne.

Next His Majesty brought all his personal attention to bear on establishing the same principle of uniformity . . . in the distribution of the land tax . . . he recognized that . . . the *vingtièmes*, instead of being assessed as they should be on all the land in his kingdom in true proportion to the value of the crop, suffer an infinity of exceptions which are tolerated rather than regarded as legitimate . . . that the results of this general tax, instead of providing the government with vital information about the produce of the kingdom and the relative wealth of each province, serve only to demonstrate the offensive inequality between their various contributions. . . .

His Majesty has judged that the way of remedying these defects simply by the application of the rules of a strictly distributive justice, of restoring the original intentions behind the tax, of raising it to its true value without increasing anyone's contribution (indeed granting some relief to the people), and of making every kind of privilege incompatible with its mode of collection, would be to replace the *vingtièmes* with a general land tax which, covering the whole area of the kingdom, would consist of a proportion of all produce, payable in kind where feasible, otherwise in money, and admitting of no exception, even as regards his crown lands, nor of any other distinctions other than those resulting from the varying fertility of the soil and the varying harvests.

The church lands would necessarily be included in this general assessment which, to be fair, must include all land as does the protection for which it is the price. But in order that these lands should not be overburdened by continuing to pay the *décimes* which are collected to fund the debt of the clergy, the king, sovereign protector of the churches of his kingdom, has decided to provide for the repayment of this debt by granting the clergy the necessary authorization to make the repayment [by selling off feudal rights, etc.]. . . .

Complete freedom of the grain trade . . . with the one exception of deferring to the wishes of the provinces when any of them think it necessary temporarily to suspend export abroad. . . .

The abolition of the *corvée* [forced labour on the public highways] as performed in person and the conversion of this excessively harsh exaction to a monetary contribution distributed more justly and spent in such a way that it can never be diverted to other purposes.

Internal free trade, customs houses removed to the frontiers, the establishment of a uniform tariff taking the needs of commerce into consideration, the suppression of several taxes which are harmful to industry or lead too easily to harassment and the alleviation of the burden of the *gabelle* [the obligation to purchase so much salt from the state] (which I have never mentioned to His Majesty without his being deeply grieved that he cannot rid his subjects of it altogether).

These, gentlemen, are so many salutary measures which enter into the plan upon which His Majesty will enlarge and which all conform to the principles of order and uniformity which are its basis.

Archives Parlementaires (AP), vol. I,
pp. 189–98.

13 Memorandum on the establishment of provincial assemblies, presented to the Notables on 23 February 1787

Necker (finance minister, 1776–81) had instituted experimental provincial administrations, but these had had several defects:

First, being composed of members originally nominated by the king – with the power to co-opt their colleagues and successors, they offered all the problems of the usurpations to be feared from permanent bodies [e.g. the *parlements*] without possessing the advantage which could be expected of them, namely that of representing all the landowners of the province and of inspiring all the confidence they would have received if they had been freely elected by their fellow citizens.

Second, it seems equally to contradict the whole purpose of these institutions that their president should be permanently appointed and always taken from the same order of society [the clergy]. The hope of being able to reach the highest office no matter what one's social condition stimulates the desire to be worthy of the ambition. . . .

Third, it is contrary to the principles of the government that bodies designed merely to inform it by their observations and determine the distribution of taxation should have any executive or judicial authority. . . .

To rectify all these defects and more perfectly fulfil His Majesty's aim, he has seen fit to institute, in all the provinces of his kingdom where the Estates are not convoked, assemblies which will always be elective, will be renewed every three years, will not have the title of 'administration', will, without being too large, represent all the landowners, be composed of members taken from all social conditions without distinction, and which will, finally, not have any pretext to arrogate any portion of executive authority. . . .

AP, vol. I, pp. 201–2

14   Memorandum on the land tax

. . . The most glaring anomalies manage to vitiate the tax system. . . .

There are towns which have bought exemption, those which have settled for a lump sum; some provinces have their taxes farmed out, others collect them through their own Estates and others have bought exemption.

One cannot take a step in this vast kingdom without encountering different laws, conflicting customs, privileges, exemptions . . . rights and claims of all kinds: and this dissonance, worthy of the barbarian centuries or those of anarchy, complicates administration, clogs its wheels . . . and everywhere multiplies expense and disorder.

. . . His Majesty therefore proposes:

1 To suppress the two *vingtièmes* and the four *sous pour livre* as from 1 January of this year. In future they will no longer be collected except on goods not susceptible to a tax in kind, as enumerated in the edict of May 1749.
2 As it is unjust that land devoted to pleasure should be more favourably treated than that employed in useful cultivation, chateaux, parkland, closes, houses and all kinds of land shall be subject to the tax but only in respect of the surface area they occupy; they will be assessed at the rate of the best land in the parish.
3 A proportion of the crop will be levied in kind on all cropbearing land no matter who owns it and whatever their order and position. But as all land is not of equal value, the various qualities of land will be

differentiated. On the best land, a twentieth of the crop will be levied; on the next category, a twenty-fifth; on the next, a thirtieth; and on lands of the worst quality, a fortieth.

4 The classification of these different qualities of land will be made by the parish assemblies, using as a basis the price of leases. They will put in the first category land leased at more than 20 francs an *arpent* [roughly an acre]; in the second, those leased at between 10 and 20 francs; in the third, those leased at between 5 and 10 francs; and in the fourth those leased at less than 5 francs.

5 Finally, acting in the same spirit of justice which prompts him to suppress all exceptions to a tax owed by the land itself, the king is resolved to exempt the first orders of his state (whom His Majesty wishes to maintain in the distinctions they merit) from all personal taxes; and, indeed, to enable them to enjoy this the more completely, he desires that in future the *capitation*, whose nature and title seem incompatible with their status, shall no longer apply to the nobility, the magistrature and the clergy of the frontier provinces who pay it at the moment; nor in general to all the clergy of France which has bought exemption and may not in any circumstances be troubled concerning this matter.[5]

AP, vol. I, pp. 204–5

15   Mirabeau[6] to Calonne, Paris, 13 June 1786

The first in a series of letters from Mirabeau to Calonne in which Mirabeau seeks preferment from the minister and also shows that he shares Calonne's conception of the monarchy, rejecting privilege as impeding the power of the state. This is borne out by his subsequent career (see 57 and 96).

. . . When can I come to see you, Monsieur, to show you an . . . important study concerning the great and truly sublime matter which you have pondered with such genius and patriotism? It is absolutely necessary that we read it together so that you can show me all the changes and additions to make. . . . This institution . . . will be the most firm rampart of royal authority, likewise the most abundant source of credit and the unshakable foundation of national prosperity. . . .

Public Record Office, PC 1/125.48

---

5 This concession was declined by the privileged orders.
6 Honoré Gabriel Riquetti, comte de Mirabeau, 1749–91. Writer of many books and pamphlets before the Revolution, orator in the National Assembly, and above all ministerial aspirant.

16 Memorandum from Calonne to the king, late August 1786, entitled 'Observations on the difference between Estates-General and Assemblies of Notables'

An Assembly of Notables, such as was held in 1558, 1583, 1596, 1617 and 1626, ought not to be confused with a meeting of the Estates-General. They are essentially different in every respect.

In the first place members of the Estates-General were not chosen by the king but by each of the three orders who chose their deputies, whereas with Assemblies of Notables the king individually summons those whom he sees fit . . .

Secondly, the difference is even more marked and appreciable when it comes to the purpose of the two kinds of assembly and subject matter of their deliberations. With Estates-General the three orders presented the sovereign with *cahiers* containing their complaints and grievances concerning all the matters they thought they should examine and they deliberated both on what they thought best for the reform of abuses and the good of the state and on the requests which had been made of them in the name of His Majesty.

With Assemblies of Notables it is the king himself who decides the matters on which he permits discussion: discussion only bears on points that he has raised. His Majesty is not looking for national consent for the raising of any taxes; he is merely expressing, in the most solemn manner, the desire to concentrate all the light which can be brought to bear on the execution of his aims.

. . . For the rest, Assemblies of Notables, without being the occasion of great expense and a fecund source of difficulties, as are Estates-General, share their advantage of sparing the government the protests of the sovereign courts and of depriving them of the pretext for treating everything which does not meet with their immediate approval as surprises against the king's religion.[7] In this respect they would be desirable today even if they were not necessary.

AN, K163 no. 103

17 Memorandum from Calonne to the king, November 1786, entitled 'Objections and replies'

The *Avertissement* is foreshadowed by Calonne's evident intention to mobilize public opinion and bring it to bear on opponents. He is acutely conscious

---

7 The French equivalent of the English concept of the king's being misled by evil advisers.

that the *parlements* have more hold on public opinion than does the government. The provincial assemblies are an attempt to remedy this.

The memorandum takes the form of imaginary objections to the proposals, together with Calonne's replies. No more eloquent exposition of the obstacles to reform is to be found than in the Tenth Reply.

Sixth Objection. Say what you will, it is impossible to balance revenue and expenditure without increasing the one and decreasing the other. Indeed it must be agreed that it is above all by increasing the revenue that balance can be achieved . . . accordingly one must expect complaints and confess that there will be grounds for complaints since it is recognized that the slightest addition to existing taxation would make its burden intolerable.

Sixth Reply. Doubtless there will and must be a great, a very great increase in revenue to cover the present deficit; but this will be produced by means . . . which will not aggravate the burden of the least affluent. . . . If, therefore, any vain complaints arise they can only come from a part of the privileged categories shameless enough to oppose its sectional interests to the general interest and to complain of contributing to the common purse in proportion to its possessions. But, as we have already observed, their voice will be drowned by the general voice which must necessarily prevail, especially when, by the establishment of the assemblies, which in the same proposals are to be set up at district and provincial level, the government acquires the help of that national interest which at present is without effect but which, properly directed, is capable of smoothing over all difficulties.

Tenth Objection. Why can all these proposals not be effected without employing the unwonted apparatus of an Assembly of Notables, the use of which has been abandoned for so long that it would perhaps be dangerous to revive?

Tenth Reply. The eradication of inveterate abuses, the suppression of unjust abuses, altering what the Estates-General of the kingdom have prescribed for reasons which no longer exist and winning the confidence of the nation . . . all this and the new order which will result together constitute an operation so vast, so elevated and so exceptional that it is indispensable to employ proportionately impressive and majestic forms. Are we going to deliver over such high interests to *parlementaire* debates, to the clash of sectional rivalries, to delays which are unseemly in such matters? We must silence the pretensions of the clergy, forestall the complaints of the nobility, ensure the swiftest registration [by the *parlements*], counter-balance the protests of a few provinces by the satisfaction of the majority and register the national interest in order to oppose it to all the sectional interests. This can only be done surely and effectively by a solemn assembly in which the sovereign authority, having deigned to buttress itself with the counsel of the persons most worthy to enlighten their king and to represent his nation, will make known its wishes in so majestic a manner that it will be impossible to think that they will ever be susceptible to any change. . . .

AN, K164 no. 4

18 Memorandum from Calonne to the king, December 1786, entitled 'Ideas submitted for the king's decision concerning the necessity, timetable, composition and form of the Assembly of Notables'

With the composition of the Assembly, Calonne's dilemma is that he does not want it to seem merely a puppet body and yet the vested interests of the members prescribed by tradition makes opposition likely. Moreover only a handful of the provincial mayors summoned actually turn out to be members of the Third Estate whilst the 'liberal' court nobility is less liberal than Calonne envisages and even more dominated in debate by the *parlementaires* and the clergy.

Timetable

It is possible and necessary that the Assembly open on 24 January. . . . The slightest delay would wreck the whole plan and render its execution impossible for next year, perhaps even for ever.

His Majesty will be convinced of this if he deigns to consider that the collection of the tax in kind, which is the first and foremost of the operations proposed, requires invitations for tenders in all the parishes of the kingdom.[8] They must be allocated at the beginning of April in order to be sufficiently ahead of every kind of harvest and must be preceded by posters and announcements on three consecutive Sundays – a process which must therefore begin towards the middle of March. The natural timespan of the Assembly of Notables, assuming its session to be uninterrupted, plus time for sending the edicts to all the courts (immediately after the closing of the Assembly), and for their registration,[9] will occupy more than six weeks. Thus from 24 January to the middle of March there would only be exactly the time necessary to complete this great matter, and there is not a moment to lose or we shall fall into the most appalling difficulties which would be such that there is no foreseeable remedy. That is why I so strongly urge 24 January and a prompt dispatch of the letters [of convocation].

---

8 The idea was to sell the king's share of the crop on the spot, not to transport it bodily to Paris.
9 Elsewhere Calonne makes it clear that this was to be by *lit de justice*.

Composition

As it is customary to summon the first presidents and procurators-general of the sovereign courts, and as there are at present 13 *parlements* and two *conseils supérieurs* which, including as always the *chambre des comptes* and the *cour des aides* of Paris, brings the total of sovereign courts to 17, the sovereign courts will provide the Assembly with 34 members, or even with 36 or 37 if, as seems natural, we maintain the Parlement of Paris in its prerogative of having two or three more than the others.

This number of magistrates from the courts, which must be counter-balanced in the Assembly, seems to require that the Assembly be larger than those held in periods when there were fewer *parlements*. It would not be right that those who already have the advantage of being versed in public affairs should also have that of greater numbers.

Moreover, it is impossible to believe that they will be entirely contented with such an assembly and as, from another point of view, the clergy must also find in it a source of complaint, it seems necessary that the members drawn from the nobility or the Third Estate should be in sufficient numbers for the king's proposals to find more supporters than opponents.

AN, K677 no. 102

19   Miromesnil to the king, 28 December 1786

The most striking thing about this letter is that its sentiments are diametrically opposed to Calonne's. First, compare the active role Miromesnil envisages for the Notables with the passive one attributed to it by Calonne (**16**). Second, compare no. 1 of the matters which Miromesnil considers have been treated 'superficially' with Calonne's famous indictment of the status quo at the beginning of   document **14**. The two ministers are clearly conducting a dialogue of the deaf. Miromesnil's point no. 2 raises the question of whether Calonne had (unsuccessfully) proposed some form of dissolution of the monasteries. Miromesnil had been in a minority of one in the ministerial committee: that is why he asks for the secretaries of state to be included – they all support his views.

I very humbly beseech Your Majesty to permit me to submit to his wisdom a few observations I was going to make yesterday in the committee but that I could not develop without causing dissensions which, out of respect, should be avoided in the presence of Your Majesty. . . . I was going to beseech Your Majesty to decide upon the character he wished to give to the Assembly he intends to convoke, that is to say whether he intends to convoke this Assembly merely in order to convey his decisions, without permitting. any representations, or whether he intends to consult it and consequently allow it to make very humble representations concerning the different matters you would present to it. In the first case, the utility of the Assembly will not be great. In the second, it is necessary to foresee the various objections which could be raised in order to be prepared to parry them and to resolve the problems. Then the Assembly could be useful. If Your Majesty's intention is such that I presume it to be, with my knowledge of your justice and kindness, you must have in front of you, before the opening of the Assembly, a complete plan of the operation you are meditating in your wisdom.

1 The method to be employed for raising the land tax throughout your states. The difficulties it may encounter when applied to Brittany and Languedoc, bearing in mind that you have just allowed these two provinces to settle for a lump sum payment [abonnement]. The measures to be taken in respect of Burgundy and Navarre and the little Estates of the provinces adjoining Navarre . . . such as Bigorre, Provence, which has its own individual regime, Flanders, Artois, the Cambrésis, in short all those of your provinces which have Estates or their equivalent, etc. All these highly important matters have been treated only very superficially in our discussions and in the committees where Your Majesty has graciously listened to us. . . .

2 The matter of the debt of the clergy and the dues owed to the church lands demands close scrutiny. I shall not repeat what I took the liberty of telling you yesterday but I doubt whether Your Majesty is inclined to apply to France the principles of government of a power [Austria?] which is certainly very respectable but whose territories [états] bear no resemblance to your kingdom. . . .

5 The matter of the abolition of the gabelle is very desirable, but exceeds my competence. I can only refer to the calculations of the controller-general. I hope they have not been arrived at without due consideration and I trust that this is the case.

6 The organization of the provincial assemblies is likewise beyond my ken. It strikes me as a little complicated and I fear difficulties in the application.

7 Drafting the various laws which you will be promulgating will require close attention. They must be clear and precise, easy to understand and to implement. It is difficult, I would even say impossible, that three people should be sufficient for the task. It will therefore be necessary for you to second some members of the council to us for drafting these laws. Finally, I think it would be characteristic of your wisdom to include the secretaries of state also in the discussions which seem to me indispensable in an operation important alike for your repute and for the welfare of the state.

AN, K163 no. 8.22

20   Miromesnil to the king, 1 February 1787

I have the honour of placing before Your Majesty the bulletin of yesterday's proceedings in the Parlement.

I enclose a private letter from the first president which seems to confirm what I had learned from another source and reported to Your Majesty concerning the intrigue on foot to get the Parlement to give a mandate to the first president and the other magistrates summoned to the Assembly of Notables.

AN, K163 no. 8.26

21   Calonne to the king, undated but *c.* 26 February 1787

Meeting instant and outright opposition to his land tax, Calonne attempted to hold the line by the *supplément d'instruction* which placed the following principles beyond discussion: 'The tax which is to replace the *vingtièmes* must be applied to all land without exception; it must be exactly proportionate with the harvest and vary with it.' The *supplément* was read out to each of the Assembly's seven working committees on 28 February by their chairmen, the princes of the blood. It had little effect.

I have learned much more than I knew when I had the honour of seeing Your Majesty last night. I can now no longer doubt that the clergy and all the disaffected deputies think that the land tax is sure to be rejected unanimously. They are wrong but it is greatly to be feared that they have carried the vast majority with them: all the princes believe so, as do the members of the council, and need to be enlightened. It seems that Your Majesty's views on the matter under discussion [the land tax] should be made known in order to prevent this move which, quite typically, has been decided on even before the examination [of the memorandum]. I have said all this to the princes, but they want the instructions in writing and approved by Your Majesty in person.

Consequently I have already drafted a *supplément d'instruction* in accordance with what Your Majesty has already indicated. I entreat Your Majesty to read it, sign it with his approval and authorize me to give a copy to each prince. I have these copies, to the number of seven, ready and waiting and I only need Your Majesty's order for them to be read out at the start of each committee. The point is of capital importance; otherwise, by an inconceivable stroke of mischance, the Assembly might suddenly adopt a course of action which would enrage the people and dishonour it in the sight of all Europe. If Your Majesty will allow me to give him a more detailed verbal report, I beg him to let me know.

AN, 297 AP 3.65

22 Extracts from the debates of the second committee of the Assembly of Notables, that chaired by the king's second brother, the comte d'Artois[10]

(a) On provincial assemblies

At the place [in the memorandum] where mention is made of the disadvantages of always reserving the chair to people of the same social order, the archbishop of Toulouse said: 'There are really only two orders in France, the people and the nobility; the latter embraces the clergy and the magistracy . . . equality is fine in republics such as at Philadelphia; it can also work under a despotism, such as that at Constantinople [but not in France]. . . . The great families are at once the support of the people and the bulwark of the monarchy. In France, the presidency of all national assemblies should be reserved for the superior order. They would not take part in assemblies if they risked being presided over or merely giving precedence to citizens of a lower order, and then the assemblies would become riotous.'

Le Blanc de Castillon [procurator-general of the Parlement of Provence] approved the sentiments of the archbishop of Toulouse and said: 'The people should be separated from the upper orders by the reservation of dignity and power to the latter. The proposed plan has two defects: that of having exaggerated the popular element in the parish assemblies; and that of giving the *intendant* too great an authority in the provincial assemblies: republicanism and despotism.'

(b) On the land tax

Le Blanc de Castillon: The king does not have the competence to institute a percentage tax but only to ask for a fixed sum to meet specific requirements. Such a tax could not be accepted by the *parlements*, who possess only a subsidiary and fiduciary power in the absence of the Estates-General. Accordingly, only the Estates-General could give the necessary consent to such a tax. An Assembly of Notables which gave its blessing to the institution of such a tax would be exceeding its powers and would be dishonoured in the eyes of the nation.

Angran d'Allerai [lieutenant-civil of the Chatelet]: [A *permanent* tax should not be payable by everyone] . . . *Roturiers* have the resources of the crafts, labour and commerce of which the gentleman and the cleric cannot avail himself. It would not be just that whilst the nobleman fights, the magistrate judges, the minister governs, and the priest celebrates divine office, there should not be reserved to him some privilege.

---

10 Charles Philippe, comte d'Artois, 1757–1836, later Charles X of France, 1820–30. Supports Calonne's radical reforms but later becomes the soul of the counter-revolution.

The superior orders would really be troubled by equality. The intention is to create a bastard republic within the monarchy and my sworn loyalty to the constitution compels me to oppose this. . . .

There should be no permanent tax without privileges, though I agree that it is just that for a temporary tax none should be claimed. Louis XIV did not think he had the right to establish the *dixième* and it was only the theologians who persuaded him that since he could dispose of the lives of his subjects, *a fortiori* he could dispose of their property.

A percentage tax infringes the rights of property. . . . The proprietor, having paid what he owes for the needs of the state, must always preserve the right to use and abuse, *uti et abuti*, the rest. [Otherwise, a man could be accused, by extension, of making inefficient use of his property.]

Bibliothèque de l'Arsenal, Ms. 3978,
fos. 39–40, 243, 420–4

23 Conversation between the king and Castries, 28 February 1787

Castries: All the orders of the state summoned to hear the projects of your controller-general are, unanimously, going to bring their disapproval to the foot of the throne; all privileges . . . [will be] overturned . . . ruin and disorder [brought] to every part of your kingdom . . .

Does Your Majesty want to constrain the *parlements*? If so, he must destroy them. Does he want to arm a hundred thousand men, does he want to leave a stain on his reputation? Your monarchy is absolute but not despotic.

Louis: Ha! You know perfectly well that I do not intend to govern like a despot but I disagree with you and I have thought about it a lot: the land tax is the most just and the least onerous of taxes.

Castries: Perhaps in the state of nature you would be right. But so many agreements, rights, even abuses have arisen that what would have been justice would not be so today. The collection of a tax in kind would be impossible and would cost a quarter of its yield.

Louis: But I assure you, you are absolutely wrong on all this.

'Journal du maréchal de Castries',
fos. 346–7

24 The *Avertissement*

[Having outlined the reforms]: What difficulties can weigh against such advantages? What possible grounds for alarm could there be?

People will pay more! Doubtless, but who? Only those who do not pay enough; they will pay what they owe as a fair proportion and no one will be wronged.

Privileges will be sacrificed! Yes, as justice demands and necessity requires; would it be better to load even more on to the non-privileged, the people? There will be loud squeals! That was to be expected: can one ever act for the general good without ruffling certain individual interests? Can one reform without protests?

But can one doubt that in the end every other consideration will yield to the voice of patriotism, to the recognition due to a sovereign who collaborates with his peoples on the best way of assuring stability ... to that sentiment of honour so strong in the Frenchman's breast?

Already the first orders of the state have agreed that the land tax should be applied to all lands without exception and in proportion to their yield.

Already they have offered to relinquish for the relief of the people certain personal exemptions [from the *capitation*] which the king had seen fit to grant them.

Already the walls of the Assembly have resounded with thanks for His Majesty's projects.

It would be wrong that reasonable doubts, that observations inspired by zeal, that the noble expressions of candour should give rise to the idea of a malevolent opposition. It would be doing the nation an injustice and showing it a lack of understanding to doubt for a moment the coincidence between its desires and those of a king whom it cherishes and whom it sees animated solely by the wish to make his people happy.

> *Collection des Mémoires presentés à l'Assemblée des Notables par M. de Calonne ... précedé d'un Avertissement* (1787)

25 Exchange between Castries and the king, 2 April 1787

Most remarkable in this altogether remarkable exchange is Castries' accusation – not denied – that Louis is putting Calonne up to it and has even prompted the *Avertissement*, parts of which he is thought to have written.

Castries: I do not know if Your Majesty knows what is going on, the way in which M. de Calonne's scandalous pamphlet [the *Avertissement*] has been distributed throughout Paris and the indignation it has caused?

Louis: Yes, I know: all that has been exaggerated.

Castries: How can one exaggerate seditiously distributing it to all the *curés* of Paris and disseminating it amongst all the people? Would Your Majesty not be alarmed to see his subjects worked up against each other? I must warn Your Majesty that things are going to become more and more difficult for him because of the increasing outcry against his controller-general.

Louis: All that is the work of intrigue.

Castries: But is it Your Majesty who is causing M. de Calonne to act so imprudently?

Louis: Ha! I have eight days.[11]

Castries: What we must provide for, sire, is the debt of the state.

Louis: That's true.

Castries: I much doubt that it can be done by the means M. de Calonne is employing.

'Journal du maréchal de Castries',
fo. 353

26   Miromesnil to the king, 4 April 1787

I most humbly beseech Your Majesty to permit me to submit to his wisdom certain reflections inspired by a considered reading of the observations of the committees [of the Assembly].

I confess, Your Majesty, that I have seen nothing indicative of a spirit of automatic resistance to every proposal. Allow me, Sire, to give you an account of what I noted on each topic.

The first is the creation of provincial assemblies. All the committees appear unanimously to want these assemblies but in truth in a form different from that proposed. They ask that the precedence accorded to the clergy and nobility from time immemorial be maintained.

The second matter is the land tax payable in kind. I note that they are all agreed on one essential point: that all the orders of the state, all your subjects of whatever condition, are liable to the tax in question in proportion to their property. But they invoke your justice in favour of the *pays d'état* [provinces with local Estates] whose customs you have confirmed, as did the kings your ancestors, and with whom you have just concluded new agreements. They invoke your kindness in beseeching you to respect the forms . . . established for the various *corps* and provinces of your kingdom, in so far as these forms and usages do not conflict with your desire that each man, of whatever order, should pay in proportion to his property. . . .

They fear that the deficit in your revenues has not been sufficiently demonstrated. This observation ought not to displease Your Majesty since

11 Louis XVI never gave a straight answer to a straight question. Here the reference is to the Easter recess when Calonne attempted to win over the provincial mayors in the Notables, wining and dining them at a great rate.

frankness, when you are gracious enough to consult them, is an act of obedience which they owe you. . . .

AN, K163 no. 8.30

27(a)   Miromesnil to the king, 5 April 1787

In 1781 the minister Necker had published his celebrated and fraudulent *còmpte rendu au roi* which suggested that in a 'typical' year royal revenue exceeded expenditure by some 10 million francs. Joly de Fleury succeeded him in May 1781. He established that Necker's figures were wrong and that there was a deficit of about 50 million and told the king [letter of July, BN, *fonds* Joly de Fleury, naf, 1438, fo. 217]. To justify his demands for increased taxation Calonne had, implicitly, to challenge the *compte rendu* which antagonized Necker's following in the Notables – a 'powerful and fanatical sect', as Calonne calls it in document **33**. Miromesnil and Joly de Fleury maliciously and dishonestly seek to envenom this conflict and to undermine the king's confidence in Calonne. The peroration of this, Miromesnil's last letter to the king, is accurate in depicting Calonne – and indeed the king – as being in opposition to the entire political world.

On reaching Paris, where I found my daughter's condition so alarming that I have little hope of keeping her, there was a letter waiting for me from M. Joly de Fleury which I think I should send to Your Majesty.

M. de Fleury maintains that he greatly doubts whether there was a deficit when you entrusted him with the administration of the finances; and he has just informed M. de Calonne of this. He maintains that the loans he raised could not have caused a deficit because of the increase in your revenues produced by the third *vingtième* and the two *sols pour livre*.

I confess that this circumstance struck me and that M. de Calonne should not fear enlightenment from any quarter. . . . Would it not be possible for Your Majesty to charge some experienced and scrupulously honest members of his council, together with the two keepers of the royal treasury and the senior officials in the finance department, with an examination of all the statements which the controller-general showed you and had you show the late M. de Vergennes and myself but which we were not as competent to check as the two keepers of the royal treasury would have been?

I confess to you, Sire, that I fear – particularly after all that has happened in the last eight days and after my conversation of Monday evening with M. de Calonne, of which I have already apprised Your Majesty – he wants you to dismiss the Assembly without concluding anything. . . . I see that he is seeking to turn you against the bishops, against the nobles, against your ministers. He is making a kind of appeal to the people which may have dangerous consequences. Finally I draw alarming conclusions for your happiness and the rest of your reign.

I throw myself at your feet and beg of you, Sire, not to blame me for these promptings of my heart. It is totally devoted to you, to your *gloire*, to the prosperity of your state.

AN, K163 no. 8.32

27(b)   Miromesnil's dismissal

The same day that this letter was written, Miromesnil was dismissed by Louis XVI; so also was Breteuil, a fact we learn from Lenoir who was to have replaced him as minister for the *maison du roi*:

This minister [Breteuil] was momentarily dismissed in 1787: M. de Montmorin was ordered to go and ask him for his resignation as well as M. de Miromesnil, but the queen had the order concerning M. de Breteuil revoked.

Bibliothèque municipale d'Orléans,
Lenoir papers, Ms 1423, *Mélanges*,
39

28   Memorandum of Loménie de Brienne, 17 April, together with the marginal annotations of Louis XVI

The incisiveness of Louis's remarks is noteworthy – particularly his lucid exposition of the theory behind the land tax and his devastating criticism of Brienne's woefully optimistic and naive assumptions (e.g. about economies and, especially, interest rates). On the basis of these comments alone, a reassessment of Louis's ability is necessary.

Brienne's text: This Assembly was convoked in the belief that its endorsement would overcome all foreseeable obstacles.

Louis's comments: Yes.

Text: The absence of such endorsement would have roughly the same effect as straight opposition. If, on the other hand, it supported the plans that the government adopts it is permissible to believe that the *parlements*, the individual Estates and the provincial assemblies will accept them almost unchallenged.

Comments: That was the idea. Your inclusion of the provincial assemblies under this heading is out of place. First, they have not yet been created. Secondly, when they have been they will only be empowered to supervise the execution of what has already been decided and to apportion taxation fairly; but they will not even possess the power of simulated consent belonging to the other provinces.

Text: . . . The Assembly may have rejected the means proposed but it has always applauded the king's objectives.

Comments: I have never doubted the Assembly's zeal for the central objective which is to bridge the deficit in the way least onerous to the people.

Text: The king has established that the deficit is 113 million francs, of which 10 [million] are for unforeseen expenditure.

He has proposed, in order to bridge this deficit:

1 Economies to the tune of 20 million.
2 An addition of 50 million to the land tax.
3 A stamp duty of 20 million.
4 An annual delay of 25 million in debt repayment.

Comments: The addition [to the land tax] has correctly been put at 50 million altogether, but only the tax on parklands and other pleasure lands is new: the rest must come from those who do not pay a fair amount. Thus if 50 million were found to exceed present requirements, it would not be on these new 50 million that the reduction would be made but on the total amount of 100 million – which will happen in any case when the second *vingtième* expires [in 1790]. . . . Suppose 60 or 80 million would suffice instead of 100, one could perhaps ask [the Notables] to concentrate on establishing the means for a fair distribution of taxation on a given base which would be raised or lowered in proportion to recognized requirements. Once this base was established, it would serve for ever, whether we were removing taxes or whether we were forced by a war to impose new ones.

Text: Economies are indispensable. They are dependent on the king, the Assembly can only ask for them. . . .

[Brienne doubts whether 70 million of extra taxation is 'absolutely necessary'; money could be saved by cheaper methods of tax collection; in addition:] if the crown, by putting itself in such a position that it no longer needed to borrow money or could borrow at a more favourable rate of interest, managed to service the debt more cheaply and successively diminished the rate of interest, then I wager that 50 or 35 or 40 million at most would suffice to cover the deficit.

. . . The king must communicate to the Assembly both the statements [of revenue and expenditure] and his plans, and induce it to adopt or at least to accept them.

It is obvious that these proposals cannot be the same as those which have been presented to the Assembly.

Comments: He will do all that is in his power but there are several economies which can only be implemented successively and all told we will be lucky to save as much as 20 million without running down the army and the navy.

Naturally the king is far from desiring such a burden of taxation if it is not necessary; on the contrary he would be delighted to lower existing taxation: remember what is said at the beginning of the memorandum about palliatives being worse than the disease.

... It is hard to believe that these various economies together would reach 30 million – it would be far less. Of course there is a substantial saving in reducing the rate of interest, but that can only be done when your credit is good and when you have enough money to dictate terms to the purchasers of stock.

I need more information here and an indication of the way in which the statements and projects should be communicated to the Assembly so that the life of the Assembly may not be unduly protracted and success may be assured.

... As regards the provincial assemblies, the clergy and nobility will be reserved the right to preside and it will be easy to arrange the other points whilst preserving for the *intendant* the right of control and supervision. This hope may be held out to them.

> *Journal de l'Assemblée des Notables de 1787 par le comte de Brienne et Etienne Charles de Loménie de Brienne, archevêque de Toulouse*, ed. P. Chevallier (1960), pp. 79–83

29   Further thoughts of Louis XVI: extract from Brienne's diary, 21 April

This morning the following note in the king's handwriting was handed to me for my perusal and comments (before this evening's [ministerial] committee if possible).

... It is hard to believe that 72 million from the *vingtièmes* will suffice; we might perhaps make do with 80. The Assembly will see from the statements the approximate size of the tax needed.

We must allow another eight million which will be necessary to service the debt this year as the new taxes cannot be raised in time; but this under the seal of secrecy.

The tax will be for a fixed amount; it will be apportioned by province for the first year in the same proportion as for the *vingtièmes*; it will be for the provincial assemblies to restore equality if there are initial errors. ...

What we could perhaps allow the clergy would be to pay the total of its taxation into the hands of its treasurer who would then hand it over directly to the royal treasury, though this would perhaps involve additional expenditure. But in any case it is essential that the assessment of the church lands, as of the other landed proprietors, should be carried out in the provincial assemblies.

The statements will be communicated to the Assembly of Notables. They will see the various items of revenue and expenditure for several years and for a typical year and consequently the balance between revenue and expenditure. But they cannot enter into the details of the various sections. That does not lie within their competence and would lead to interminable debates. . . .

A final session to collate the opinions of the committees would certainly be highly desirable and would lend great weight to the proceedings. But are you sure it would succeed? You could explore the ground.

Journal de l'Assemblée des Notables de 1787, pp. 89–90

30 Entry in Castries' diary for 20 May 1787

The committees have enveloped their half acceptance of the tax in so many words that those who refuse and those who consent are indistinguishable. Their opinion must be extracted from 50 pages of print.

'Journal du maréchal de Castries', fo. 368

31 From the section on provincial assemblies in Brienne's speech during the last session of the Assembly of Notables, 25 May 1787

This extract is given for its bearing on the heated question of voting in the Estates-General of 1789. Why did the method adopted for the provincial assemblies arouse controversy at the level of a national assembly?

The first two orders will have the presidency and the precedence which they have always enjoyed in national assemblies. . . .

Since one and the same interest ought to animate the three orders it might be thought that each should have an equal number of representatives. The first two have preferred to be merged together and consequently the Third Estate, being assured of comprising by itself as many votes as the clergy and nobility together, will never have to fear that any sectional interest will influence their votes. It is, moreover, right that this portion of His Majesty's subjects, so numerous, so important and so worthy of his protection should at least receive through the number of its votes compensation for the influence which riches, offices and birth necessarily impart.

In accordance with the same principles, the king will order that the votes will not be counted by order but by head. The opinion of a majority of orders does not always express that real majority which alone expresses the true feeling of an assembly. . . .

AP, vol. I, p. 233

32   Brienne to Calonne, Versailles, 17 June 1787

Monsieur, I showed the king the letter you took the trouble to write to me. His Majesty replied that he had already given his orders and that he did not wish to make any changes. You do me the justice of believing that I am well disposed towards you and far be it from me to disturb the repose you have planned for yourself. However, you cannot be ignorant of the fact that large sums of money have left the royal treasury without the king's authorization; you do not know what became of them and you should not be surprised by His Majesty's displeasure. It would have been wrong of me to conceal from him that which he should know about in the interest of his service; and, as there is no doubt here, I have not sought clarification from you.

If there had been only doubts, you will understand how eagerly I should have dispelled them and indeed the pleasure I would have experienced in so doing. . . .

                                                                    AN, 297 AP 3.112

33   Calonne to d'Angiviller, director-general of the king's buildings, late July 1787

Dear friend, you will understand how heart-rending it is to leave behind everything which is most precious to me in the world; but can I remain in this kingdom when I am publicly stripped of the insignia of the Order [of the Saint-Esprit] with which His Majesty invested me and when by this rigorous treatment, hitherto unprecedented, I seem to be regarded as a criminal? Can I remain when the archbishop of Toulouse, informing me himself of the king's displeasure as the direct result of his own reports, adds that I ought not to be surprised – without however saying of what he accuses me – and declines my offer of explanations, having, he says, no doubts? Finally can I remain when the press announces that every aspect of my administration is going to be investigated by a commission of the council and when at the same time I have every reason to suppose that I will be allowed no right of reply? My enemies must inculpate me in order to justify the deception they have practised on the king.

They know that the public has no difficulty in believing accusations, especially when levelled against ministers; they are counting on the resentment of the Parlement; they are certain to carry the finance committee: in M. d'Ormesson,[12] who has not been brought into this committee without design, they are sure of having a *rapporteur* who has thoroughly made up his mind against me in advance.

---

12 Calonne supplanted d'Ormesson as controller-general in November 1783 and placed two spies in his household.

... [The archbishop] talks vaguely about considerable sums leaving the royal treasury without authorization and he wants to make a crime out of something practised at all times[13] by employing sophistry capable of deceiving those who are ignorant of the administrative process. ...

How harsh it is, my friend, to be reduced to self-justification! Would you expect it after all that I have done, all that I have sacrificed? What if, in the midst of the vast operations which absorbed all my physical and mental faculties in the last period of my ministry, I let slip some measures which can be criticized as to form but not motive? What if I was too complaisant over matters of small consequence or too trusting towards people I was entitled to believe were honest? ...

May His Majesty also review all that has happened since the convocation of the Notables when my ruin was resolved and when unhappily opposition to everything I presented in the very name of His Majesty seemed to furnish an infallible means to this end! A combination of every kind of obstacle, a union of all the injured vested interests; the baleful preponderance of the clergy; the manoeuvres of a powerful and fanatical sect [Necker's followers]; the perfidy of my main collaborator [Miromesnil]; the best intentions denigrated; a war of hair-splitting; unseemly railing against the minister; the insinuation that his dismissal was the only way of terminating the affair and finally the false alarm instilled into the king by the incredible allegation that in eight days' time there would not be a sous left in the royal treasury.

What would he say today, that worthy and much-lamented friend [Vergennes] whose last and only too prophetic words I shall never forget? Would that he himself had been able to execute the commission he bequeathed me! He would have spoken better than I. Perhaps the plots which he had run to earth would not have materialized if he had lived; or, in any case, if the king had kept him he would not have been deprived of all the ministers who were truly loyal to him.

AN, 297 AP 3.19

---

13 i.e. the use of *acquits de comptant* by which secret expenditure was exempted from the normal accounting procedures. Calonne gave the money to agents such as the abbé d'Espagnac to prop up stock on the Bourse during the critical period when the Notables were assembled.

|4|

The edicts of 8 May 1788

Without the endorsement of the Notables, Brienne was left to get Calonne's modified proposals through the *parlements* as best he could. The legislation concerning the provincial assemblies limped through, but the land tax and the stamp duty were rejected, the *parlements* calling the king's bluff, declaring their own incompetence to approve taxation and demanding the Estates-General. The summer was consumed in these disputes, Brienne vainly trying to assert his authority by having himself declared 'principal minister' (**34**) and the Parlement exiled to Troyes (15 August–20 September). Finally a compromise was reached whereby the Parlement would be recalled, the new taxation abandoned and the Estates-General summoned before 1792. In return the Parlement would endorse a massive loan of 500 million francs, to be staggered over five years. The Parlement was to solemnize this arrangement on 19 November.

This session of the Parlement has come to be known as the *séance royale* because of the unusual procedure adopted. In a normal session, the *parlementaires* gave their opinions and then voted; in a *lit de justice* the king ordered registration without opinions or votes. On 19 November it seems that a free session was intended but that after the *parlementaires* had given their opinions (with the balance of the debate probably in favour of registration) the keeper of the seals, Lamoignon, whether panicking or stung by some of the speeches, whispered to the king to proceed to registration without counting the votes.

Not surprisingly the status of this hybrid session was the subject of acrimonious dispute. The king's cousin, the duc d'Orléans,[1] whom many were soon to accuse of aspiring to the throne, said that the session was a *lit de justice* – the kiss of death for a loan – and was exiled to his estates (**35**). The king himself told the Parlement (**36**) that a vote was only necessary in his absence, as being 'the only way of informing me of the result of your debates'. He added, significantly, that if he were bound by a majority vote

1 Louis Philippe, duc d'Orléans, 1747–93.

'the monarchy would no longer be anything but an aristocracy of magistrates' – the first use of the word 'aristocracy' in its pejorative, revolutionary sense.

That the *séance royale* was bungled was probably due to the fact that, at heart, both sides repented of the compromise. Certainly they both now prepared themselves for a final battle. A letter of 24 April 1788 from Marie-Antoinette to her brother Joseph II of Austria (**37**) gives the radical essence of the government's plan: 'to confine . . . [the *parlementaires*] to the function of judges and to create another assembly which will have the right to register taxes and general laws for the [whole] kingdom'. However, the queen's letter also contains scruples as to method and doubts as to the plan's ultimate success.

For their part the *parlementaires*, aware of the imminence of the blow and uncertain whether they would ever meet again as the Parlement (**46**, third paragraph), finally disclosed the content of the Fundamental Laws of the Kingdom, concerning which they had hitherto been notably reticent (**38**). Apart from the first law, the Salic Law, this document is very much a *pièce d'occasion*. It is instructive to contrast it with the statement of Louis XVI's objectives at the *lit de justice* of 8 May. In particular, the Parlement stresses the sanctity of provincial customs and the duty of local *parlements* to modify royal legislation so as to conform with them; whilst Louis asserts: 'A great state needs one king, one law, one registration' (**47a**). It now seems doubtful whether France possesses an agreed constitution.

For his part in drafting the declaration of Fundamental Laws, the king ordered the arrest of Duval d'Eprémesnil[2] and of Goislard de Monsabert for another inflammatory resolution. They took refuge in the Parlement during the night of 4/5 May and the next six documents (**39–44**) concern the king's attempts to seize them. The documents form a series of letters between the king, Breteuil, the minister for Paris, and his deputy de Crosne, lieutenant-general of police, the duc de Biron, colonel of the French guards – the principal military force in the capital – and Captain d'Agoult, also of the guards, who had the mission of entering the Parlement and arresting the two men.

The position of the French guards is interesting because the defection of the regiment the following summer contributed to the fall of the Bastille. There is no sign of disloyalty throughout the difficult summer of 1788. However, the duc de Biron is obviously doubtful whether the king will ultimately succeed in his struggle with the *parlements* (**39**). Accordingly he refuses to give Breteuil more than 50 guards to supplement the police without direct orders from the king ('otherwise the Parlement could take me to task'). Indeed even the king's formal orders, drafted by a minister, are not enough: 'It is necessary that in such a situation the colonel of the guards know the king's personal intentions.' This shifting of responsibility directly on to the king is a sign that the regime and not just the government is at

2 Jean Jacques Duval d'Eprémesnil, 1746–94, later a deputy for the nobility to the Estates-General and a leader of the aristocratic party (see **81**).

stake. Breteuil also is surely worried by his responsibility when he asks the king to send him in his own handwriting a copy of the blank order signed 'Louis' which Breteuil had filled in and despatched, in accordance with normal procedure (**41**).

Meanwhile the various 'chambers' of the Parlement assembled together and summoned the peers of France, who were honorary members of the Parlement of Paris, to lend weight to their proceedings. The king's orders to the peers not to attend (**40**) were largely disobeyed. The Parlement refused to yield up their two brethren and d'Agoult unfortunately did not know them by sight. Accordingly, Breteuil sent him a M. Archier, who did (**41 and 42**). However, as Breteuil had feared, Archier, fearing 'to incur the eternal wrath' of the Parlement, pretended he could not see d'Eprémesnil and Monsabert. Finally, having made his point and spun out the drama to the limit, d'Eprémesnil gave himself up (**43 and 44**).

Two days later the king held his long-awaited *lit de justice* at Versailles, whither the Parlement had been summoned amid heavy police precautions (**45 and 46**). The essence of the measures that were unveiled (**47**) was to deprive the 13 *parlements* of their right of registering new legislation and confer it instead on a new body – the plenary court – which would effect a central registration for the whole country. Hitherto the king had had to negotiate with each of the *parlements* separately and they had often modified his legislation in accordance with local customs, with the result that the legislative process was unduly protracted and general legislation for the whole country impossible. It is noteworthy that although the government speeches delve into the mists of time, their argument is essentially rationalist rather than traditionalist in character. Lamoignon also (**47b**) seeks severely to restrict the judicial competence of the *parlements*, well knowing the power their judicial functions have given them over such a litigious society.

Reaction to the May Edicts in the country is hard to gauge. There was relative calm in Paris and Biron wrote to Breteuil complaining of the excessive deployment of troops (**49**). On the other hand, document **50** would suggest that even the main beneficiaries of the judicial reforms – the 16 tribunals which were elevated to the status of *grands baillages* – accepted their promotion reluctantly; though how far this was due to fear of *parlementaire* reprisals in the event of government defeat will never be known. The picture painted by Marie-Antoinette for her brother (**51**) may be near the truth, though somewhat rosy because of her personal identification with Brienne's ministry. At all events, Brienne resigned at the end of August, shortly to be followed by Lamoignon, and their reforms, the last of the *ancien régime*, went with them. Necker,[3] their successor, merely put the regime in the hands of the official receiver – the Estates-General, which were to meet in 1789.

3 Jacques Necker, 1752–1804, banker, finance minister 1776–81 and 1788–90.

34 Brienne made principal minister: circular letter sent by the king to all the ministers on 27 August 1787

The basic attribute of a principal minister under Louis XVI was that of censoring all important information which the other ministers gave the king. Brienne was the only minister to enjoy the title, though Maurepas before and, to an extent, Necker afterwards played the role.

The present situation demanding that there should be a common centre in the ministry to which all the parts should relate, I have chosen the archbishop of Toulouse as my principal minister and I am writing this letter to notify you. Consequently my intention is that with important matters where I must be informed – either by you and him together or in your working session with me[4] – you give him prior notification.

'Journal du maréchal de Castries', fo. 392

35 The *séance royale* of 19 November: Marie-Antoinette to her brother Joseph II of Austria, 23 November 1787

... On Monday [19 November] the king went to the Parlement to register two edicts: the first for loans to be spread over a five-year period in order to repay loans with a fixed date for redemption. There was a majority of opinions in favour of registration, but the king presides over the Parlement as he presides over his council, i.e. without being bound by the majority opinion.[5] Consequently, after everyone had given his opinion, the king, without counting the votes, said: 'I order the registration.' The duc d'Orléans dared to protest and say that this form was illegal.[6] The king left with his brothers and the duc d'Orléans remained in the Parlement; then – and this is what proves his evil intent – he produced from his pocket a protest written out in advance. He failed to have it adopted in its entirety but he managed to have a resolution passed declaring the registration illegal as to form. The king has exiled him to Villers-Cotterêts and forbids him to see anyone but his family and household. Two councillors in the Parlement, M. Fréteau and the abbé Sabattier, had spoken with lack of respect in the king's presence; they have been conveyed to two fortresses. I am grieved that we are obliged to employ such authoritarian measures: unfortunately they have become necessary and I hope they act as a deterrent.

4 Each minister had a weekly *travail* or working session with the king.
5 The Bourbon kings did in fact abide by the majority advice of their council.
6 Orléans said that the king should have ordered registration 'at his express command' – the formula employed for a *lit de justice*.

The second edict is to give civil status to Protestants by recognizing their marriages and baptisms; it is expected to pass without difficulty. There was not time to opine on this matter.

What causes me a lot of distress is that the king has announced that he will hold the Estates-General five years from now. There is such a demand for the Estates that the king was advised to summon them on his own initiative whilst he still had the choice. This would also have ensured that they were more manageable than has sometimes been the case.

> *Lettres de Marie-Antoinette*, ed. M de la Rocheterie et le marquis de Beaucourt (2 vols., 1896), vol. II, pp. 108–9

36 Louis XVI's reply of 17 April 1788 to the Parlement's remonstrances of 11 April against the *séance royale*

I have read your remonstrances and I want to reply to them so explicitly that you can have no doubt as to my intentions nor allow yourselves to deviate from them.

There was no need for you to talk to me about the rules of registration and the freedom of voting. When I come to hold my Parlement it is to hear a discussion of the law I bring with me and to decide on its registration with fuller knowledge. That is what I did on 19 November last.

I listened to everyone's opinion.

It is only necessary to count votes when I am not present at your deliberations; in such a case a majority is the only way of informing me of the result of your debates.

When I am present, I judge of this myself.

If a majority vote in my courts constrained my decision, the monarchy would no longer be anything but an aristocracy of magistrates, as detrimental to the rights and interests of the nation as to those of the sovereign.

It would indeed be a strange constitution which equated the king's legislative volition with the opinion of one of his officers and which subjected the legislator to as many opinions as there were different deliberations in the various courts of law in his kingdom.

> *AP*, vol. I, p. 284

37 Marie-Antoinette to Joseph II, 24 April 1788

We are about to make great changes in the *parlements*. For several months the king's orders and replies [to the *parlements*] have displayed unswerving consistency and firmness of principle. The *parlements* are stunned and worried but persist nonetheless with seditious resolutions and remonstrances. The idea is to confine them to the function of judges and to create another assembly which will have the right to register taxes and general laws for the [whole] kingdom. I think we have taken all the measures and precautions compatible with the necessary secrecy; but this very secrecy involves uncertainty about the attitude of large numbers of people who can make or break the operation. It is very irksome to be obliged to institute changes of this nature, but it is clear from the state of affairs that delay would diminish the resources for preserving and consolidating the king's authority.

Lettres de Marie-Antoinette, vol. II,
p. 115

38 The Parlement's view of the Fundamental Laws or constitution of France: resolution proposed by Duval d'Eprémesnil, 3 May 1788

The court, with all the chambers assembled and the peers present, amply warned by public knowledge and notorious fact of the *coup d'état* which threatens the nation by striking at the magistrature . . . and leaves the nation no other resource but a precise declaration by the court of the maxims it is charged with maintaining . . .

Declares that France is a monarchy governed by the king in accordance with the laws.

That of these laws several are fundamental and that these include:

The right of the reigning house to succeed to the throne in the male line according to primogeniture to the exclusion of females and their descendants.

The right of the nation to grant taxation freely in Estates-General regularly convoked and of fixed composition.

The customs and capitulations of the provinces.

The irremovability of magistrates.

The right of the courts in each province to verify the king's legislative volition and to proceed to its registration only in so far as it is conformable to the basic laws of the province as well as the Fundamental Laws of the state.

The right of every citizen, whatever his offence, to appear only before his peers as defined by law.

And the right, without which all the others are of no avail, to appear before the competent judge immediately after arrest no matter on whose orders.

The said court protests against any future violation of the above principles.

AP, vol. I, pp. 284–5

39   Biron, colonel of the French guards, to Breteuil, 5 May 1788

Monsieur, the marquis du Sauzay is with me at this moment. He came to report the conversation he had with yourself and M. de Crosne. He told me that you want the regiment of guards to furnish the lieutenant-general of police with such detachments and patrols as he may have need of this evening in the vicinity of the Palais [de Justice]. You will appreciate that this request is open-ended and that without more information I cannot give such an order, especially as, if things become more serious, it is indispensable that I receive orders from the king informing me of his intentions. If there are ugly incidents, the Parlement could take me to task and I could only defend myself by exhibiting the orders I had received from the king. So this evening I could give you five patrols each consisting of ten men under a sergeant, which would suffice to assist the watch if it is insulted. You speak to me of one or two detachments without telling me of their purpose. It is necessary that in such a situation the colonel of the guards know the king's personal intentions (*ait le secret du Roi*) in order to carry out His Majesty's orders with best effect.

If matters become more serious and it becomes necessary I will, despite the poor state of my health [Biron was dead within the year], go to Versailles myself to take the orders which His Majesty has always given me directly in such circumstances.

AN, O^1 354 no. 54

40   Breteuil to d'Agoult, captain in the guards, 6 May

. . . Please read my letter to the chamber so as to inform the peers who are present that if they had been at home in the evening they would have received a letter which the king ordered me to write to them informing them that the king's intention is that they should abstain from participating in the Assembly of Chambers if invited by the Parlement until further orders. I sent this letter yesterday evening to all the peers and those who were not at home will find it on their return.

AN, O^1 354 no. 61

41 Breteuil to the king, Paris, 6 May, 7.45 a.m.

. . . I have at this moment, Sire, in my ante-chamber an officer of the *robe courte* [guards] called Archier who assures me that he knows M. d'Epré-mesnil perfectly by sight. I trust that I am carrying out Your Majesty's wishes in giving him an order signed 'Louis' and, beneath, your secretary of state to go to M. d'Agoult and enter the Grand' Chambre with him in order to point out M. d'Eprémesnil. I beseech Your Majesty to be so good as to send me in your own handwriting the order I have just given to M. Archier so that if the Parlement asks me to show them your original order I can have it sent to M. d'Agoult.

AN, O^1 354 no. 51

42 Breteuil to d'Agoult, 6 May, 9.30 a.m.

I am sending you M. Archier with an order from the king to follow you into the Grand' Chambre [of the Parlement] and point out M. d'Eprémesnil to you. M. Archier is an officer of the *robe courte* [guards] and has assured me that he knows M. d'Eprémesnil's features well, so you need have no fear that he will make a mistake in designating him to you. I would just ask you not to allow this officer of the *robe courte* to take fright at the moment when you decide to introduce him into the Grand' Chambre because I fear that he may be seized with such terror at incurring the eternal wrath of these gentlemen that he may either say that he does not recognize d'Epré-mesnil or genuinely miss him. . . .

AN, O^1 354 no. 62

43 D'Agoult's report of the arrest of d'Eprémesnil, Paris, 6 May, 10.30 a.m.

After the king's repeated orders to arrest M. Duval d'Eprémesnil, the baron de Breteuil sent me an officer of the *robe courte* to indicate M. d'Epré-mesnil so that I could arrest him. I entered the Grand' Chambre and once more intimated the king's orders; the man instructed to designate the said magistrate was unable to do so. Having retired, I was summoned once more into the Grand' Chambre and then M. d'Eprémesnil stood up and disclosed his identity. He harangued the Assembly and asked me whether I had orders from the king obliging him to follow me. I replied that he knew the king's orders and that he could only refuse on pain of disobedience. He asked me whether he would suffer ill-treatment. I replied that he could rest content because he was obeying without resistance and that I should be the person escorting him; he announced that he was ready to follow me. I escorted him immediately to M. de Crosne to hand him over to the prevotal police.

AN, O¹ 354 no. 64

44   Breteuil to the king, 6 May, 11.00 a.m.

Sire, M d'Eprémesnil has been arrested and will leave the Hôtel de la Police, where he is now, to be conveyed to the Isles Sainte-Marguérite. I have the honour of sending you the report which the marquis d'Agoult sent me. No one could have displayed greater firmness and discretion than he brought to bear in carrying out this commission.

I cannot find anyone in the police who knows M. Monsabert. He is a young man who has only been in the Parlement a few years without distinguishing himself in any way. I have arranged with M. d'Agoult that he should re-enter the Grand' Chambre without delay and require that M. Monsabert be handed over to him or should disclose his identity. I expect that he will do this of his own accord after this new summons. I think that the boredom of all these gentlemen will bring about this result. I thought I would be carrying out Your Majesty's intentions by authorizing M. d'Agoult to allow all these gentlemen to leave freely as soon as he has arrested M. Monsabert. But I have told him that Your Majesty's intention is that the doors of the Palais should be shut immediately and remain so all day. Likewise enough troops will remain in the Palais to prevent any crowds gathering. There is still perfect calm.

AN, O¹ 354 no. 63

45   Crosne to Breteuil, 7 May

I have received the letter you did me the honour to write informing me that the king is to hold his *lit de justice* at Versailles tomorrow, Thursday, at nine o'clock in the morning. As you wished, I am giving orders to prevent any disturbances along the streets by which the Parlement, the *cour des aides* and the *chambre des comptes* will pass.

AN, O¹ 354 no. 72

46   Crosne to Breteuil, 7 May

I have just been informed that the guards of the *robe courte* have managed, but only with great difficult, to clear the courtrooms in the Palais of the crowds of young men who had gathered there and that the doors of the courts have been closed and order restored . . . but there is every reason to believe that the departure of the Parlement tomorrow will give rise to a large crowd and that the tumult will begin again.

It is therefore at all events greatly to be desired that you send the maréchal de Biron and the comte d'Affry the orders signed by the king they require, so as to be able to take possession of the interior of the Palais should circumstances require.

It was reported to me that several members of the Parlement, at the end of this morning's audience, told the booksellers inside the Palais that today they had held their last session and several cleared their accounts with them. General consternation reigns among all the *boutiquiers* in the halls. This morning there was a rumour that tonight the registers and archives of the Parlement would be put under seal. Consequently clerks [etc.] of the Palais have carried out vast quantities of documents.

I forgot to have the honour of informing you this morning of the precautions I have concerted with the commander of the fire brigade yesterday to put out any fires in the vicinity of the Palais. At night we have doubled the number of firemen attached to the guards of the Palais, the Mint and the Isle de Saint-Louis, and an officer spent the night in the Palais. The same precautions have been taken this evening and will be continued.

AN, O¹ 354 no. 74

47 The May Edicts

(a) From the speech of Louis XVI at the lit de justice of 8 May

I wish to transform a moment of crisis into a period of prosperity for my subjects: to begin the reform of the judicial hierarchy, starting with the tribunals which should be its foundations, and to secure swifter and cheaper justice for litigants. . . .

Above all I want to impart to all parts of the monarchy that unity of direction, that *ensemble* without which a great kingdom is weakened by the very number and extent of its provinces.

The regime I intend to inaugurate is not new. There was only one Parlement when Philip the Fair made its residence at Paris permanent. A great state needs one king, one law, one registration.

Tribunals with restricted competence judging the majority of cases.

Parlements to whom the most important cases are reserved.

A single court, which is the repository of laws common to the whole kingdom, entrusted with registering them.

Finally Estates-General summoned not just once, but whenever the needs of the state require.

Such is the restoration which I have meditated out of love for my subjects and today consummate for their welfare.

My one aim will ever be to make them happy.

My keeper of the seals will develop my intentions more fully.

(b) From Lamoignon's speech on the administration of justice

[Having dwelt on the disadvantages for litigants of the extensive jurisdiction of the Parlement of Paris, covering over a third of France, Lamoignon continues:]

Consequently the king has decided to reorganize his *baillages*; he authorizes them all to judge without appeal cases where the sum involved does not exceed 4,000 francs.

At the same time, above this primary level of the *baillage*, His Majesty has chosen to enlarge the competence of the tribunals in the most sizeable towns in your jurisdiction; and, with the title *grands baillages*, they will judge without appeal criminal cases and civil suits where the sum involved does not exceed 20,000 francs.

(c) From Lamoignon's speech on the plenary court

Gentlemen, even before this court contained such a large number of magistrates, Francis I, Henri II, Henri IV and Louis XIII were aware of the danger of admitting young magistrates to the deliberations of the *parlements* on public affairs.

They considered that, being excluded from judging important cases, *a fortiori* they should not participate in discussions concerning the state where force of numbers would carry the day.

Struck by the same disadvantages, His Majesty is implementing today what his predecessors conceived.

From the Parlement of Paris, the king will only admit the Grand' Chambre to the court [the plenary court] which he is restoring for the verification and publication of his general legislation.

But in his desire to render this court as worthy as possible both of his own confidence and that of the nation, the king will add this eminent section of the magistrature to the princes of his blood, the peers of his kingdom, the great officers of his crown, the prelates, the marshals of France and other qualified persons – governors of provinces, knights of his orders, a magistrate from each of his *parlements*, members chosen from his council, two magistrates from the *chambre des comptes* and two from the *cour des aides* of Paris.[7]

AP, vol. I, pp. 294–9

48(a)   Breteuil to de Crosne, 9 May 1788

[Breteuil expressed the king's satisfaction at the measures de Crosne has taken to maintain order in the capital on 8 May and continues:] It only

---

7 The similarity between the proposed body and the Assembly of Notables is striking and it is reasonable to doubt whether the plenary court would have been any more tractable than the Notables had been.

remains for me to recommend that you neglect nothing that will enable you to be informed of such assemblies and conventicles as may be held at the houses of individual . . . [*parlementaires*] to discuss present events.

AN, O¹ 354 no. 80

48(b) Breteuil to de Crosne, 10 May 1788

The King has ordered me, Monsieur, to tell you to see M. [name illegible], councillor in the Parlement, living in the place Royale, and tell him that His Majesty has been informed that there has been a fairly large gathering at his house of councillors from the suppressed Parlement and that if these assemblies recur His Majesty will take it very seriously and will make him feel the weight of his displeasure.

AN, O¹ 354 no. 89

49 Biron to Breteuil, 26 May 1788

In your letter of the ninth you did me the honour of instructing me that the same level of guards and patrols should be maintained until further notice. Accordingly the detachments of the regiment of guards sent to the Palais have hitherto been regularly relieved every day; but this continuous service day and night for three weeks is excessively tiring for the regiment. Many soldiers have fallen ill and more are succumbing daily. Considering the calm that obtains at the Palais, the Châtelet and throughout Paris, I beseech you to propose to His Majesty that he progressively reduce the size of detachment to enable the regiment to endure these duties as long as His Majesty is pleased to continue them.

AN, O¹ 354 no. 102

50 Judicial reactions to the *coup d'état* of 8 May

From a report of 1 June 1788 listing the tribunals which had accepted or rejected the May Edicts or whose attitude was not yet known. There follow the *arrêtés* of three typical *baillages royaux* concerning their promotion to the status of *grand baillage*.

Langres: Resolved that . . . [this tribunal] saw with sorrow that the Parlement was unable freely to participate in the registration of the edicts; will gladly see the king restrict the jurisdiction he has granted to the court; that because the cessation of justice is the greatest of misfortunes, for this reason alone the court has decided provisionally to fulfil the functions confided to it.

Orléans: The edicts were presented . . . at the king's most express command [i.e. by *lit de justice*]. They were registered in virtue of the orders of the *intendant*, as bearer of the king's commands, without any voting by the judges. It is declared that the judges' presence . . . and the warrant of the *intendant* do not imply any adhesion on the part of the judges to anything which could be subversive of the principles of the monarchy.

Decided to send remonstrances to the king as represented by the keeper of the seals . . .

Poitiers: Resolved by the judges that out of respect and submission . . . they will move to the reading and registration of the edicts; that His Majesty should be petitioned to consider again the means of reconciling the maximum advantage to the provinces in respect of the administration of justice with the conservation of the ancient form of the Parlement and to take into consideration the past services of the officers of the suppressed tribunal, etc.

AN, O¹ 354 nos. 108–9

51 Marie-Antoinette to Joseph II, 16 July 1788

. . . The *parlements* are giving full rein to their opposition to the new edicts; a portion of the nobility, especially in Brittany, has joined them and every day brings forth rebellious and seditious declarations. It is grievous to be obliged to employ the way of force, the extent of which cannot be calculated in advance. But it has become necessary and the king is resolved to maintain his edicts and his authority. There is unrest in Dauphiné but less than in Brittany and the provinces in general, excepting the towns where there are *parlements*, seem satisfied with the new edicts. At Rouen and Nancy there have been attempts to stir up the people but with so little success that the resolutions of the two *parlements* were booed and ridiculed. What distresses me is that if we were forced to go to war [see 7] we should also be forced to convoke the Estates-General and that, perhaps, before calm had been entirely restored. . . .

Lettres de Marie-Antoinette, vol. II,
pp. 118–19

52 The Pope to Louis XVI, 9 September 1788

When Brienne resigned, Louis asked the Pope to make him a cardinal – a routine request which was at first refused in the following, very singular letter.

Our most dear son . . . our brother, the archbishop of Rhodez, our nuncio, has informed us that the minister to whom you wanted us to give the purple was capable of the blackest ingratitude towards you . . . that whilst you entrusted him with the welfare of your peoples, he has made them miserable – that he has not blenched from ordering the blood of his fellow-citizens, of your faithful subjects, to be shed; that he has profaned the Temple of the Lord by billeting soldiers there and announced in your name, dearest son, that you would not honour your engagements [a reference to the decree of 16 August suspending payments until 1 September, thereafter resuming them half in paper, half in specie]. . . .

Whilst admiring your goodness, dearest son, we must point out that if the sweetest prerogative of kings is to pardon, their first duty is justice. When Jesus Christ drove out with whiplashes those who had dared profane the Temple of the Lord, he did not think it right to give them compensation.

Forfend it God, dearest son, that we should seek to turn you against the man whom you honour with your confidence . . . rather we prefer to feel that he will repent of his own accord . . . that, covered in sackcloth and ashes, his head bowed to the ground in front of the cathedral church of Sens [Brienne had exchanged the archbishopric of Toulouse for the more lucrative one of Sens], he will beg forgiveness of God and men for his transgressions.

AN, K161 no. 38

|5|

Preparations for the Estates

Faced with mounting opposition throughout the summer of 1788, Brienne turned with serious interest to the idea of the Estates-General. At the *séance royale* he had promised these by 1791; now, by the *arrêt du conseil* of 8 August, the date of their meeting was advanced to May 1789. However, Estates which had been yielded to aristocratic pressure could be expected to consolidate the gains made by the nobility and clergy. Only an alliance with the Third Estate could prevent this. Consequently Brienne, as he tells us in his memoirs **(54)**, intended to challenge the traditional organization of the Estates. He threw down this challenge in the *arrêt du conseil* of 5 July, inviting opinion from all sides on how the Estates should be organized, given the modifications in society since the Estates had last met in 1614. Censorship of the press was lifted for this exercise, whilst Lamoignon's letter to Breteuil **(53)** shows the importance attached to the matter.

Brienne intended to alter the traditional organization of the Estates in two important respects. First, he wanted to increase the number of deputies for the Third Estate from just over a third to half the total. Second, he did not intend using the ancient electoral unit of the *baillage* but instead to have the deputies to the Estates elected by the new provincial assemblies from amongst their number. In the provincial assemblies, not only were half the members drawn from the Third Estate but each member represented a geographical rather than a social constituency and naturally the votes of individuals were counted, 'by head', rather than the bloc vote of orders. By extending this system to the Estates-General, Brienne hoped to secure, in the words of the *arrêt* of 5 July, 'an Assembly truly national in its composition'.

When Necker succeeded Brienne, there was a marked change in royal policy towards the Estates. On the one hand Necker intended to let the Estates decide everything: the mere fact of his appointment – and his advancing the date for their meeting to 1 January **(55)** – convinced people that the Estates really were going to be summoned. (With victory achieved the ramshackle alliance against the May Edicts fell apart, the Third Estate, whose 'awakening' dates from this period, demanding double representation and voting by head in the forthcoming Estates.) On the other hand, whether out of respect for the ancient rights of the nobility and clergy or whether because of an exaggerated sense of their power, Necker rejected Brienne's policy of straight alliance with the Third Estate. An imaginative policy would have been to uphold Lamoignon's judicial reforms, leave the Parlement in exile, and announce, and to the sound of trumpets, double representation for the Third Estate and voting by head. Necker did none of these things. Instead he recalled the Parlement, vainly hoping by the royal declaration of 25 September to prevent *parlementaire* reprisals against those who had co-operated in the judicial reforms (**55**). The reply of the Parlement (**56**) shows how deceived he was in this hope. But the sting of the reply was reserved for the last clause of the last sentence which stipulates that the Estates-General should be organized 'according to the forms observed in 1614'. This was intended and taken to mean that there should be neither double representation for the Third Estate nor voting by head.

The Parlement's popularity vanished overnight. For all his claim to be the interpreter of public opinion, Necker was slow to realize this fact. Instead he responded to the Parlement's pronouncement by deferring the Estates until May and meanwhile reconvening the Assembly of Notables to advise him. The futility of this procedure is succinctly stated by Brienne (**54**, penultimate paragraph), for the Notables, by five of their working committees to one, advised against *doublement*. To the voice of the Notables was added that of four of the six princes of the blood who had presided over these working committees. The king's brother, the comte de Provence, and the duc d'Orléans (he of the *séance royale*) did not sign. The memorandum of the princes (**58**) is notable for its vivid apprehension, at this comparatively early stage, of the essentials of the revolutionary mentality (which appears to the princely signatories as some galloping disease) and of what the Revolution would accomplish. No one has a quicker eye than the conservative for the implications of change.

The Notables having given their advice, the matter was examined at length by the king and his ministers in the *conseil d'état* (**59**). The attitude of the king and queen, their resentment against the nobility and clergy, shows that Necker could have pursued a much bolder policy from the outset: alliance with the Third Estate was not just traditional royal policy, it had received a special emphasis ever since Calonne's series of memoranda to the king in 1786. Nevertheless, Necker remained cautious and the *résultat du conseil* (**60**) gives the Third Estate double representation without settling the question of voting procedures in the Estates. Indeed the use of the old electoral machinery would imply a preference for voting by order.

At the end of the *résultat* was printed Necker's report on which it had been based. Necker concludes with some constitutional promises which the king had vouchsafed to 'the ministers honoured with his confidence'. Here the king promises: no taxation without the consent of the Estates-General, which will meet at regular intervals, and restriction of *lettres de cachet*[1] and

---

1 A *lettre de cachet* was technically merely an order given under the king's small seal; its most famous use was for detention without trial, usually being issued at the request of the head of a family to restrain one of its members from dishonouring it.

press censorship. It might be observed that such a sweeping surrender of royal authority (which had been more specifically demanded by the aristocracy) might not have been necessary if the king had openly identified himself with the Third Estate.

53 Lamoignon to Breteuil, 6 July 1788

I enclose the draft of an *arrêt du conseil* ordering a search in all the archives of each province for transcripts and documents concerning the Estates-General and the consequent elections thereto. I beg you to be so good as to have this order despatched with all possible expedition.

AN, O^1 354 no. 107

54 Extract from the memoirs of Loménie de Brienne

[The exiled *parlementaires* sought a compromise with the government.] . . . I refused all the proposals which required sacrifices I did not consider reasonable. Moreover my opinion – witness all the king's pronouncements – was that such sacrifices should be made to the nation and not to bodies which I have ever regarded as the enemies of the nation, usurpers of its rights, solely concerned with their own interests and veritable scourges in a well-ordered state. Therefore I came to a decision and said to myself: 'We must have done and think no more of delaying the Estates-General.' Perhaps by announcing their convocation we would diminish that general concern for the *parlements*. Once a date for the Estates had been fixed, the plenary court, which had aroused such ignorant indignation, would be rendered redundant. At the same time, however, all that had been done to reform the administration of justice was so useful, so intrinsically just, that the Estates would add to it rather than detract.

I had already made preparations for holding [the Estates]. . . . Rheims had been selected as the place for their meeting; the king was to reside at Saint-Thierry.

I will go further, lest there remain any doubt concerning my sincere wish to hold the Estates in the month of May following as stated in the *arrêt du conseil* [of 8 August]: concerning the manner in which they should be convoked, I had requested information – not from a new Assembly of Notables [the procedure adopted by Necker in November 1788], composed of the privileged orders whose mentality I knew only too well and who, when assembled, could only be disposed against the Third Estate and consequently dangerous – but from the provincial assemblies who, composed as I desired the Estates to be and voting as I wanted them to vote, would have given a uniform opinion and removed all difficulties.

From this it is clear that my preference was for a double representation for the Third Estate and voting by head – principles I had introduced in the provincial assemblies and that were being adopted in all the provincial Estates being set up. Indeed my ultimate intention was to establish as many of these provincial Estates as time permitted. Those for Dauphiné had already been agreed and after I . . . [left the ministry] were set up along the lines I had indicated. Franche-Comté was going to follow the same lines and I would have counted on overcoming the opposition of the nobility. Normandy was beginning to stir. Part of the kingdom would have been endowed with provincial Estates along the lines of the provincial assemblies with double representation and voting by head. They would have nominated their deputies [to the Estates-General]; elections by the *baillages* would not have taken place; the other provinces would have been obliged to follow suit. Brittany alone, which it was impossible to overcome, would have resisted but would have been bypassed as happened in the event; and certainly the Breton nobility was so imbued with prejudices and prepossessions, was so stubborn and pig-headed in its resistance, that it was impossible to foresee anything but trouble and disorder from that quarter.

Published in J.-L. Soulavie, *Mémoires
historiques et politiques du règne de
Louis XVI* . . . (6 vols., Paris, 1801),
vol. VI, pp. 240–4

55 Royal declaration registered by the Parlement on 25 September 1788

1 It is our wish and command that the assembly of the Estates-General take place during January of the following year.

2 Consequently we enjoin all the officers of our law courts without exception to continue to exercise the functions of their offices as formerly.

3 It is likewise our intention that no change should be made in the hierarchy of law courts . . . subsisting before last May.

4 Notwithstanding, we ordain that all judgements, whether civil or criminal, given by the tribunals created at that time be implemented according to their form and tenor.

5 We do not, however, intend thereby to deprive litigants of the right of appeal against such judgements.

6 We impose strict silence on our *procureurs-généraux* and other *procureurs* in matters relating to the execution of the previous edicts.

7 Everything contrary to our present declaration is abrogated.

AP, vol. I, p. 389

56 Resolution of the Parlement concerning the preceding declaration

The court, continuing in the principles which inspired its resolutions of 3 and 5 May last . . . orders that the said declaration be registered on the rolls of the court to be implemented according to its form and tenor but with the following provisos: that it cannot be argued from the preamble or any of the articles of the said declaration that the court needed to be restored in order to resume functions which violence alone had suspended; the court cannot be prevented, by the silence imposed on the king's *procureur-général* in matters relating to the execution of the ordinances, edicts and declarations of 8 May last, from taking cognizance of offences with which the court would have been obliged to deal; that it cannot be argued from articles 4 and 5 that the judgements mentioned there are not subject to appeal or that any of those who have not been examined and sworn in by the court, according to the ordinances, resolutions and regulations of the said court, should be allowed to exercise the functions of judge in the lower tribunals. Finally the said court, in conformity with its resolution of 3 May last, maintains its insistence that the Estates-General designated for next January be regularly convoked and composed and that according to the forms observed in 1614.

AP, vol. I, p. 389

57 Mirabeau to Montmorin, the foreign secretary, 28 December 1788

This letter, together with his earlier one to Calonne (9), establishes the continuity between Mirabeau's revolutionary philosophy and that of the royal ministerial reformers during the pre-Revolution. Its keystone is that an alliance between the king and the Third Estate against corporate rights and privileges will strengthen not diminish royal authority. When Mirabeau rehearsed this argument during the Revolution it seemed paradoxical but in the earlier period commonplace.

. . . I do not want either you or your friends to be able to think ʳhat I am deserting them. M. de Lamoignon has been denounced and the time has come to offer him my services. I am charmed by his character, I esteem his intentions, I abhor the way in which he is being hounded and I execrate, more than he does himself, the body [i.e. the Parlement] which, not content with having vanquished him, wants to immolate him also. I know the designs of these implacable bodies, their intrigues, in a word their conspiracy – because the plan of attack they are now preparing against the government is a conspiracy against the nation. I offer myself unequivocally to M. de Lamoignon for his personal defence if he has need of me and I beg you to tell him so. That is the first object of my letter.

However, there is a more important one, Monsieur le comte; you love the king, as you should both as a man and as a minister. Myself, as a citizen, I tremble for royal authority which is more necessary than ever even as it stands on the brink of ruin. Never was crisis more difficult nor more pregnant with opportunities for licence; never did the coalition of the privileged pose so formidable a threat to the king and to the nation; never did national assembly threaten to be so unruly as that which is about to decide the fate of the monarchy, that to which everyone is rushing with such precipitation and mutual suspicion.

However, is the ministry, which has rushed into this fatal pass through having striven to postpone the Estates-General rather than prepare for them, working on ways of removing the threat of being dominated by them, or rather of making their co-operation fruitful?

Well! I have such a programme, Monsieur le comte. It is based on that of a constitution which will save us from the conspiracies of the aristocracy, the excesses of democracy and the profound anarchy into which the government, through having wanted to be absolute, has plunged both us and itself. . . . Do you want to see the plan? Will you show it to the King? . . . Without at least the secret assistance of the government I cannot be elected to the Estates-General. . . .

> *Correspondance entre le comte de*
> *Mirabeau et le comte de La Marck,*
> ed. A. de Bacourt (2 vols., 1851),
> vol. I, pp. 238–9

58 The memorandum of the princes of the blood

When Your Majesty forbade the Notables to discuss the memorandum submitted to them by the prince de Conti, Your Majesty declared to the 'princes of his blood that when they desired to communicate to him that which might be useful to the good of his service and that of the state, they might address him'.

The comte d'Artois, the prince de Condé, the duc de Bourbon, the duc d'Enghien and the prince de Conti consider it their duty to respond to this invitation from Your Majesty.

It particularly behoves the princes of your blood to tell you the truth: by rank, they are the first of your subjects; by their condition, your natural advisers; by their rights, most interested in defending yours; and they consider likewise that they owe you an account of their feelings and of their thoughts.

Sire, the state is in peril. Your person is respected, the virtues of the monarch assure him of the nation's homage. But, Sire, a revolution is being prepared in the principles of government; it is being accomplished through the turmoil in men's minds. Institutions which were considered sacred and which have enabled this monarchy to flourish for so many centuries have been put into question or even decried as unjust.

The writings which have appeared during the Assembly of Notables; the memoranda which have been submitted to the princely signatories, the demands formulated by various provinces, towns or *corps*; the subject matter and style of these demands and memoranda all herald, all prove that there is a deliberate plan of insubordination and of contempt for the laws of the state. Every author sets himself up as a legislator; eloquence or a facile pen – even devoid of study, knowledge or experience – seem sufficient authorization to regulate the constitution of empires. Whoever advances a bold proposition, whoever proposes to change the laws is assured of readers and sectaries.

So fast does this deplorable mania develop that opinions which a short while ago would have appeared most reprehensible today seem reasonable and just . . . Who can say where the audacity of opinions will stop? The rights of the throne have been called into question; opinion is riven over the rights of the two orders of the state; soon the rights of property will be attacked; inequality of wealth will be represented as something which needs to be reformed; already it has been proposed that feudal dues be abolished as representing a system of oppression, a barbarous survival.

Derived from these new theories, from the intention to change rights and laws, is the claim advanced by several sections of the Third Estate that their order should have two votes in the Estates-General whilst each of the two leading orders continues to have but one.

The princely signatories will not repeat what has been developed by several committees [of the Notables], namely the injustice and danger of innovations in the composition of the Estates-General; the host of resultant claims; the ease with which, if votes were counted by head and not by order, the interests of the Third Estate – better defended by the existing arrangements – would be compromised by corrupting members of the Third Estate; the destruction of the equilibrium so wisely established between the three orders and of their mutual independence.

It has been demonstrated to Your Majesty how important it is to preserve the only method of convoking the Estates which is constitutional, the mode hallowed by law and custom: the distinction between the orders, the right to deliberate in separate chambers, equality of votes [between them] – these unchangeable foundations of the French monarchy. . . .

These principles have been developed and proved, it would seem, irrefutably.

It only remains for the princely signatories to add the expression of feelings inspired by their attachment to the state and to Your Majesty.

They cannot conceal their fears for the state should the claims of the Third Estate be successful and the dire consequences of the proposed revolution in the constitution of the Estates: they perceive a sad vista unfolding; they see each king altering the rights of the nation according to his personal inclinations: a superstitious king giving extra votes to the clergy; a martial king showering them on the nobility, his comrades-in-arms; the Third Estate, now obtaining a majority of votes, then being punished for its success by these changes; each order, depending on the period, the oppressor or the oppressed; the constitution rotten or unstable; the nation perpetually divided and henceforth always weak and unhappy.

But there are yet more immediate misfortunes. In a kingdom where for so long civil dissensions have not existed it is painful to pronounce the word schism. However we must expect this if the rights of the first two orders suffer any change. In this case one of these orders – or both of them perhaps – could refuse to recognize the Estates-General and thereby avoid confirming their degradation by appearing before the Assembly.

At any rate, who can doubt that we shall see a large number of gentlemen challenging the legality of the Estates-General, issuing protests and having them registered in the *parlements*, even addressing them to the assembly of the Estates? Henceforth what is decided in this Assembly would no longer, in the eyes of a portion of the nation, have the force of national consensus; and imagine the hold on the people of protests tending to dispense them from paying taxes granted by the Estates! Thus this Assembly, so desired and so necessary, would be nothing but a source of troubles and disorder.

But even were Your Majesty not to experience any obstacles in carrying out his intentions, could his noble, just and tender spirit consent to the sacrifice and humiliation of this brave, ancient and respected nobility which has shed so much blood for king and country . . . ?

In speaking for the nobility, the princes of your blood are speaking for themselves. They cannot forget that they form part of the body of the nobility, from which they should not be distinguished; that their highest title is that of gentleman: Henri IV said this and they delight in repeating his noble sentiments.

Let the Third Estate, then, stop attacking the rights of the first two orders – rights which are no less ancient than the monarchy and should be as unalterable as its constitution. Let them content themselves with requesting the reduction of their share of taxation which may be too great. Then the first two orders, recognizing in the Third Estate citizens who are dear to them, will be able, out of the generosity of their hearts, to renounce any prerogatives which have a pecuniary value and consent to carry their full share of public taxation.

The princely signatories ask to set the example of all the sacrifices which can contribute to the good of the state and to cement the union of the orders composing it.

AP, vol. I, pp. 487–9

59   Barentin's account of the ministerial discussions leading to the *résultat du conseil*

Barentin,[2] who succeeded Lamoignon as keeper of the seals and headed the 'aristocratic' faction within the ministry, recounts how the king, before taking the final decision in the council on the composition of the Estates-General, presided over a series of preliminary ministerial committees consisting of Necker, himself (as minister responsible for the Estates and also as Necker's antagonist) and two other ministers, different on each occasion.

The king, who was present at each of these committees, did not display the slightest sign of impatience although they lasted for four or five hours, and on each occasion he heard the same things repeated since the two ministers summoned were different every time. His Majesty made frequent observations but it was impossible to divine his opinion.

The separate committees preceded a general one at which the queen was present and which occupied two sessions. . . .

The discussion was very heated, everyone believing that the destiny of the state depended on the course of action he had espoused. M. Necker and M. de Montmorin [the comte de Montmorin, foreign secretary] multiplied their wiles, returning to the wrongs they attributed to the clergy and the nobility at the time of the edicts of 8 May and contrasting their behaviour with the obedience of the people: past experience was sufficient guide to the future; royal authority had everything to fear from two powerful orders and everything to gain from uniting with the people; the slightest favour was enough to tie it to the interests of the crown. These ideas were calculated to have a powerful effect on the minds of the king and queen and fed the prejudices of both against the clergy, the nobility and the *parlementaires*.

It seemed that the king, having heard and digested everything, had only to pronounce. Nevertheless he wanted to count the votes again. I adhered firmly to my original opinion, as did M. de Villedeuil [Laurent de Villedeuil, minister for the *maison du roi*]. M. de Nivernais [the duc de Nivernais, minister without portfolio] was less firm, playing the subtle courtier and not coming to a positive conclusion; M. de Puységur [the comte de Puységur, minister for war] wavered. The king pronounced for double representation. He did not consider the suggestion of increasing the number of towns allowed to send deputies either sufficiently frank or sufficiently decisive.[3]

2 Charles de Paule de Barentin, 1736–1819, pursued a career in the Parlement and the *cour des aides* before becoming keeper of the seals, 1788–9. He disposed the king against the Third Estate in the Estates-General.

3 This compromise, suggested by Barentin and briefly accepted by Necker, would have given the Third Estate more deputies than the other two orders taken separately but less than their combined total.

The queen maintained total silence; it was however easy to see that she did not disapprove the double representation of the Third Estate.

> *Mémoire autographe de M. de Barentin, chancelier et garde des sceaux, sur les derniers conseils du roi Louis XVI*, ed. M. Champion (1884), pp. 71–3

60 The *résultat du conseil*, 27 December 1788

The king, having heard the report delivered in his council by the minister of his finances concerning the forthcoming convocation of the Estates-General, has adopted its principles and objectives and ordains as follows:

1 That the deputies to the forthcoming Estates-General will be at least a thousand in number.
2 That this number will be determined, as far as possible, by virtue of the population and taxation paid by each *baillage*.
3 That the number of deputies for the Third Estate will be equal to that of the other two orders combined and that this proportion will be established by the letters of convocation.
4 That these preliminary decisions will serve as the basis for the work necessary in drawing up without delay the letters of convocation and other related arrangements.
5 That the report delivered to His Majesty will be printed after the present *résultat*.

Necker's report

Having given his advice about elections to the Estates-General, Necker concludes with some important *obiter dicta* concerning the powers of the Estates.

Sire, as you have told the ministers honoured with your confidence, you intend not only to carry out your promise not to impose any new taxes without the consent of the Estates-General of your kingdom but also not to extend the life of an existing tax except on this condition. You further desire to guarantee the periodic return of the Estates-General by consulting them as to the interval which should be fixed between convocations and by lending a favourable ear to their suggestions on how to give these provisions permanence and stability.

Your Majesty also wants to prevent, in the most efficacious manner, the havoc which the malpractices or incompetence of his ministers could wreak in his finances. You intend, Sire, to work out with the Estates-General the best ways of achieving this aim. . . .

Your Majesty, bringing his attention to bear on all the measures capable of contributing to the public good, intends to meet the entirely legitimate demands of his subjects by inviting the Estates-General themselves to consider the great debate which has arisen on the subject of *lettres de cachet*, in order that Your Majesty may, with the aid of their reflections, come to a perfect understanding of what rules should be observed in that part of the administration. Your only wish, Sire, is for the maintenance of order and you want to leave to the law everything with which it can deal.

According to the same principle, Your Majesty is impatient to hear the views of the Estates-General on the degree of freedom to grant to the press and on the publication of books relating to administration, government, and any other public matter.

Finally, Sire, you prefer, and with reason, the lasting deliberations of the Estates-General of your kingdom to the transient advice of your ministers; and when you have tried the wisdom of the Estates-General you will not hesitate to give them a stability capable of inspiring confidence and to safeguard them from a change of heart on the part of the kings your successors.

AP, vol. I, pp. 496–8

|6|

The cahiers de doléances *and the elections*

The *cahiers de doléances* drawn up by their constituents for the guidance of the deputies to the Estates-General, show a remarkable uniformity in demanding precisely what the king has already conceded in the *résultat du conseil* (though possibly because everyone has read Necker's report, which becomes the basis for the constitutional demands). Thus documents **61** and **62** seem radical indeed until one realizes that the most radical demands had already been granted by the king, namely consent by the Estates to taxation, meeting of the Estates at fixed intervals and modification of *lettres de cachet*.

One common demand in the *cahiers* owes a particular debt to Necker: measures to prevent financial malpractices by ministers. Indeed Necker's bitter polemical battle with Calonne gave rise to a rather simplistic view of the financial crisis: if Necker's *compte rendu* was accepted, which it was, then it followed that Calonne had embezzled the difference between Necker's assessment of 1781 and his own of 1787 – four billion livres. This was the line Necker had to take and Brienne also, as we have seen, to discredit Calonne with the king. However it was a Faustian bargain for it engendered a distrust of *all* governments and hence of the regime. Nothing was more scandalous than a public debate as to whether the king had authorized a mistake in 1781 or in 1787.

The *cahiers* were the yardstick by which Louis XVI judged the achievements of the Revolution. This is understandable since they were as near as you could get to the authentic voice of the nation. But this was to ignore the fact that after they had been drafted and after the Estates had met there occurred what Robespierre[1] called 'a revolution as marvellous as it was unexpected',[2] namely the storming of the Bastille. From a personal point of

---

1 Maximilien François Marie Isadore Robespierre, 1758–94, lawyer, deputy to the Estates-General, member of the Commune August–September 1792, *conventionnel*, member of the 'great' Committee of Public Safety.
2 Robespierre, *Oeuvres complètes* (ed. M. Bouloisseau, G. Lefebvre and A. Soboul) (10 vols, 1912–67), vol. IV, p. 89.

view Louis objected to the fact that he was denied a role in the legislative process, 'in contempt of the *cahiers*', like document **61** (paragraph 5) and document **62** (paragraph 5). However, document **62** (paragraph 6) would deny him the right of dissolution enjoyed by the king of England.

In general the demands of the *cahiers* were less radical and less bitter than the revolutionary outcome. The *parlements* come in for strong criticism for venality and slow and expensive procedures and for preserving tax evasion by the nobility. Nevertheless they are assigned a role, albeit a reduced one, in the new order. They will register (but unmodified and immediately) legislation passed by the king and the Estates conjointly; and when the Estates were not in session (and nobody envisaged the continuous assemblies of the Revolution) they would exercise their traditional role of verification and registration, subject to ratification by the Estates. In view of the criticism of the *parlements*, so recently the popular heroes, it should come as no surprise that so few *parlementaires* were elected to the Estates-General, despite the fact that they were one of the few groups with any experience in public affairs.

Criticism of the nobility is muted, its tax exemptions are attacked, but then their surrender had been widely trailed. The exemptions enjoyed by the *haute bourgeoisie* are as heavily attacked (**67**). The court nobility are attacked by the provincial (**64**). There is resentment against the feudal system (**67–69**) and document **68** advances the (contentious) view that once they had been surrendered, the question of voting in the Estates by head or order would become irrelevant – contentious because the division of society into orders, which the voting expressed, went deeper than the level of vested interests; but see also document **62** (clause 12).

Alliance between the king and the Third Estate is eloquently advocated in the potted history of the *vingtième* in document **66**. Other things being equal, at a certain stage in the development of parliamentary institutions the king's power is increased (that is why he summons them), the best example being that of Henry VIII of England; but skilful management is called for.

All, however, was not sweetness and light as Robespierre's contribution to the electoral campaign in Artois (**70–71**) makes clear.

61　A combined *cahier* of the three orders of the *baillage* of Fenestrange

The universal cry which goes up from the nation . . . announces that the moment has finally come to determine its constitution.

The efforts which ministerial despotism have made over several centuries to annihilate it and raise its tyranny on its ruins and which in this decisive moment will crush us forever under its yoke unless we have the strength to resist it, imposes on us the overriding law of claiming our rights and employing all our efforts finally to give a stable form to the French constitution.

Consequently we instruct our deputies to insist with all their might that the following fundamental articles of our constitution should be settled before any other matters.

1 That the liberty of the individual be safeguarded by the abolition of all *lettres de cachet*, letters of exile, and proscribing judgements by special commissions and any other kind of arbitrary orders and that no citizen can be arrested without appearing immediately before his natural judges.

2 That it be recognized by an authentic and everlasting charter that the nation alone has the right to tax itself, that is to say to grant or withhold subsidies, to regulate their extent, employment, basis, assessment and duration and to raise loans.

3 That periodic and regular meetings of the Estates-General should be permanently guaranteed, as often as present needs require and thereafter every three years to review the state of the kingdom ... and if the convocation of the national assembly should not have taken place within the period stipulated by law, that the provincial Estates be authorized to oppose the collection of taxes and even that the *parlements* be authorized to prosecute anyone who continues to collect them for misappropriating public funds.

4 That no general law whatsoever be introduced except in the Estates-General and by mutual co-operation between the king's authority and the consent of the nation; and that these laws should be sent before the Parlement of Paris, attended by the princes and peers, during the same session of the national assembly, to be inscribed on the registers without the Parlement's being able to make any changes whatsoever; but that the Parlement continue as before to be entrusted with seeing to the execution of the laws of the kingdom, with the maintenance of the constitution and with recalling its principles by sending remonstrances to the king whenever it judges that these rights are threatened.

5 That ... ordinary administrative and police laws will, when the Estates-General are not in session, be provisionally sent for free verification and registration by the courts, as has always been the case, but that they should only have the force of law until the next session of the national assembly where they will need to be ratified to have the force of law.

6 The confirmation of the capitulations and treaties which unite the provinces to the crown, as well as the guarantee of all private property.

7 That the ministers whom the nation accuses of having exercised in the king's name acts of arbitrary authority or of having misappropriated public funds, shall be judged by the Estates-General or by the national tribunal they choose.

62   General cahier of the three orders convoked at Vesoul (Franche Comté)

... We the members of the three orders of the *baillage* of Amont ... united by the identity of interests established between the three orders by the nobility and clergy's complete and authentic surrender of all pecuniary exemptions in relation to taxes or public charges present and future, have resolved to draw up the *cahier* of our grievances ... together ...

In consequence whereof we hereby give our deputies to the Estates-General of the kingdom meeting at Versailles on 27 April 1789 the following instructions and powers ...

3 In order to preserve the personal safety and liberty of all citizens, the deputies will demand that the Estates-General pass a perpetual and irrevocable law preventing the future use of *lettres de cachet* and preventing any person vested with public authority from having a domiciled citizen arrested without bringing him before the appropriate judge within 24 hours.

4 Ministers shall not on any pretext be able to hinder the exercise of the legislative power, nor infringe personal liberty or property by any arbitrary order, even if signed by the king.

5 No general law shall be reputed such in France unless it has either been proposed by the king and accepted by the Estates-General or passed by the Estates-General and sanctioned by the king.

6 As the legislative power should have an independent, free and non-continuous activity, it is for the Estates-General themselves to determine the date of their dissolution and of their assembly in the future. ...

9 No court of whatever description – even the executive commission of the Estates-General – which can be claimed to represent the assembled nation or take the place of the Estates shall ever be established.

10 The deputies will demand recognition of the right belonging to the nation to give its consent to taxation, to regulate the way in which it will be spent and to scrutinize the way in which it has been spent by means of annually published accounts. ...

12 Voting by head shall be demanded. ...

16 Each departmental minister shall be obliged to give the Estates-General a strict account of his use of the funds at his disposal, for which he will be held personally responsible. ...

23 The deputies will demand the establishment of provincial Estates throughout the kingdom, their form and organization to be prescribed by the Estates-General, and such that all the members shall be freely elected with no one able to claim any rights, privileges or honours. ...

31 The life of every tax shall be limited to six months after the day fixed for the next convocation of the Estates-General; no new tax may be

collected in the interval between Estates-General and without their consent ... no loan, direct or indirect, may be sought without the consent of the Estates-General which will be invited to examine the best way of providing for the expenses of an unforeseen war.

AP, vol. I, pp. 773–4

63　The *cahier* of the clergy of Saintes

Reform of tribunals

The venality of judicial offices has long attracted lively criticism. Several Estates-General have asked for its suppression.

There are also complaints about that the judicial process is too slow, too expensive and too complicated. . . .

In some *parlements* – and notably that of Paris – a custom has arisen which merits great attention, namely that of only admitting nobles as judges. This practice shuts the door to many honourable and capable men. It is strange that nobility is required for offices which themselves confer nobility.

The territorial jurisdiction of the Parlement of Paris is too large.

Once the Estates-General have met they will surely find a way of reconciling the rights and pretensions of the courts of magistrates with the right of the monarch and the constitution of the monarchy.

AP, vol. V, p. 664

64　The *cahier* of the nobility of Bouzonville

The Third Estate complained of the Ségur ordinance of 1781 which restricted commissioned entry into the army to those with four generations of nobility. However, the measure was regarded by the provincial nobility as inadequate compensation for being themselves denied entry to the higher ranks.

Since the ministry of M. de Saint-Germain [1775–7] as a result of the ordinances issued by the council of war, the profession of arms has become almost humiliating for the provincial nobility which the council restricts to subordinate tasks by proclaiming that the court nobility is pre-eminently destined to command armies, in contempt of seniority and of the merit of the services performed by gentlemen who are poor, it is true, but often scions of houses no less illustrious than those whom their fortune enables to incur the necessary expense of being presented at court . . . the military career has become a matter of money; governorships and commands are its prerogative . . . a child scarcely out of college arrives, with a display of luxury humiliating for the others, to teach a captain of grenadiers what he has learnt from his father. . . . With tears in their eyes and grief in their heart, the nobility begs His Majesty to leave the higher ranks open to merit.

E. Champion, *La France d'après les cahiers* (1907), p. 172

65   The *cahier* of the Third Estate of Paris *intra muros*

1 That the town resume its ancient and natural right of electing its own *prévôt des marchands*; that this first municipal officer be drawn from the nobility, the *robe* and the bourgeoisie without distinction; that his name be changed to that of mayor of Paris.

3 That the odious wall, by means of which the king's tax farmers have imprisoned the capital, despite the prodigious efforts of the Parlement and the energetic patriotism of the municipal officers, be demolished from top to bottom at the expense of the said tax farmers.

4 Entreat the king to spend his winters in his good city of Paris. . . .

6 Diminish the terrifying proliferation of carriages, limit their terrifying speed, and at a time when everyone is talking about liberty, at least allow the poor pedestrian to defend his life.

7 Build the pavements which have been so long desired and as an interim measure install traffic-calming devices in the main streets. Only ever allow single-file traffic. All cabriolets should be fitted with a bell – even those belonging to princes, so that this new music becomes the safeguard of the citizen.

8 No proprietor should be allowed to build houses of more than four storeys, that streets may cease to be dirty valleys where the sun penetrates with regret.

12 Reduce the incredible number of petty assassins who, with the aid of a wig and a licence, wielding often only the razor, undertake to treat the most complicated illnesses and to whom the blood of the people seems to have been abandoned.

24 Diminish the vast number of free art and other schools and of scholarships to colleges which depopulate the countryside and workshops which are of much greater social utility than this crowd of unemployed clerks. ....

40 Introduce measures to limit the number of bankruptcies and make it impossible for a merchant whose business in the rue Saint-Honoré has failed to launch another which will fail in the faubourg Saint-Germain.

49 The final wish of the citizens of Paris is that the Estates-General, regularly convoked every three years, should in future be held in the capital where His Majesty can be surrounded by his loving subjects, just as well as at Versailles.

AP, vol. V, p. 525

66   The *cahier* of the Third Estate of Nemours

Chapter Four: Vingtièmes

The *vingtième* is the only rational tax – at least in theory – and the only one which, according to the spirit and letter of the edict establishing it . . . is meant to be proportionate to income. It is regrettable that this equity resides only in the word and not yet in the deed.

In 1750 M. Machault [controller-general] . . . judged that [the clergy] did not have a valid claim to exemption from a tax which was to be levied on the whole nation. He demanded that ecclesiastical property be valued. The clergy then saw fit to declare . . . that they only owe the state their prayers. The friends of M. de Machault replied: 'If the clergy only owes the state its prayers, then the state only owes the clergy alms.' The quarrel was very lively and strongly contested on both sides. M. de Machault was dismissed.

It took 37 years before another minister [Calonne] dared to attempt the same enterprise which in the event was just as fatal to him and served only to bring to office a prelate [Brienne, archbishop of Toulouse] who had it proclaimed by the *arrêt du conseil* of 5 June last that the amount paid by the clergy should only be proportionate to its zeal. It was certainly in his interest to manage the king's finances satisfactorily. Yet he did not think, even as prime minister, that he could obtain anything from his own order beyond the 900,000 for which he had thanked them. . . . [Yet he knew from the calculations of the Assembly of Notables that if the clergy paid on the same basis as the nobility they should pay 22,000,000.]

These facts demonstrate how much the power of the king is augmented by the help of that of the nation. No sooner was it certain that the Estates-General would meet than the clergy declared on all sides that it would be happy to contribute not only to the *vingtièmes* . . . but even to the replacement tax for the *taille* which would be assessed on all the orders; in a word that it would renounce all fiscal privileges. So that which 80 years' work had not managed to achieve, and which had cost two ministers their credit and place, found itself accomplished without difficulty the instant it pleased the king to say: 'To me, my people!' It must please him to see that this word is more effective than 'Guards, ho!' and much cheaper. . . .

The *vingtième* was levied on the property of the poor to the last penny. There is perhaps not a single property of the nobility, the *noblesse de robe* or even those citizens of the Third Estate distinguished by their wealth or by their offices which is taxed at the true rate. There was no need of collusion for this to happen. The vice lies in the general lack of public spirit which allows the tax assessors to believe that one cannot tax a man fairly without giving offence and creating a redoubtable enemy, however little influence the offended one possessed.

The Third Estate cannot but observe with sadness that this state of affairs was inevitable, since all the companies of magistrates supported it with all their power . . . that they made it a condition of all the prorogations of the *vingtième* and of all the augmentations proportionate to this tax, necessitated by the war[3] that the assessment should be made from the old tax rolls whose partiality was well known.

The Third Estate demands that the same equality . . . should be established between all the provinces as between all private citizens; that the *abonnements*[4] of all the *pays d'états* and the princes should likewise disappear.

AP, vol. IV, pp. 118–19

67 The *cahier* of the parish of Vitry-sur-Seine

1 We demanded as a matter or urgency that the tax band of the land at Vitry be altered . . . all the adjoining lands are in the second band whilst ours, inferior as it is [half liable to flooding, half stony] . . . has been placed in the first band.

4 The total suppression of all privileges whatsoever. Our parish . . . contains fifty bourgeois properties with the best land of the locality, whether houses, paddocks and land without paying any taxes. Moreover these privileged men profit from the misery of the inhabitants of the parish to buy up the land and houses which come on to the market by offering a price which no parishioner can give, given that he is burdened with paying annually taxes from which the privileged are exempt. And if these privileges are not stopped in their tracks, Vitry, which is on the doorstep of Paris, will soon find itself three-quarters populated by *valets* of independent means who assume the honourable title of *bourgeois de Paris*, and let or buy a manor.

Another sort of privilege are the exemptions from parish dues, which we expressly ask to be abolished. It is the most well-to-do inhabitants of the parish who, to get out of paying these dues, buy an office in the town militia, or the mint, or in the administration of the *gabelle*, the *aides*, etc. With the result that nine or ten of the richest . . . are exempt.

7 Total destruction of all rabbits.

9 Total abolition of . . . the right to keep a dovecote.

10 Herds to be forbidden entry to meadows from 1 March. . . .

12 The price of bread to be fixed at a lower price . . . and better quality, for it is often the case that the worse the bread the more it costs.

13 The export of grain to be absolutely forbidden.

---

3 France was involved in the War of American Independence, 1778–83; a third *vingtième* was introduced in 1782 on the condition that it be collected on the old rolls.

4 Exemption bought by a lump sum payment.

14 Introduction of national weights and measures.
15 Grain to be sold by weight [as opposed to volume].
18 Suppression of the *aides*: wine is a product of the land . . .
19 Suppression of the *gabelle*.

AP, vol. V, pp. 601–3

68   The *cahier* of Les Arcs, Provence

The division between the orders, each with its rights, objectives and conflicting interests, is a great misfortune for the nation and a great obstacle to the general good . . . If the rights were equal, all would have the same will. . . . The majority of the clergy and the nobility has made a giant leap towards this accord by consenting to pay a proportionate amount of all public taxes. There remains a great bone of contention between the orders in the shape of feudal rights which burden the persons and the property of the Third Estate; if it were possible to reconcile differences on this matter too, equal voting and even deliberation by order or by head would become almost irrelevant.

Champion, *La France d'après les cahiers*, p. 100 n. 1

69   The *cahier* of the inhabitants of Montauroux and Les Adrets

The inhabitants protest against the *banalité* – the obligation to have their produce pressed at the *seigneur's* mill.

The inhabitants live so far from the mills that they spend four or five hours taking their olives and their grain there and as long returning. They are obliged to cross rivers and dangerous torrents sixteen times. Several people have been drowned, since it is not possible to construct bridges. The inhabitants have even noted with sadness that a few years ago the *seigneur* built two new mills but restricted their use to foreigners.

Champion, *La France d'aprés les cahiers*, p. 145

70   Extracts from two of Robespierre's election pamphlets

F. Furet has argued that the full-blown Terror of 1794 was implicit in the language of 1789. These extracts, written before the Estates had even met and when France was not at war and Robespierre's life was not remotely threatened would seem to bear him out.

(a) From Les ennemis de la patrie démasqués par le récit de ce qui s'est passé dans les assemblées du Tiers Etat de la ville d'Arras *(Arras, 1789)*

Citizens the nation is in danger! Domestic enemies, more dangerous than foreign armies, are secretly plotting its ruin . . . What does it matter to me that . . . they are already considering the martyrdom of all the defenders of the people?

(b) From Au peuple de l'Artois par un habitant de la province *(March, 1789)*

This short passage contains three characteristic Robespierre themes: beware new patriots, beware traitors and construct a political biography of politicians; and the germ of a fourth: the need for purges.

Distrust new-minted patriots, those who go around proclaiming their mercenary devotion [to the people], and hypocrites who despised you yesterday and who flatter you today to betray you tomorrow. Question the past conduct of candidates: it must stand guarantee for their future conduct. To serve one's province worthily one must be without reproach.

71   Robespierre casts a damper: the duc de Guines, governor of Artois, to Laurent de Villedeuil, minister for the interior, 20 April 1789

[The nobility and clergy having renounced their fiscal privileges, a vote of thanks was proposed.] A barrister [Robespierre] got up and said that one owed no thanks to people who had done no more than renounce abuses. This motion was adopted by the majority. This order [the third] being in general badly composed, one presumes that it will present obstacles to the desired union and that the assembly will last a long time.

AN, B. II. 7

THE CONSTITUTIONAL MONARCHY

|1|

From Estates-General to National Assembly, May–July 1789

A comparison of the king's objectives as outlined in Part I, with the 'August Decrees' passed by the National Assembly in 1789 (**95**), in particular the abolition of fiscal privilege, provincial autonomy, seigneurial justice and venality of office, and a further comparison of the king's constitutional promises in the *résultat du conseil* (**60**) with the demands of the *cahiers* (**61–69**), would lead one to expect that the Revolution would have been accomplished peacefully. This expectation of a creative partnership between king and Estates is increased by an examination of document **74** which shows the intentions of the Breton deputies of the Third Estate as expressed to Bertrand de Molleville,[1] the former *intendant* of Brittany. In Brittany the royal policy of alliance with the Third Estate against the nobility in the local Estates had been particularly pronounced throughout the reign of Louis XVI and, having responded to this policy at provincial level and noted the king's general pronouncements – the *Avertissement* (**24**), the *arrêt* of 5 July (**53**) and the *résultat du conseil* (**60**) – these deputies came to the meeting of the Estates-General at Versailles intending 'to do all in their power to establish the king's authority in such a manner that the nobility and the Parlement might never have the power of injuring it'. This attitude must have been general with the deputies of the Third Estate, though the Breton deputies were among the most radical: their club – the Breton Club – was the nucleus of the celebrated Jacobin Club.

For his part, the king's attitude towards the Third Estate seemed to be favourable. In the *résultat du conseil* he had granted them a double representation but had left the Estates themselves to decide the question of voting procedures. In order to prejudge this question and bring about voting by head rather than by order, the Third Estate insisted that the credentials of all the deputies of whatever order should be 'verified' by the Estates as a whole sitting together in one room. And the king himself told the queen's circle of friends, the Polignac group, who were most hostile to the pretensions of the Third Estate: 'But it is not clear that the Third Estate are wrong.

---

1 Antoine François Bertrand de Molleville, 1747–1818, minister for the marine October 1791–March 1792.

Different forms have been observed each time the Estates have been held. So, why reject verification in common? I am for it' (**75**).

However, the Third Estate were to be deceived in these hopes and this deception more than anything produced that sense of betrayal and that climate of distrust and violence which are characteristic of the next five years of the Revolution. It is largely attributable to a failure of communication between the king and the Estates. The king was naturally taciturn and enjoyed leaving people to guess his intentions (**72**). No attempt was made to influence the elections to the Estates and, once they had met, Necker considered any attempt to 'manage' them as 'repugnant to the purity of his principles' (**74**, last paragraph). No guidance on the question of voting procedures was given either by the king or by Necker in their speeches opening the Estates.

Moreover, whilst Necker and his ministerial supporters Montmorin and Saint-Priest[2] pursued a policy of abstention, his opponents, led by Barentin, undeterred by their setback over the *résultat du conseil*, consistently urged the king to support the nobility against the Third Estate (**77–79, 83, 85, 86** and **90**). Barentin, as keeper of the seals, had special responsibility for the holding of the Estates-General and he was powerfully supported by the king's younger brother, the comte d'Artois, by the princes of the blood and by the Polignac group (**75** and **81**). Barentin's method was to deny the Third Estate access to a king who was basically 'in favour of verification in common' (**75**). The deputies of the Third Estate, worried by the month-old deadlock in the Estates, wanted to send a deputation to the king to explain their position and discover his. Barentin claimed that everything presented to the king should first be vetted by himself; the Third Estate refused this, claiming that 'communication between the king and the nation should be without intermediaries'. Denied an opportunity to explain themselves, the Third Estate were driven to proclaim themselves the National Assembly (**78**) – Barentin would not allow them to explain this to the king either (**79**) – and to a radical assumption of power, constituent as well as fiscal. This in turn forced the government to intervene by the *séance royale* of 23 June and a battle was joined which could and should have been avoided.

In fact both Barentin and Necker wanted the king to intervene at this juncture; both were annoyed by the declaration of the National Assembly; both wanted the Estates to vote on matters of common interest 'by head' and on matters relating to individual orders 'by order'. How Necker defined common interest is not known, because his draft proposals for the *séance royale* are lost, but he felt the changes were substantial enough, when he feared he would fail to carry the day, to advise the king to cancel the *séance* (**80**) and, when it went ahead, to absent himself from the ceremony. However, Saint-Priest's letter to the king in support of Necker's proposals (**82**) suggests that these were not sufficiently favourable to the Third Estate to guarantee their acceptance, quite apart from the Third Estate's likely objections to the king's 'sovereign intervention at this juncture'.

2 François Emmanuel Guignard, comte de Saint-Priest, 1735–1821, minister without portfolio 1788, appointed minister for the *maison du roi* after the fall of the Bastille.

The debate in the royal councils between the 'hawks' and the 'doves' was won by the former because they had a clearly defined position. Necker did not; nor – witness Saint-Priest's letter – could he guarantee success. In fact, since the departure of Brienne and Lamoignon the previous autumn, the council had not possessed an unequivocal advocate of the traditional policy of alliance between the king and the Third Estate. The *résultat du conseil*, popular though it was at the time, had really been a meaningless and misleading compromise; even now Necker told Malouet that he considered the nobility 'a great weight in the balance' and his proposals for the *séance royale* would apparently have led to a bicameral parliament – with a 'House of Lords' and a 'House of Commons' – which nobody wanted. Thus the case for alliance with the Third Estate went by default: French kings were not expected to take personal initiatives but to rule by counsel and there was no one present to advise such an alliance, though the indications are that it would have proved palatable. The Barentin faction, moreover, was able to take advantage of Louis's grief at the death of the dauphin on 4 June to withdraw the king from Versailles to the seclusion of Marly, where they were able to work on him at leisure: document **81** gives an idea of the pressures he had to withstand.

Of the *séance royale* in its final form (document **84**) it can be said that if the king had continued his alliance with the Third Estate, the sweeping constitutional concessions he granted would not have been necessary but that, as things stood, they were not sufficient. The proposals would have led to an aristocratic, de-centralized, limited monarchy and, as such, they were to hold a key position in the doctrines of the Counter-Revolution. But the most revealing aspect of the articles is the opening sentence: 'The king wishes the ancient distinction between the three orders of the state to be preserved in its entirety as being indissolubly linked to the constitution of his kingdom.' The fundamental issue here – and it is really the fundamental issue in the French Revolution – is whether the ancient distinction between the three orders be preserved, not just in the Estates-General but in society at large. It was not so much that the nobility did not want to sit next to the Third Estate because they would then be outvoted on, say, matters of feudal privilege, but simply that they did not want to sit next to *roturiers*. Had it not been said of them during the Assembly of Notables: 'They would not take part in assemblies if they risked being presided over or merely giving precedence to citizens of a lower order' (**22a**)? And here was the bourgeois Bailly president of the National Assembly. Similarly, it was this attitude of the nobility's which rankled with the Third Estate – so much so that within a year they had comprehensively abolished hereditary nobility and sought to destroy all visible reminders of its previous existence (**97**). This is why Necker's bicameral solution would never have been accepted, since it would not only have 'preserved the ancient distinction' but given it a new lease of life.

The *séance royale*, carried out in a deteriorating situation with the clergy about to go over to the Third Estate (**62**), was a fiasco. The very criers refused to proclaim the new laws, claiming that they had colds (**79**), whilst the Third Estate defied the king's orders and remained in occupation of the main chamber. On 27 June the king ordered the deputies for the clergy and nobility to join the Third Estate, Barentin having tried in vain to prevent this by asking the king to summon an extraordinary session of the council and reminding him that he 'owed it to himself . . . and to the legitimacy of his authority not to allow it to weaken or suffer any revolution during his reign' (86).

But the conflict did not end with the union of the orders. The decision had already been taken at Marly, concurrently with that to hold a *séance royale* – the first orders are dated 22 June – to concentrate troops in the area of Paris and Versailles. The purpose of these troop movements is obscure. Necker did not know it nor, he thought, did the king (87). The correspondence between the commander-in-chief, Broglie,[3] and his field commander in Paris, Besenval,[4] lieutenant-colonel of the Swiss Guards (88–90 and 92), shows that their plans were purely defensive and limited to protecting key points in the capital: the Bank, the Treasury, the Bourse, the Bastille and the Invalides. Indeed document 88 reveals doubts about the loyalty of some of the troops and contingency plans to abandon Paris and fall back on Versailles.

The Parisians, however, were expecting a coup against the capital, coupled with the forcible dissolution of the National Assembly, for which they took the replacement of Necker by Breteuil on 11 July to be the signal. This event sparked off disturbances in Paris which culminated in the storming of the Bastille on the 14th. In fact they need not have been alarmed by Breteuil. As minister for Paris at the time of the *coup d'état* of 8 May 1788 he had shown himself reluctant to take personal responsibility for repressive measures, insisting on holograph orders from the king (44) even though the king's support was assured. In 1789 this support was very doubtful. As Necker observes in document 87: 'They [the new ministry] also had to contend with the peculiar difficulties of inducing the king to act in a manner very contrary to his natural dispositions, and from these debates, disputes, and over-persuasions, necessarily resulted indecision and feeble half measures.' Small wonder that Breteuil 'paid a great deal of attention to installing himself in his *hôtel* and in forming his secretariat'[5] – and made no plans. Nor were his fears unfounded. The fear among the king's agents of execution in 1788 that the Parlement would 'take them to task' if they were unsuccessful became a reality in 1789 when, in November, Barentin, Broglie and Besenval were tried for the new crime of *lèse-nation*.

The rising in Paris resulted in the resignation of the Breteuil ministry and the return of Necker, whose fading reputation had been refurbished by the non-implementation of his measures. But the king's authority in Paris had been irreparably smashed: a municipal revolution had removed his control of the Hôtel de Ville whilst a new bourgeois militia, the National Guard, had assumed responsibility for the policing of the capital. The new situation is symbolically represented in document 93 when Saint-Priest, minister for the *maison du roi* and for Paris in Necker's third ministry, receives a rude shock

---

3 Victor-François, maréchal-duc de Broglie, 1718–1804; minister for war, 13–15 July 1789; exceptionally, Louis XVI handed over command of the troops round Paris and Versailles to him in June 1789.
4 Pierre-Victor, baron de Besenval, 1722–94.
5 J. F. X. Droz, *Histoire du règne de Louis XVI* . . . (2 vols., 1858–9), vol. II, p. 299.

on going to Paris 'in order to take possession of the municipal administration of the said city'.

72 The king to the duc de Liancourt, undated (but 15 March 1789)

The king made no attempt to influence the elections to the Estates-General and did not even reveal his position, as the following letter shows. Liancourt had been elected as a deputy to the Estates-General by the nobility of the *baillage* of Clermont-en-Beauvaisis and had sent the king the *cahier* of his *baillage*, which constituted his mandate, in case the king should consider that he had contracted obligations incompatible with his position as grand master of the wardrobe. The king offers him no guidance.

I am returning the papers which you sent me yesterday. When I saw you this morning I had not yet managed to read them; I know your heart and I have always had occasion to rely on your devotion to me; I do not doubt that in the assembly of Clermont you acted according to your Christian conscience and when I ordered the convocation of the Estates-General I permitted all my subjects to tell me everything they thought was for the good of the state. When the Estates-General are met, I shall treat with them concerning the high matters which will be there presented but before then I must not reveal my attitude towards individual deliberations provided they are conducted according to the rules.

AN, K. 679 no. 10

73 Louis XVI to Necker, *c.* 1 May 1789

This important letter shows Louis's insistence on playing a part in the legislative process. The somewhat awkward last sentence of the first paragraph probably means that the promises the king has made in the *résultat du conseil* (consent to taxation, etc.) do not need to be ratified by the Estates to have force of law.

Monsieur, I enclose your speech. I can tell you without flattery that I took great pleasure in re-reading it. I have just made a few minor corrections along the lines I have already indicated. At the beginning I have added *at the request* of the Estates because, as they cannot make law on their own, we must say that it is at their request, in accordance with their wishes, or something similar. In the second section, I still want to change the phrase with *Legislative Authority* compared to the promises the king has made [in the *résultat du conseil*]. . . .

I am not sure that the little compliment for the ministers won't excite ridicule. I think it would be best left out. The rest is really only minor points.

> *Recueil de documents relatifs aux séances des Etats-Généraux de 1789,* vol. I, ed. G. Lefebvre and A. Terroine (1953) and vol. I(2) ed. G. Lefebvre (1962); vol. I(2), p. 180

74   A missed opportunity: contact between Bertrand de Molleville and the Breton deputies

Some days after the opening of the Estates-General, the desire I had to know the particulars of what was passing carried me to Versailles. I was accosted, in the street, by three deputies of the Third Estate of Brittany. They expressed much regret that they had not been able to find me sooner, and requested a rendezvous, to confer with me upon very important matters. It was then about seven o'clock at night, and I proposed to accompany them to their lodgings. They agreed to this proposal so much the more willingly, as they expected, that evening, some of their colleagues, members of the Breton Club. . . . I accordingly went with them to their inn, where our company was soon increased by the addition of seven or eight persons, amongst whom were four deputies whom I had known in Brittany.

After I had been introduced to those who were strangers to me, Champeaux Paslane, deputy from Saint-Brieux, told me that since their arrival he and his colleagues had been extremely solicitous to see me, in order to take my opinion upon the conduct which they ought to maintain. 'We are here', he said, 'as if we had fallen from the clouds, in an unknown country, where an order of things exists of which we had no idea. We are unacquainted with the court and the ministers, we know not what they desire of us, and we hope that you will direct us. You know our reliance upon you, and you may believe that we shall pay the same regard to your advice here that we had in Brittany.' They all united in the same request, accompanied with the same assurances. I inquired what were their sentiments, and in what way they expected me to direct them. They assured me that their intention was to do all in their power to establish the king's authority in such a manner that the nobility and Parlement might never have the power to injuring it. I greatly approved of these sentiments; but I observed that as I was not in the ministry I could not take upon me to direct them; that it was M. Necker to whom they ought to address themselves; and that I would speak to him, if they authorized me. They answered that they were not fond of going to M. Necker because there was always a crowd at his house; and that if they were often seen with him they would be suspected of being sold to the court; but that if I would be their interpreter with M. Necker, and transmit them his instructions, they would always strictly conform to them. I promised to wait upon M. Necker next day, and to bring to them his answer. They then consulted me upon the choice of their president; and they knew so little of the court that they had determined to choose the duc d'Orléans, from the idea that they could not make a choice more agreeable to the king. I convinced them of their error; and M. Bailly was named president.

I went next day to inform M. Necker of the disposition of these deputies; but not being able to see him, I desired M. Coster, his first secretary, to acquaint him with my business. When I went, next day, to receive M. Necker's answer, M. Coster told me that the minister declined all private communication with those deputies as repugnant to the purity of his principles, since it might be considered as tampering with them, or a species of corruption.

> A. F. Bertrand de Molleville, *Private Memoirs Relative to the Last Year of the Reign of Louis the Sixteenth*, trans. G. K. Fortescue (2 vols., 1909), vol. I, pp. 157–9

75 The king of the Third Estate: extract from the memoirs of the comtesse d'Adhémar[6]

We [the queen's circle of friends] never ceased repeating to the king that the Third Estate would wreck everything – and we were right. We begged him to restrain them, to impose his sovereign authority on party intrigue. The king replied: 'But it is not clear that the Third Estate are wrong. Different forms have been observed each time the Estates have been held. So why reject verification in common? I am for it.'

The king, it has to be admitted, was then numbered among the revolutionaries – a strange fatality which can only be explained by recognizing the hand of Providence. Meanwhile Paris was unquiet and Versailles scarcely less so. The comte d'Estaing,[7] who was shortly to be commander of the National Guards of that town, was already playing an important role. The king freely listened to him . . .

The king, deceived on the one hand by the Genevan [i.e. Necker] . . . paid no attention to the queen's fears.

---

6 I am indebted to Professor Norman Hampson of the University of York for drawing my attention to the existence of these remarkable memoirs. They are ghosted from notes left by the comtesse, a leading member of the Polignac circle.
7 In the Assembly of Notables, d'Estaing had outspokenly defended the *Avertissement*.

This well-informed princess knew all about the plots that were being woven; she repeated them to the king, who replied: 'Look, when all is said and done, are not the Third Estate also my children – and a more numerous progeny? And even when the nobility lose a portion of their privileges and the clergy a few scraps of their income, will I be any less their king?'
This false perspective accomplished the general ruin.

> Comtesse d'Adhémar, *Souvenirs sur Marie-Antoinette, archiduchesse d'Autriche, reine de France et sur la cour de Versailles* (4 vols., 1836), vol. III, pp. 156–7

76   Robespierre to Buissart, 24 May 1789

... I have made no special mention of the chamber of the nobility. It scarcely merits the honour. It is divided into three parties, the *parlementaire* party, which would immolate the whole human race to preserve the power of the *parlements*; the party of the *grands seigneurs* of the court who combine all the sentiments conjured up by the pride of aristocrats with the servile baseness of courtiers; and that of the reasonable men which is small in number and not all of whom are exempt from the prejudices of the nobility. Numbered among this party, which is called that of the minority, are M. de la Fayette[8] and the duc d'Orléans. In general the chamber of the nobility contains few men of talents. D'Eprémesnil daily heaps extravagance on extravagance to the point where he destroys his credit even with his own party. When our deputies proceeded to the chamber of the nobility to announce our decisions to appoint commissioners [to discuss verification procedures] he protested heatedly against the title of 'Commons' which we have taken and which he presented as an English insurrection. He opposed with all his strength the renunciation of pecuniary privileges which the majority of the members of the nobility want to present to us, not out of patriotic motives but in the hope of negotiating more successfully with us at the expense of the rights of the nation, once they have made this illusory sacrifice which is no longer dependent on their will and which must no longer be a gift of the corps of the nobility but a constitutional law which the Estates-General alone ought to pass.

> Robespierre, *Oeuvres*, vol. III, pp. 41–2

8 Marie Jean Paul Motier, marquis de La Fayette, 1757–1834, soldier, deputy, commander of the Paris National Guard.

77   Barentin, keeper of the seals, to the king, 12 June 1789

The deputations from the chamber of the Third Estate to the other two orders [once more urging them to 'verify their powers' together] have been received. Both replied that they would discuss the matter. The Third was determined to wait for a reply.

They have passed a resolution to send an address to Your Majesty.

M. Bailly, the *doyen* of the Assembly [of the Third Estate] has just left me, having requested that I ask Your Majesty when he will be good enough to receive him and whether it will be alone or with other deputies and to what number. I replied to the *doyen* that I would take Your Majesty's orders but that it was not the form to present you with anything you had not seen in advance and that consequently he must give me the speech or address. He observed that the draft had not been absolutely finalized and that moreover he could not take it on himself to communicate it; he would have to discuss the matter with the other members of the deputation and if they preferred not to take a decision there might be no way of avoiding consulting the Assembly which might decide against this prior communication because it could lead to difficulties; it might also claim that communication between the king and the nation should be without intermediaries.

> *Lettres et bulletins de Barentin a*
> *Louis XVI, avril–juillet 1789*, ed. A.
> Aulard (1915), no. 37

78   Barentin to the king, 17 June

The vote was taken this morning and the Assembly has constituted itself the National Assembly by a majority of 490 to 90.

The Assembly immediately declared its present *doyen*, M. Bailly, president, but I think only provisionally and by acclamation until a regular election has been conducted.

Then they turned to the reply they should make to the nobility on the subject of their proposal concerning grain [the nobility had proposed that the three orders should concert action for relieving rural poverty].

The president read out a draft reply. He was beginning with the words 'I have the honour to reply, etc.', when a storm of protest erupted against the words 'I have the honour'. The National Assembly, they said, cannot have the honour. After a few moments, M. Bailly observed that he was speaking for himself and that in that case he ought to employ the word honour. More protests that his distinction was not valid. Then he proposed a new formula and this reply was roughly as follows: 'I am charged in the name of the National Assembly sitting in this chamber to reply that the deputies for the nobility have been constantly beseeched and invited to have their powers verified in common. The National Assembly will continue to hope that they will present themselves here to work together and in particular to consider ways of relieving public hardship.'

Lettres et bulletins de Barentin à
Louis XVI, no. 47

79   Barentin to the king, 19 June

The result of the deliberations of the three orders[9] will show Your Majesty that nothing has happened to impede his plans [for a *séance royale*] but that there is no time to lose in executing them and that Your Majesty should give orders that it is his pleasure that no order enter [its chamber] tomorrow; for once the clergy had left, there was some commotion and an attempt to force the *curés* to change their minds. There was a large number of people assembled for the purpose and it is important to render further developments impossible.

If the resolution passed by the nobility contains nothing which could displease Your Majesty I should consider it valuable, indeed absolutely essential, to the success of his further plans that he receive the deputation. There is a great difference between it and that of the Third Estate. The Third Estate asks to communicate to Your Majesty deliberations of which he cannot approve, whilst the nobility, on the contrary, is coming to present its respectful homage . . . and to represent to Your Majesty its alarm about the state of affairs now that the Third Estate has set itself up as a National Assembly. There is nothing to prevent its being received and danger in not admitting it.

Lettres et bulletins de Barentin à
Louis XVI, no. 48

80   Necker to Louis XVI, 20 June 1789

I have the honour of sending Your Majesty a note via the person whom I mentioned to Your Majesty yesterday under the seal of secrecy.

I have been made to realize that there are several drawbacks to a *séance royale* which I had overlooked and it is thought that an ordinary letter [inviting the orders to deliberate together on certain topics] would be better, but there is not a moment to lose. I will explain myself more particularly to His Majesty if he sees fit to give me his orders.

Recueil de documents relatifs aux
séances des Etats-Généraux de 1789,
vol. I(2), p. 180

---

9 On sitting with the Third Estate; this was rejected by the clergy by 137 votes to 128 and by the nobility by 172 to 60.

81 The chevalier de Coigny to the bishop of Soissons, 20 June 1789

This letter by one of the Polignac circle is transcribed by the comtesse d'Adhémar.

We are overjoyed here and I think that you will be as glad as we are when you learn of the decision which has just been taken. We are saved and the men of faction ruined for thus has the king decided and assuredly he will not go back now.

We had come to Marly in great agitation, we saw clearly where we were being led and we would have been lost if that rabble of the Third Estate had thought it could lay down the law to us. The good duchesse [de Polignac], who is so active and busy you would not recognize her, had fully comprehended that we could not fall asleep in a situation where we were staking everything; accordingly she saw fit to summon us all to the queen last night.

We spoke fervently to Her Majesty, we brought home to her the fact that nothing less than the overthrow of legitimate authority was at stake; that she was the principal target and that unless she aided us we would no longer answer for anything. M. d'Eprémesnil, who has been admitted for some time to our inner circle, gave her an elegant lecture. When he had finished, our pleasant prince [the comte d'Artois] gave him a playful box on the ear and said: 'You big child, if you'd always been so good we wouldn't have put you in disgrace and you'd have had a sweetie' [he had been one of the main *parlementaire* opponents of the crown in the period 1787–8].

This pleasantry cheered us up and made our gathering less sombre. It was then agreed that we should urge the king to curb the popular usurpations. The prince de Condé and the prince de Conti had been alerted and they were ready to come to the council whenever they should be summoned. For we judged that in such circumstances it was fitting that all the royal family should seem to be united in the same opinion.

This morning the queen and the king's brother went to see the king and asked him what he was planning to do; he seemed as usual very uncertain and said that really the matter was not worth worrying about; that as the previous Estates-General had not all acted uniformly as regards the protocol of their ceremonial, one could let them arrange it as they liked.

The conversation went on some time in this vein. Then the queen, unable to contain herself, depicted the throne overturned by the men of faction and the formation of a flagrant conspiracy aimed at changing the order of succession, adding that none of what was being done was for the good of the people but to aid a guilty prince [the duc d'Orléans] in seizing the crown.

Just when this princess was at her most impassioned, a secret deputation from the Parlement of Paris was announced. It was accompanied by the keeper of the seals, and M. d'Eprémesnil was also there. It had come to beg the king to dissolve the Estates-General whose existence was compromising the existence of the monarchy; at the same time it gave assurances that the Parlement, to arrest the tempest, would not hesitate to register such fiscal legislation as might be sent before it and would furthermore promise in advance to do anything which His Majesty wanted.

M. d'Eprémesnil in turn spoke forcefully; he drew attention to the existence of the plot, supplied proof and, in his boldness, went so far as to give the king to understand that in years to come he would be held responsible for all the ills that befell. His Majesty, struck by these words, gave a start and looked at the orator with surprise mingled with displeasure. The keeper of the seals in turn warned the king that it was dangerous to suffer the audacity of the Third Estate any longer. He said that all these barristers, lesser judges and country *curés* just wanted a general uprising, that already they were encroaching on the royal prerogative and that it would be culpable to tolerate their excesses.

Meanwhile M. le cardinal de La Rochefoucauld accompanied by the archbishop of Paris appeared in their turn. With emotion, they threw themselves at His Majesty's feet as soon as they entered and beseeched him in the name of Saint Louis and the piety of his august ancestors to defend religion, cruelly attacked by the *philosophes* who counted among their sectaries nearly all the members of the Third Estate.

Then our dear duchesse, carrying Monseigneur le dauphin and leading Madame Royale by the hand, pushed them into the arms of their father beseeching him to hesitate no longer and to confound the plans of the enemies of the family. The king, touched by her tears and by so many representations, gave way and intimated his desire to hold a council on the spot; the princes were informed and the council met immediately without summoning the controller-general (who knows nothing of this). Everything is settled: the king will issue a declaration which will satisfy the nation, will order the deputies to work in their respective chambers and will severely punish the meddlers and intriguers. You may rest assured that he will not budge and a *séance royale* is announced; it is there that the plan I tell you of will be unfolded . . .

Comtesse d'Adhémar, *Souvenirs*, vol.
III, pp. 170–5

82   Saint-Priest, minister without portfolio, to the king, undated (but 22 June 1789)

Yesterday Your Majesty deigned to ask my advice concerning the project presented by M. Necker and in particular the proposal to command the first two orders of the state to join with the third and vote by head on matters which do not concern the individual interests of each order and certain other stipulated issues. Their Royal Highnesses, your brothers, were of the opposite opinion. They thought that the constitution of the kingdom should in no way be changed and they applied this principle to the form of deliberation in question. Assuredly, Sire, it would be safer for my colleagues and myself, as individuals, if the opinion of their Royal Highnesses had been adopted in preference to ours. Having satisfied the promptings of our conscience we would not have to fear that the [i.e. Necker's] proposed project might not have the success we hope for. Because, Sire, I shall not conceal from Your Majesty that I fear lest the Third Estate, in its present exaltation, may claim those matters which are so justly reserved in the project for deliberation by order. I even fear that they will complain about the sovereign intervention of Your Majesty at this juncture, so heated do the members of the Third Estate appear, having already been led to exceed the limits of their mandates and of justice itself. Our one hope in that eventuality would be the verdict which the nation reached. But would Your Majesty find that resource, as slow as it is uncertain, in time to parry the numberless difficulties which might intervene? It is that, Sire, with which your ministers are threatened and all of us have disregarded this very natural anxiety because our zeal for the service of Your Majesty overrides all personal considerations on our part. At present there are only four of us who are *ministres d'état*[10] and we are men of age and experience, versed in the affairs of the kingdom at home and abroad; and our unanimous advice is in favour of the proposal made by one of us.[11] The young hotheads, eager for change, regard ancient laws as superannuated prejudices: but what we take into the most serious consideration, Sire, is the weight of present circumstances: the ship of state is threatened with wreck; it is a matter of avoiding it and this time we cannot do it by facing the storm. As at sea we must be able to lose ground in order to make it up later when this is dictated by justice and the good of the state. Despite its faults, I love the French constitution as well as anyone; but I confess that what I have seen practised hitherto in this kingdom has almost entirely consisted of the authority of every kind exercised by our kings for nigh on two centuries. I was as surprised as anyone at the return of the Estates-General and, although I do not disapprove, it is to my way of thinking an innovation or should I rather say a veritable renovation. But why should these Estates, after so long an interval, be still subjected so strictly to the form of deliberation practised in 1614 as though it had always operated invariably in the kingdom . . . ?

10 Only those ministers who were invited to sit in the *conseil d'en haut* were technically *ministres*. The other three were La Luzerne (marine), Montmorin (foreign affairs) and Necker.
11 This opinion was resisted by Barentin and Laurent de Villedeuil (*maison du roi*).

It's an old saying, Sire, but there's nothing constant under the sun. We must ply with circumstances – it is in reality they which govern states. The safety of the people should be the supreme law: your people, Sire, are led astray by new opinions. They have not erred from their devotion to your august person, which is extreme but – and I must not conceal it from Your Majesty – even this devotion is in large measure based on your well-known readiness to sacrifice even your own royal prerogative for the general good. Ought the right of the orders to deliberate separately be more sacred? No, Sire, I have no hesitation in saying so. It must give way to the needs of the moment, to the need to make the Estates-General work, to revive credit through public confidence, to provide for indispensable expenditure, to calm the people whilst they are experiencing a period of high food prices and are threatened with shortages.

People talk of upholding the constitution at all costs. But even if we closed our eyes to the terrifying scenario to which the strict application of this principle could lead, we should still need the means with which to act. Your Majesty has an army – it has to be paid. The royal treasury is empty: cannot these people see this army, almost from the start, reduced to free billeting and requisitions? Once discipline was slackened, would Your Majesty be able to rely on his troops? I pause before the sketch of this sad picture without including the advantage which rival powers may take of our internal troubles.

Sire, adopt the proposals which your ministers offer you. If it meets with resistance among the various orders it may perhaps only need patience and time will overcome difficulties. If, by misfortune, the result should be schism in the assembly, the people will see that their deputies have exceeded all limits without a sword having been drawn. Such is my preference. I make bold to transmit it directly to Your Majesty without having shown it to anyone, submitting it to your prudent consideration and august indulgence.

Recueil de documents relatifs aux
Etats-Généraux, vol. I(2), pp. 196–9

83   Barentin to the king, 22 June 1789

. . . Your Majesty will find enclosed the new draft [of the articles for the *séance royale*] which he charged M. Vidaud de La Tour to prepare. It has the advantage both of firmly maintaining the constitution and of opening up an avenue of conciliation which, without the king's dictating it, will have the same effects.

Lettres et bulletins de Barentin à
Louis XVI, no. 53

84   The *séance royale* of 23 June

Declaration of the king concerning the present session of the Estates-General

1 The king wishes the ancient distinction between the three orders of the state to be preserved in its entirety as being indissolubly linked to the constitution of his kingdom; and that the deputies freely chosen by each of the three orders, forming three chambers, deliberating by order but able, with the sovereign's consent, to agree to deliberate together, may alone be considered as constituting the body of the representatives of the nation. Consequently the king declares null and void the decisions taken by the deputies of the Third Estate on the seventeenth of this month and any subsequently adopted as being illegal and unconstitutional. . . .

7 His Majesty, having exhorted the three orders, for the good of the state, to meet together for the present session of the Estates only, and to deliberate in common on matters of general interest, wishes to make known his intentions concerning the manner in which they should be effected.

8 The following will be expressly excluded from the matters which may be discussed in common: matters relating to the ancient and constitutional rights of the three orders, the form of organization to be given to future Estates-General, feudal and seigneurial properties and the profitable rights and honorific prerogatives of the first two orders.

9 The separate consent of the clergy will be necessary for all provisions tending to affect religion, ecclesiastical discipline, secular and regular orders and associations. . . .

11 If, with a view to facilitating their union, the three orders decide that the matters they are to discuss in common shall only be carried by a two-thirds majority, His Majesty is disposed to authorize this form.

15 Good order, public decency and indeed freedom of debate require that His Majesty forbid, as he does expressly, any person, other than the members of the three orders comprising the Estates-General, from attending their discussions, whether they be together or in separate chambers.

*Declaration of the king's intentions (*volontés*)*

1 No new tax will be imposed or any old one extended beyond the date stipulated by legislation without the consent of the representatives of the nation.

2 Neither future taxes nor old ones will be extended beyond the period elapsing before the next meeting of the Estates-General.

3 Since loans necessarily lead to an increase of taxation, none will be contracted without the consent of the Estates-General but with the proviso that in case of war or other national peril, the sovereign will be able to borrow up to 100 million francs without delay. For it is the king's express intention never to allow the safety of the realm to be dependent on anyone.

5 A statement of revenue and expenditure will be published annually in a form proposed by the Estates-General and approved by His Majesty.

6 The sums assigned to each ministry will be determined in a regular and permanent manner and the king submits to this general rule even the sums assigned for the upkeep of his household.

8 The representatives of a nation which is mindful of the laws of honour and probity will in no wise violate public confidence and the king expects them solemnly to underwrite the debt of the state.

9 When the explicit intentions of the nobility and clergy to renounce their fiscal privileges have been given deliberative effect, the king's intention is to implement them so that there should no longer subsist any form of privilege or distinction in the payment of public taxation.

12 All forms of property without exception will be respected for all time and His Majesty expressly includes as property: tithes, *cens, rentes*, feudal and seigneurial rights and duties and, in general, all rights and prerogatives, both useful and honorific, belonging to lands and fiefs and categories of people.

14 His Majesty's intention is to determine, on the advice of the Estates-General, what employments and offices will continue in future to have the privilege of conferring and transmitting nobility. Notwithstanding, His Majesty, in virtue of the rights inherent in his crown, will continue to grant patents of nobility to those of his subjects who show themselves to be worthy of this reward through service to the king and the state.

15 The king, desirous of guaranteeing the personal liberty of every citizen on a permanent basis, invites the Estates-General to suggest the most workable way of abolishing the orders known as *lettres de cachet* whilst yet preserving the public safety and taking the precautions necessary to safeguard, in certain cases, the honour of families, to nip sedition in the bud and to preserve the state from the harmful effects of criminal intelligence with foreign powers.

16 The Estates-General will examine and communicate to His Majesty the most satisfactory way of reconciling freedom of the press with the respect due to religion, morality and the honour of the citizen.

17 In the various provinces or *généralités* [the unit administered by an *intendant*] of the kingdom provincial Estates will be established with the following composition: two-tenths clergy – with some seats automatically reserved for the episcopal order – three-tenths nobility and five-tenths Third Estate.

18 The members of the provincial Estates will be freely elected by the respective orders and some property qualification will be necessary to vote or be elected.

19 The deputies to these provincial Estates will deliberate in common on all matters, in accordance with the usage observed in the provincial assemblies which these Estates will replace.

29 The king desires that the laws which he promulgates whilst the Estates are in session and in accordance with their desires and wishes should not meet with any delay or obstacle in their registration and execution throughout the kingdom.

35 His Majesty, having summoned the Estates-General to join him in deliberating great matters of public welfare and everything capable of contributing to the good of his people, declares most expressly that he wishes to preserve intact and unimpaired the organization of the army and also all authority and disciplinary powers over the soldiers which the French monarchs have always enjoyed.

[In other articles the king invited proposals for abolishing the *taille* (art. 10), *franc fief* (art. 11), internal customs barriers (art. 25), the *gabelle* (art. 26), *aides* (art. 27), the *corvée* (art. 30), *mainmorte* (art. 31), and *capitaineries* (art. 32). He concluded with the following speech:]

Gentlemen, you have just heard a statement of my provisions and my objectives; they conform to my lively desire to act for the good of all and if, by a remote mischance, you were to abandon me in such a fine enterprise, I should effect the good of my peoples alone; alone I should consider myself their true representative and knowing the content of your *cahiers*, in the knowledge of the perfect harmony subsisting between the wishes of the vast majority of the nation and my own beneficent intentions, I will have all the confidence which so rare a harmony should inspire; and armed with this I will go forward courageously and steadfastly towards my goal.

Reflect once more, gentlemen, that none of your projects, none of your arrangements can have the force of law without my explicit approval; thus I am the natural guarantor of your respective rights and all the orders of the state can rely on my equity and impartiality; any mistrust on your part would be a great injustice. So far it is I who have done everything for the welfare of my peoples and it is perhaps rare that the solitary ambition of a sovereign should be to persuade his subjects to agree together at last so that they can accept his gifts.

I order you, gentlemen, to disperse immediately and each of you to proceed tomorrow morning to the chamber assigned to his order, there to resume your deliberations. In consequence whereof I order the grand master of ceremonies to prepare the chambers.

AP, vol. VIII, pp. 143–6

85   Barentin to the king, 24 June 1789

... I have given orders for the proclamation of the laws emanating from
Your Majesty yesterday: they have not yet been proclaimed and several
criers, upon being asked why they were not crying, replied that they had
colds.

Lettres et bulletins de Barentin à
Louis XVI, no. 55

86   Barentin to the king, 25 June 1789

The conduct of the chamber of the Third Estate, its heated deliberations
yesterday, its resolution of the previous day, its apparent contempt for Your
Majesty's wishes, all demonstrate how necessary it was for Your Majesty to
preserve the principles of the monarchy. But it is not enough, Sire, to have
enshrined them, they must be maintained; and the more they are flouted,
the more it is the duty of a king to reclaim those who have wandered from
the truth. Far be it from me to propose to Your Majesty any act which
could go against the kindly intentions of his heart, but at the same time he
owes it to himself, to those of his subjects who are truly loyal to him and
finally to the legitimacy of his power not to allow his authority to weaken
or suffer any revolution during his reign. These various important considerations and several points which seem to demand immediate attention
would seem to require that Your Majesty hold a council. If he were pleased
to indicate one for this evening we would be able to deal with what had
happened in the various chambers today and to propose to Your Majesty
what seemed best in the grievous crisis in which we find ourselves and the
state: only the pooling of ideas can indicate the road to follow.

Lettres et bulletins de Barentin à
Louis XVI, no. 58

87   Necker on the troop movements

The ... intelligence that the court was drawing troops to Versailles and
that several regiments were already on their march soon gave rise to a fresh
alarm. Most of the ministers of state, and I was one of them, were kept in
ignorance of these orders till their effects became matter of public notoriety.
The minister at the head of the war department spoke of the transaction as
a measure of caution rendered necessary by the seditious movements that
had recently taken place in Versailles and Paris. This seemingly natural
explanation, however, became suspected as soon as it was known that
maréchal Broglio had received orders to come to court. For my own part, I
was never made perfectly acquainted with the plans that were in agitation;
the whole was a system of secrets within secrets and I believe the king

himself was unacquainted with the final view of his advisers, who probably intended to reveal them only by degrees, and according to the pressure of circumstances. . . .

But no foresight, no wisdom, distinguished the enterprises of the new ministry which had made such liberal promises and whose abilities were supposed to be equal to any concurrence of circumstances. They also had to contend with the peculiar difficulties of inducing the king to act in a manner very contrary to his natural dispositions and from these debates, disputes, and over-persuasions, necessarily resulted indecision and feeble half-measures, which combined the mischiefs of both systems, without any of the advantages of either.

> J. Necker, *On the French Revolution*
> (2 vols., 1797), vol. I, pp. 213–14,
> 223–4

88   The duc de Broglie to the baron de Besenval, lieutenant-colonel of the Swiss Guards, Versailles, 1 July 1789, 12.30 p.m.

I have just received the letter which you did me the honour of sending at nine o'clock this morning. I read it immediately to His Majesty who ordered me to instruct you that if the warnings you have been given of a rumoured attack by the populace today on the Discount Bank and the Royal Treasury materialize, the king consents that you assemble all the forces on which you can rely to safeguard the Royal Treasury and the Discount Bank and that to this end you implement the arrangements proposed in your letter and that you confine yourself to defending these two positions, the importance of which you fully realize and which fully deserve all your attention at a time when we are unfortunately not in a position to look to everything.

I shall order the marquis d'Autichamp to remain in his command at Sèvres and then, if it becomes necessary, to bring up the Salis regiment as reinforcement to protect Versailles, falling back on the palace if necessary.

The comte de Puységur [minister for war] will send you an adjutant.

> Published by P. Caron in 'La tentative
> de contre-révolution de juin–juillet,
> 1784', *Revue d'histoire moderne* 8
> (1906), p. 25.

89   Broglie to Besenval, 5 July 1789

M. de Crosne has just asked me, Monsieur, for assistance in maintaining order in Paris should it be troubled tomorrow by the common people if they cannot obtain bread at the morning market and he has requested me to authorize you to employ the Swiss regiments arriving in the course of the day at the Champ de Mars to restore order, if need be and only if the regiments of guards and the Swiss regiments already in Paris are insufficient for this task. As this request is solely intended to afford protection to the citizen and to prevent disorder, I fully authorize you to comply with it, employing that habitual circumspection which you have evinced over the last three months which will prompt you to issue the officers commanding the detachments you may be called upon to employ with the most precise and limited orders so that the troops may only act as protectors and scrupulously avoid getting entangled with the people – unless to prevent arson or excesses and pillage which threaten the safety of the citizen.

I trust that you will not have to employ these means and I desire it more than I can express: I am perfectly sure that these are no less your own sentiments.

Caron, 'La tentative de contre-révolution', p. 25

90   Fears for the safety of the Bastille: Broglie to Besenval, 5 July, 3.30 p.m.

. . . To return to the matters in your letter, I will say straight away that there are two sources of anxiety concerning the Bastille: the person of the commandant and the nature of the garrison there. To obviate these difficulties I have engaged His Majesty to instruct the comte de Puységur to confer with M. de Villedeuil [minister for the *maison du roi* and Paris] and recommend a good senior officer to whom he can entrust the command of the Bastille and send there as commandant; and you must despatch to this post (today if you can but certainly tomorrow after the arrival of the Swiss regiments who are to camp on the Champ de Mars) 30 men from these regiments to act as a garrison – and see that they are under a very firm officer; and as soon as the artillery regiment arrives you must send in a small detachment of gunners to examine whether the cannons are in good order and to use them if it comes to that – which would be extremely unfortunate but happily is wildly improbable. . . .

Caron, 'La tentative de contre-révolution', p. 26

91   Barentin to the king, 8 July 1789

. . . M. de Mirabeau then proposed a very strong motion to the effect that Your Majesty be beseeched to withdraw the artillery and troops and send them back to the places from which they were taken. He proposed the establishment of a bourgeois militia, both in Paris and Versailles.

Things were very heated in the Assembly and there were threats to denounce those who had given Your Majesty such a perfidious counsel as to call in troops. I am only giving Your Majesty a faint impression of all the dangerous principles advanced in this session and of the fatal consequences for royal authority to which they could lead: their every act seems to reveal a fixed intention to lay hold of it.

> *Lettres et bulletins de Barentin à*
> *Louis XVI*, no. 73

92   Broglie to Besenval, 11 July 1789

The bureaux [of the war office] have sent out their orders so imperfectly and the schedule we have been given for the movement of the troops bears so little relation to the routes that were sent them that they are not arriving on the expected days with the result that they find neither staff officers to receive them nor food and lodgings prepared; all this will sort itself out gradually. . . .

As I am apprised from many quarters that there is reason to fear a violent insurrection at daybreak tomorrow, I beseech but also enjoin you – as the king writes to bishops – I instruct you therefore, on the pretext of military exercises, to bring up the battalions of Swiss Guards which are at Rueil and Courbevoie . . . before dawn. . . .

If there is a general insurrection we cannot defend the whole of Paris and you must confine yourself to the plan for the defence of the Bourse, the Royal Treasury, the Bastille and the Invalides. . . .

> Caron, 'Contre-révolution', pp. 27–8

93   Saint-Priest on the collapse of royal authority in Paris after 14 July

Necker [on his return from exile] appeared before the National Assembly and received an ovation. Next, he wanted to go to Paris to enjoy a triumph and show himself at the Hôtel de Ville. As the capital fell within the jurisdiction of my ministerial department, I thought the occasion would be propitious to accompany him in order to take possession of the municipal administration of the said city. This was a false step but Necker readily accepted my offer. We left in his carriage, escorted by the National Guard of Versailles . . . Finally we reached the Hôtel de Ville. Upstairs we found a table at the head of which were two armchairs which I thought had been put there for Necker and myself, both of us being *ministres d'état*. The mayor, Bailly, offered one to Necker and, without ceremony, took the other, indicating to me the first place on the benches along the table where the new town councillors, who had been elected without the king's participation, were sitting. I had, for the sake of peace; to suffer this insolence on the part of the mayor, hitherto my subordinate (with the title *prévot des marchands*), who took his orders direct from the minister for Paris. But royal authority in the capital had already vanished. . . .

> *Mémoires de Saint-Priest*, ed. baron
> de Barante (2 vols., 1929), vol. I, pp.
> 240–1

94   Robespierre to Buissart, 23 July 1789

. . . Noteworthy among the bodies which addressed thanks to the National Assembly [after Necker's reappointment] were the *grand conseil*, the *cour des monnaies* and above all the Parlement. Concerning the last there is an anecdote which you will perhaps not be sorry to hear. Instead of deputing a delegation to the National Assembly to present its decree, the Parlement saw fit merely to send it. A member of the Assembly made the observation that since the Parlement was merely a private body within the state, it could not address as an equal the National Assembly which represented the nation of which it formed but an infinitesimal portion and that it should have taken the trouble to present its homage in person. The duc d'Aiguillon got up and declared that speaking as a member of the Parlement [as a peer] he agreed with the previous speaker; the duc de La Rochefoucauld said the same thing; a judge in the Parlement of Aix, who is in no way a *parlementaire*, M. d'André, said: 'If it be permitted to a miserable provincial judge to speak on this matter, I would say I was of the same opinion'; finally M. d'Eprémesnil, the most ardent defender of *parlementaire* folly, who had not yet opened his mouth in the National Assembly, got up to say that he adhered to everything which had just been said. To such cowardly and hypocritical proceedings, I prefer the conduct of M. Fréteau, who tried to make some excuse in favour of his corps. . . .

Adieu my dear friend, my compliments to all my friends and to all the patriots. . . .

M. Foulon[12] was hanged yesterday by a decree of the people.

> Robespierre, *Oeuvres*, vol. III, pp.
> 48–50

---

12 Joseph-François Foulon, baron de Douai, 1715–1789, was a junior minister in the Breteuil
   administration.

2

The legislative work of the National Assembly, 1789–1791

After the July crisis, the National Assembly settled down to its self-appointed task of remodelling France and giving her a written constitution. Its legislative achievement can be divided into two categories: the first being that which was merely the culmination of the policies of centralization and standardization patiently pursued by the kings over the centuries (but with a greater sense of urgency since 1786); the second being the product of the abstract thinking of the Enlightenment. In the first category stand the August Decrees (**95**), the abolition of nobility (**97**) and the *Loi Le Chapelier* (**100**); in the second stand the Declaration of the Rights of Man and the Constitutional Articles (**101**) and the civil constitution of the clergy (**99**).

Much of the programme of the August Decrees can be found in the programme which Calonne presented to the Assembly of Notables in 1787, whilst seigneurial justice had been virtually abolished by the edicts of 8 May 1788 and venality of office in the *parlements* had been abolished in 1771, though later restored. But the king's efforts had been successfully resisted by those with vested interests in the status quo and it had taken the National Assembly, or the threat of it, to overcome them, as the *cahier* of the Third Estate of Nemours (**66**) had observed. That is the force of Mirabeau's assertion in document **96**: 'that in the course of a single year liberty had triumphed over more prejudices destructive of power . . . than royal authority could over several centuries'.

However, in 1790 and 1791 this revolution was carried a stage further. The decree of 19 June 1790 (**97**) abolishing nobility and the straight abolition of the *parlements* (**98**) was the *reductio ad absurdum* rather than the logical extension of royal policy. Mirabeau may have been right in claiming that 'this uniform surface . . . facilitates the exercise of power'. Napoleon was to discover this. But was he right in claiming: 'The notion of forming just one class of citizens would have pleased Richelieu'? For the kings, whilst attacking the political and financial privileges of the nobility, had sought to preserve their social status. Yet this was precisely what the National Assembly challenged. As early as August 1789, when the Declaration of Rights was drafted, it had asserted not only equal admissibility of all citizens to all offices (article 6) but, in its first article, that 'social distinctions can only be founded on public utility'.

Turgot had abolished the guilds in 1776, only to see them restored after his fall, and the *Loi Le Chapelier* (**100**) returns to this policy but greatly enlarges its scope. 'Trade unions' are outlawed on the grounds that 'the abolition of every kind of corporate organization for citizens of the same condition or profession is one of the fundamental bases of the French Constitution'. Le Chapelier was to try to muzzle the Jacobin Clubs on the same grounds and one may question whether his equation of a 'trade union' with a corporation such as a *parlement* is specious and ask whether his motives are constitutional or economic and political.

In the category of the National Assembly's more abstract, doctrinaire pronouncements, derived from theory rather than French experience, pride of place goes to the Declaration of Rights (**101**) and the civil constitution of the clergy (**99**). There is some indebtedness to Rousseau – 'The law is the expression of the general will' (article 6) – and more to the American Declaration of Rights. The American doctrine of the separation of powers is put in an extreme form – 'Only a society in which . . . the separation of powers . . . [is] effected has a constitution' (article 16) – and this was to have a profound influence on the development of the Revolution. The Americans have given us the word 'gridlock' and the French the experience of it: institutionalized distrust of the executive resulting in paralysis of the political process. To this theoretical distrust of the executive, endemic in the eighteenth century, was added mistrust of the incumbent king, the man Louis XVI. Further comment on his constitutional position will be offered in the next section. Many articles, however, were uncontroversial, deriving as they did from the *résultat du conseil* and the *cahiers*; such articles were: abolition of *lettres de cachet* (article 7), freedom of expression (articles 10 and 11) and consent to taxation (articles 13 and 14).

Louis XVI had been reluctant to sanction the Declaration of Rights before the constitution to which it was to stand preface had been drafted. For Robespierre this was not a problem: every clause in the constitution should be derived from the principles enunciated in the Declaration. In document **103** he refutes the idea that a knowledge of diplomacy is necessary to settle the question of the feudal rights of the German princes with land in the provinces, such as Alsace and Lorraine, which had been ceded to the king of France. Imagine then his consternation when the Assembly, in drafting the constitution, extended its mistrust of the king to the people also. As Robespierre correctly observed (**102**) elections to the Estates-General had been held under virtual manhood suffrage (they had also been completely free (**72**)). Now the Assembly proposed to restrict the political rights and access to the National Guard of those who had given the Assembly its mandate if they did not possess a qualification based on the possession of landed property. Robespierre was to inveigh against the hypocrisy and verbal juggling involved in the division into 'active' citizens, who enjoyed the vote, and 'passive' citizens who did not. The distinction was all the sharper because the constitution was to provide for election to every imaginable post and for some which it would be hard to imagine, like election of the clergy provided for by the civil constitution.

Talleyrand famously called the civil constitution 'the biggest single blunder of the Constituent Assembly'. It caused a headlong collision between two absolutist spiritual forces, the French Revolution and the Papacy. The stumbling block was not the confiscation of church lands, the dissolution of the monasteries (article 21) or even the election of bishops and *curés* (chapter II) but the new boundaries for the bishoprics which were to coincide with the departments which replaced the old provinces. For this required papal institution (specifically forbidden by clause 19): as there were 135 old bishoprics and only 83 departments, some bishops would have to resign and others be assigned new sees. Pius VI condemned the civil constitution and half the *curés* and all but seven bishops refused to take the oath that the Assembly insisted they take on 27 November 1790. Schism was thus established and with it the raw material for a civil war.

95   The August Decrees

1 The National Assembly abolishes the feudal system entirely. It decrees that, as regards rights and duties, both feudal and *censuel* [the *cens* was an annual tax paid by *roturiers* for land attached to a *seigneurie*], those relating to *mainmorte* applying to lands or persons and to personal serfdom, and those which represent them are abolished without indemnity; all the others are declared to be redeemable and the rate and mode of redemption will be determined by the National Assembly. Those of the aforementioned rights which are not abolished by this decree will continue to be collected until their owners have been compensated.

4 All seigneurial courts are abolished without any indemnity; nevertheless, the officers of these courts will continue in their functions until the National Assembly has made provision for the establishment of a new judicial system.

5 All forms of tithe and dues in lieu of them . . . are abolished, subject to making alternative provision for the expenses of divine worship, payment of priests, poor relief, etc. . . . to which they are at present allocated.

7 Venality of judicial and municipal offices is abolished with immediate effect. Justice will be administered without charge. Notwithstanding, the titularies will continue to exercise their functions and receive payment until the Assembly has made provision for their reimbursement.

9 Financial privileges, whether relating to persons or to land, in matters of taxation are abolished for all time. Payment will fall on all citizens and all lands, in the same manner and form. . . .

10 Since a national constitution and public liberty are more advantageous to the provinces than the privileges which some of them enjoy and which must be sacrificed for the sake of the intimate union of all the

parts of the empire, it is declared that all the special privileges of the provinces, principalities, *pays*, cantons, towns and village communes, whether pecuniary or of any other kind, are abolished forever and assimilated into the common rights of all Frenchmen.

11 All citizens, without distinction of birth, are eligible for all offices and dignities, whether ecclesiastical, civil or military, and no useful profession will carry *dérogeance*.[1]

16 The National Assembly decrees that in memory of the great and important decisions which have just been taken for the welfare of France, a medal shall be struck and that a Te Deum shall be sung as a thanksgiving in all the parishes and churches in the kingdom.

17 The National Assembly solemnly proclaims King Louis XVI the Restorer of French Liberty.

AP, vol. VIII, p. 511

96   Two extracts from Mirabeau's notes for the court

After castigating the court in the early days of the National Assembly, Mirabeau strove for *rapprochement* and between June 1790 and February 1791 sent the queen a series of 50 secret letters of advice, much of which was fanciful and little of which was heeded. In the following extracts, however, he offers a persuasive interpretation of the Revolution, as completing the work of the monarchy, which is utterly consistent with the views he had expressed over the previous five years (**15 and 57**).

(a) From the eighth note, 3 July 1790

... A portion of the operations of the National Assembly – and that the most considerable – is evidently favourable to monarchical government. Is it nothing to be rid of the Parlement, the pays d'états, the corporate power of the clergy, of those with privileges, of the nobility? The notion of forming just one class of citizens would have pleased Richelieu. If this uniform surface is favourable to liberty, it also facilitates the exercise of power. Several reigns of absolute government would not have done as much for royal authority as a single year of liberty.

(b) From the twenty-eighth note, 28 September 1790

... I have always said that the revolution is consummated but not the constitution; that the various points on which it is impossible to go back

---

1 If a nobleman entered a mechanical trade (except glass-blowing) or traded as a retailer (but not a wholesaler) he was supposed to forfeit his nobility. However, this was a matter of internal regulation among the nobility rather than a law of the state and the precise operation of the rules of *dérogeance* (or even whether they operated) is uncertain.

have rather strengthened than weakened royal authority, properly understood; that in the course of a single year liberty had triumphed over more prejudices destructive of power, crushed more enemies of the throne, obtained more sacrifices for national prosperity than royal authority could have done over several centuries. I have always drawn attention to the fact that the annihilation of the clergy [i.e. its corporate status], the *parlements*, the *pays d'états*, feudalism, the capitulations of the provinces and privileges of every kind is a conquest common both to the nation and to the monarch.

> *Correspondance entre le comte de Mirabeau et le comte de La Marck,*
> vol. I, pp. 355, 424

97   The law of 19 June 1790 abolishing nobility

The National Assembly decrees that hereditary nobility is for all time abolished and that consequently no one whosoever shall use or be addressed by the titles of *prince, duc, comte, marquis, vicomte, vidame, baron, chevalier, messire, écuyer, noble* or any other similar title.

Every French citizen must use only the real surname of his family. He may no longer wear livery or cause it to be worn or possess armorial bearings. In church, incense will be burned only to honour the deity and will not be offered to anyone be he never so high.

No body or individual will be addressed by the titles *monseigneur* and *meisseigneurs* nor by those of *excellence, altesse, éminence* or *grandeur*. However, no citizen may choose to make the present decree a pretext for defacing monuments placed in churches, charters, titles and other documents of importance to families, property or the embellishments of any public or private building; nor may anyone at all proceed with or require the implementation of the provisions relating to liveries and to armorials on carriages before 14 July (for citizens resident in Paris) or before the expiry of three months (for those living in the provinces).

> *AP*, vol. XVI, p. 378

98   The end of the *parlements*

On 3 November 1789 the National Assembly prolonged the summer vacation of the *parlements* indefinitely and on 7 September of the following year abolished them. Napoleon was to create a new nobility, the king came back in 1814, the *émigrés* received compensation in 1824 for their confiscated lands, but the *parlements*, that most characteristic institution of the *ancien régime*, sank without trace, mourned by few of those who had cheered their return in September 1788. Their fate had been foreshadowed when Louis XVI had been driven by their obstructiveness to convoke the Assembly of Notables.

A short extract is given below of the debate in the National Assembly on 3 November followed by the decree which, in the words of Alexandre de Lameth, 'buried the *parlements* alive'. Lameth interrupted a debate on the new administrative divisions of France to urge that the *parlements'* functions be immediately suspended lest they impede the working of the new authorities as they had the provincial assemblies in 1787–8. He continued:

The Constitution will never be solidly established as long as there exist, side by side with the National Assembly, bodies which rival its power, have been long accustomed to regard themselves as the representatives of the nation and are so formidable through the influence of their judicial power – bodies whose subtle tactics have enabled them to turn every eventuality to the increase of their power. . . .

M. *Target*: The *parlements*, it should not be forgotten, declared their incompetence to consent to taxation and they demanded the convocation of the Estates-General; perhaps it is not given to bodies which are less enlightened and more addicted to forms than nations to transcend prejudices . . . they did not see that the legislative power belongs to the citizens; that the orders derive from private interests which divide the empire and that instead of the Estates-General of 1614 we needed what we now have – a National Assembly; the time has come, the revolution is accomplished, the nation has resumed its rights forever. The Assembly will be permanent; there will no longer be any laws but those which it has passed; the most prompt obedience to them is requisite; delays, which were a resource, would today be a crime; there were then tribunes, of a kind, there are now only judges. Registration will now be no more than a transcription on to the registers. . . .

The National Assembly decrees:

1 That in the short interval before it deals with the new organization of the judicial power, all the *parlements* will continue to remain in vacation and that those which have returned from vacation will go back into that state; that the *chambres des vacations* will continue or resume their functions and hear all cases notwithstanding any regulation to the contrary until other provisions have been made on this head.

2 That the president shall withdraw to the king's presence to ask him to sanction this decree and request him to expedite all the necessary letters and orders.

AP, vol. IX, pp. 664–6

99 The civil constitution of the clergy, 12 July 1791

Chapter I: Ecclesiastical offices

I   Each department will form a single diocese and each diocese will have the same extent and the same limits as the department.

II   The seats of the bishoprics of the 83 departments of the kingdom will be fixed in accordance with the following table. . . .

All the other bishoprics present in the 83 departments of the kingdom which are not expressly mentioned in the present schedule are and will remain suppressed.

III   The kingdom will be divided into ten metropolitan provinces.

VII   On the advice of the bishop and of the district authorities immediate steps will be taken for a new division of all the parishes of the kingdom. . . .

XV   The canons of cathedral churches and the vicars superior and directors of the seminary together will form the permanent advisory body to the bishop, who will be incapable of any act of jurisdiction, concerning the governance of the diocese or seminar, without having first consulted it. Notwithstanding, the bishop, in the course of pastoral visits, may issue the appropriate provisional ordinances.

XVI   In towns where there are less than 6,000 souls, there will be only one parish; the other parishes will be suppressed and joined to the principal church. . . .

XXI   All titles and offices except those mentioned in the present constitution, all dignities, canonries, prebendaries, demi-prebendaries, chantries, whether of cathedral or collegiate churches, and all regular and secular chapters of either sex; all priories and abbeys, whether regular or *in commendam*, likewise of either sex, and all other benefices and *prestimonies* generally of whatever kind and under whatever denomination are, from the day of the publication of the present decree, suppressed without possibility of establishing anything similar.

Chapter II: nomination to ecclesiastical offices

I   From the publication of the present decree there will be only one way of appointing to bishoprics and cures, namely election.

II   All elections will be conducted by ballot; the successful candidate will have an absolute majority of votes.

III   The election of bishops will be conducted in the form prescribed and by the electoral college provided for by the decree of 22 December 1789 for the nomination of members of the departmental administration.

XV   The minutes of the election and of the proclamation will be sent to the king by the president of the electoral body to inform His Majesty of the choice which has been made.

XIX The new bishop may not ask the Pope for confirmation; but he may write to him as the visible head of the Church Universal in token of the unity of faith and of the communion he should maintain with him.

XXI Before the ceremony of consecration begins, the newly elected one, in the presence of the municipal officers, the people and the clergy, will take a solemn oath to care for the faithful of the diocese which is entrusted to him, to be faithful to the nation, to the law and to the king and to maintain with all his power the constitution decreed by the National Assembly and accepted by the king.

AP, vol. XVII, pp. 55–60

100 The *Loi Le Chapelier*, 14 June 1791

This decree takes its name from that of its proponent, Isaac-René-Guy Le Chapelier, 1754–94. He had previously been president of the National Assembly on the night of 4 August and had also proposed the decree abolishing nobility. In the summer of 1791 he was a strong advocate of increasing the king's constitutional powers.

1 As the abolition of every kind of corporate organization for citizens of the same condition or profession is one of the fundamental bases of the French constitution, it is forbidden to restore them indirectly no matter what the pretext or form.

2 Citizens of the same condition or profession, employers, master craftsmen and workers in any craft whatsoever may not, when gathered together, appoint a president, secretaries or permanent committee, keep minutes, pass resolutions or draw up regulations concerning their pretended common interest.

3 All administrative or municipal bodies are forbidden to receive or reply to any address or petition in the name of a craft or calling and they are enjoined to declare null and void such resolutions as may have been taken in this manner and to ensure that they are not carried any further.

4 If, in violation of liberty and the constitution, citizens belonging to the same professions, arts and crafts pass resolutions or contract engagements among themselves tending to refuse employment or withhold labour or to offer it only at a pre-determined rate, the said resolutions and engagements, whether accompanied or not by an oath, are declared to be unconstitutional, in contempt of liberty and the Rights of Man and null and void: administrative and municipal bodies are obliged to declare them as such. Those who instigate, draft or preside over the passing of such resolutions will be . . . fined 500 francs each and be suspended for a year from the exercise of all the rights of an active citizen and from a seat in the primary assemblies.

6 If the said resolutions or agreements, placards or circular letters contain any threats against employers, artisans, workers or day labourers coming into the locality for work or against those who settle for a lower wage, then all authors, instigators and signatories of such acts or writings will be punished with a fine of 1,000 francs each and three months' imprisonment.

7 Those who employ threats or violence against workers exercising the freedom to work and the freedom to employ granted by the constitutional laws will be prosecuted as criminals and punished according to the rigour of the law as disturbers of the peace.

8 All assemblies consisting of or instigated by artisans, workers, journeymen and day-labourers in restraint of the free exercise of the right to employ and to work on any terms mutually agreed, which belongs to all men, or to impede the police and the execution of judgements passed in this field and likewise tenders and the public allocation of different contracts, shall be deemed seditious assemblies; and as such they will be dispersed by the depositories of the public force, after being requested to do so in accordance with the law, and their authors, instigators and leaders and all those who have committed assault and acts of violence will be punished according to the full rigour of the law.

AP, vol. XXVII, p. 211

101   The Declaration of the Rights of Man

The representatives of the French people, constituted as the National Assembly, considering that ignorance, neglect or contempt for the rights of man are solely responsible for public misfortunes and the corruption of governments, have resolved to set forth the natural, inalienable and sacred rights of man in a solemn declaration, to the end that it may serve all the members of the body politic as a constant reminder of their reciprocal rights and duties; that the acts of the executive and legislative powers may be all the more respected because they can be constantly compared with the end of all political institutions; and that the demands of the citizens, grounded henceforth on simple and incontestable principles, should always tend to the maintenance of the constitution and the common good.

Consequently the National Assembly, in the presence and under the auspices of the Supreme Being, recognizes and declares the following rights as belonging to man and the citizen:

1 Men are born free and remain free and equal in their rights. Social distinctions can only be founded on public utility.

2 The aim of every political association is the maintenance of the natural and imprescriptible rights of man. Those rights are those of liberty, property, security and resistance to oppression.

3 The fundamental source of all sovereignty resides in the nation. No body nor any individual may exercise any authority which does not derive explicitly from the sovereign nation.

4 Liberty consists in being able to do anything which does not harm another: thus each man's exercise of his natural rights has no limits but those which guarantee the other members of society the enjoyment of these same rights. These limits can only be determined by the law.

5 The law can only forbid actions harmful to society. That which is not forbidden by law cannot otherwise be prevented and no one may be constrained to do anything which is not ordered by the law.

6 The law is the expression of the general will. Every citizen has the right, in person or by representation, to participate in the legislative process. The law must be the same for all, whether it punish or protect. Every citizen, being equal in its eyes, is equally admissible to every dignity, office and public employment in accordance with his ability and with no other distinction than that of his virtue and talent.

7 No man may be accused, arrested or detained except in cases determined by the law and according to the forms therein prescribed. Those who solicit, issue, execute or order the execution of arbitrary orders must be punished. But every citizen summoned or arrested in virtue of the law must obey instantly; he makes himself guilty by resistance.

8 The law must only prescribe punishments which are strictly and evidently necessary and no one may be punished except in virtue of a law which has been passed and promulgated before the commission of the crime and which is legally applied.

9 Since every man is presumed innocent until proved guilty, if it is deemed indispensable to arrest him, all force beyond what is necessary to lay hold of his person must be severely repressed by the law.

10 No one must be troubled on account of his opinions, even his religious beliefs, provided that their expression does not disturb public order under the law.

11 Free expression of thought and opinions is one of the most precious rights of man. Accordingly every citizen may speak, write and publish freely, subject to the penalties for the abuse of this freedom provided for by the law.

12 An armed public force is required to safeguard the rights of man and the citizen: this force is therefore instituted for the advantage of all and not for the private purposes of those to whom it is entrusted.

13 General taxation is indispensable for the upkeep of the public force and for the expenses of government. It should be borne equally by all the citizens in proportion to their means.

14 Every citizen has the right, in person or through his representative, to establish the necessity for a tax, freely to consent to it, to supervise the way in which it is spent and to fix its rate, basis, method of collection and duration.

15 Society has the right to demand of every public employee an account of his administration.

16 Only a society in which guaranteed rights are assured and the separation of powers effected has a constitution.

17 As the right to property is inviolable and sacred, no one may be deprived of it except when public necessity, legally established, evidently demands it and this on condition of being paid fair compensation in advance.

Constitutional Articles

1 All the powers [i.e. executive, legislative, and judicial] emanate entirely and can only emanate from the nation.

2 The government of France is monarchical: no authority in France is above the law by which alone the king reigns and it is only in the name of the law that he can require obedience.

3 The National Assembly has recognized and declared as fundamental elements in the French monarchy that the king's person is inviolable and sacred; that the throne is indivisible and that the crown is hereditary in the ruling dynasty from male to male in order of primogeniture to the perpetual and absolute exclusion of females and their descendants, the whole without prejudicing the effect of the renunciations [i.e. by the Bourbon kings of Spain of their right of eventual succession to the throne of France].

4 The National Assembly will be a permanent institution.

5 The National Assembly will be composed of only one chamber.

6 Each parliament will last for two years.

7 At the end of each parliament elections will be held for every seat.

8 The legislative power resides in the National Assembly which shall exercise it as follows:

9 No act of the legislative body may be considered a law unless it has been passed by the freely and legally elected representatives of the nation and received the royal assent.

10 The king may refuse his assent to acts of the legislative body.

11 If the king refuses his assent, this veto will only be suspensive.

12 The king's suspensive veto will end with the second parliament following that proposing the law.

13 The king may invite the National Assembly to take a matter into consideration, but the initiation of legislation appertains exclusively to the representatives of the nation.

14 The creation and abolition of offices can operate only in virtue of an act of the legislative body sanctioned by the king.

15 No tax or levy, whether in kind or money, nor any loan, direct or indirect, may be raised except by an explicit decree of the assembly of the representatives of the nation.

16 The supreme executive power resides exclusively in the king's hands.

17 The executive power may not issue any laws, even provisional ones, but merely proclamations conformable with the laws to order or bring to mind their observance.

18 The ministers and other agents of the executive are responsible for their use of the funds of their department and likewise for such infringements of the law as they may commit, whatever orders they may have received. But no order of the king's may be executed without its having been signed by His Majesty and countersigned by a secretary of state.

19 The judicial power may in no case be exercised by the king or by the legislative body but justice shall be exercised, in the name of the king, exclusively by the tribunals established by law in conformity with the principles of the constitution and the forms prescribed by law.

AP, vol. IX, pp. 236–7

102 Robespierre to Buissart, undated (dated by the recipient 9 November 1789)

The power of the clergy is destroyed by the decree [of 2 November] which has just declared that ecclesiastical possessions are placed at the disposal of the nation. The day after the *parlements* received a sure pledge of their ruin in the law which condemned them to remain on vacation. The feudal aristocracy is just about destroyed; the greatest abuses seem to have disappeared at the voice of the representatives of the nation; will we be free? I believe that it is still permissible to ask this question. The new constitution seems to me at the very least to contain essential vices which should stop good citizens shouting for joy.

The most important part of the constitution will be incontestably the worst; I speak of the organization of the municipalities, the provincial assemblies and the national assemblies. No doubt you know that a specific sum of money is being demanded of citizens for them to exercise the rights of citizens; that they must pay a tax equivalent to three days' work in order to participate in the primary assemblies; ten days' to be a member of the secondary assemblies which are called departments; finally 54 livres tax and possession of landed property to be eligible for the national assembly. These provisions are the work of the aristocratic party in the Assembly which has not even permitted the others to defend the rights of the people and has constantly shouted them down; so that the most important of all our deliberations was taken without discussion, carried off in tumult.

We are now replacing the old division of provinces and dividing the kingdom into 90 departments, subdivided into primary and secondary assemblies, without regard to the boundaries of the former provinces. This measure which at the present moment seems to me more favourable to aristocracy and despotism than to liberty has given rise to great debates; it seems to me that a representation founded on the bases I have just indicated could easily raise up an aristocracy of riches on the ruins of the feudal aristocracy; and I do not see that the people which should be the aim of every political institution will gain much from this kind of arrangement. Moreover I fail to see how representatives who derive their power from their constituents, that is to say from all the citizens without distinction of wealth, have the right to despoil the major part of these same constituents of the power which they have confided to them. I beg you, my dear friend, tell me of the likely reception of this proposal in Artois.

    . . . I expect to be here for a few months. My address is: 30 Rue Saintonge, in the Marais, chez M. Humbert.

Robespierre, *Oeuvres*, vol. III,
pp. 57–9

103   The rights of the '*princes possessionés*'

The ducs de Liancourt and de La Rochefoucauld told [Robespierre] how astonished they were that he was risking speaking on a matter of this nature without ever having read or learned anything on the subject. 'But you are at least familiar with the Treaty of Ryswick?' – 'No.' – 'Have you studied German public law?' – 'No. Public law and treaties don't come into it, only the law of peoples.'

Robespierre, *Oeuvres*, vol. VI,
p. 231

|3|

The response of Louis XVI to the Revolution

Louis XVI was blinded to Mirabeau's interpretation of the Revolution by the divisions in society which it had caused and by the circumstances in which it had been accomplished: the insurrection in July but, above all, the invasion of Versailles by the Parisians on 5–6 October and the forcible removal of himself and his family to Paris. It is noteworthy that his 'solemn protestation' to his cousin Charles IV of Spain (**104**) against his 'enforced sanction of all that has been done contrary to royal authority since 15 July' is sent, not on 15 July, but on 12 October.

The king was virtually under house arrest in the Tuileries and as such was a political nullity. All his actions and words were construed as being made under duress. Apart from the desire natural to any prisoner to want to escape, there were specific tactical reasons why he had to make a move in 1791. The constitution was due to be completed in July, when it would be presented to the king for acceptance or refusal, 'in contempt of one of the main clauses of the *cahiers* providing that *legislation would be carried out in conjunction with the king'*. This sentence from the declaration, which he left behind when he escaped from Paris on the night of 20–21 June, explains the main motive for his flight, which is elaborated by the duc de Choiseul, who was responsible for providing military escorts on the route to Montmédy in Lorraine, the king's destination. As this memoir (**106**) makes clear, Louis intended, from a place of safety, surrounded by loyal troops, to negotiate his return with the Assembly in return for changes to the constitution along the lines he indicated in his manifesto. He would then take up residence at Compiègne and translate the Assembly there (there is a receipt for the arrival of a consignment of furniture at Compiègne in December 1790 'for the Estates').[1] Whether or not deputies from the old left wing of the Assembly, like Barnave, Duport and the Lameth brothers actually connived at Louis's escape (as Robespierre believed), they would certainly have been glad of the excuse of negotiating with the king to 'terminate the Revolution', as Barnave put it, before there was a social revolution and in Duport's words, 'the land was divided'.

---

1 I. Dunlop, *Marie-Antoinette* (1993), p. 246.

A further tactical reason for departure was to halt the primary assemblies for the new legislature which were in progress in June and which, Louis notes in his manifesto, were going badly for him and which were suspended until August as a result of his flight. Robespierre gives this as Louis's reason for 'choosing this precise moment' to leave. It is noteworthy that Robespierre explains the king's flight in exactly the same terms as Choiseul, only whereas Robespierre thinks such motives blameworthy, Choiseul praises them. Thus both agree that Louis intended to renegotiate the constitution with a treasonable/sensible Assembly. 'You will have noticed', Robespierre proclaims, 'how [Louis] distinguishes between those things in the constitution which he finds offensive and those he deigns to find acceptable.'[2] Both Robespierre and Choiseul agree that the king also planned to induce the *émigrés* to return with concessions. The voice of compromise is seldom loudest in a Revolution, and whilst in the Tuileries Louis could not express it at all, so in order to make it clear to foreign governments what it was, to distinguish it alike from the *émigrés* and the Jacobins, Louis appointed the baron de Breteuil his minister plenipotentiary (**105**).

This necessary difficulty of speaking his mind makes the king's lengthy manifesto, where for once he can, an important document (**108**). Its personal nature is increased because it is elaborated without the assistance of his ministers who, for their own protection, were kept in ignorance of his plan to escape. Marie-Antoinette's influence can also be discounted: her letter to Mercy-Argenteau (**107**) outlines the very different kind of manifesto (shorter, more vengeful) she would like to have seen produced. The regime Louis wanted to see in place was not the *ancien régime* but rather one based on the *cahiers* and, to a lesser extent, the *séance royale*, of 23 June 1789. It is a plea for a strong constitutional monarchy, with the king possessing the initiative in legislation and an absolute veto, as in England. He nowhere makes an explicit comparison with England but he had a lifetime fascination for that country (whose language he taught himself against parental opposition) and followed George III's political vicissitudes avidly.

Apart from his criticism of his exclusion from the legislative process, Louis complains – for this is a somewhat bad-tempered document – that his executive powers have been effectively nullified by the Assembly's practice of forming committees to duplicate – and in the case of the finance committee effectively replace – the government departments. The administration of the kingdom is excessively decentralized and not only does the king have little control over local government but the constituted authorities are eclipsed by the local Jacobin clubs as the National Assembly was overawed by the central Jacobin Club. The analysis of the way the Jacobin network operated is particularly perceptive.

The king's flight was checked at Varennes, some 30 miles from Montmédy. He was sent back to Paris and suspended from his functions pending the completion of the constitution. The constitutional committee did try to incorporate some of the king's demands in the finished document and, arguably, paved the way by the repression of popular dissent on the Champ

2 Robespierre, *Oeuvres*, vol. VII, pp. 518–23.

de Mars (**109**). However the extreme right, pursuing a *politique du pire* in the hope of a return to the *ancien régime*, refused to co-operate in the revision, which accomplished only the granting of a bodyguard of 1,800 men to the king, and the re-classification of the civil constitution as an ordinary rather than a constitutional law, making it easier to repeal.

Louis's aim throughout the Revolution was to prevent civil war or, put more positively, to effect reconciliation, first between the orders, later between the *émigrés* and the revolutionaries – to create conditions, as he says in his declaration, in which the former can return to France – finally between the constitutional and refractory priests and their respective congregations. These, as he explains to his *émigré* brothers (**110**), are the motives which induced him to accept the constitution. This letter is basically a thorough and prophetic examination of the disfiguring impact which war, foreign and civil, will have on France. The revolutionary leaders 'will use the national guards and other armed citizens' and they will begin by massacring 'those who are called aristocrats'. The *émigrés* would need not only victory but an army of occupation to rule the country against its will. For (and here Louis seizes the essence of the Revolution): 'the nation likes the constitution because the word recalls to the lower portion of the people only the independence in which it has lived for the last two years and to the class above [the bourgeoisie] equality. The lower portion of the people see only that they are reckoned with; the bourgeoisie see nothing above them. Vanity is satisfied. This new possession has made them forget everything else.'

The Constituent Assembly was replaced by the Legislative Assembly which met on 1 October. As the king had predicted in his manifesto, it was more radical than its predecessor. The new left wing in the assembly, dominated by the group known to history as the Girondins, sought to embarrass the king by asking him to sanction decrees which he could not possibly accept. On 9 November a decree was passed enjoining all *émigrés* to return to France within two months on pain of being suspected of conspiracy, seeing their lands confiscated and being punished by death. On 29 November another decree declared that priests must take the oath recognizing the civil constitution within eight days or be 'suspected of revolt against the law and of evil intentions towards the *patrie*'. They were to be stripped of their pensions and held responsible for all religious disturbances in their neighbourhood. Louis expresses his predicament in an anguished letter to his plenipotential envoy, Breteuil (**112**).

Nothing demonstrates the audacious cynicism of the Girondins better than the fact that, just a fortnight before this draconian legislation was passed, Vergniaud and Gensonné proposed that the civil constitution itself should be repealed. The same cynicism is evinced by their policy of forcing Louis to go to war against his brother-in-law, the Emperor Leopold (who was, in fact, well disposed towards the Revolution), in the hope of revealing Louis's treachery (**113**). Louis called their bluff by appointing a Girondin ministry and on their written, signed advice (which he published) went down to the Assembly on 20 April 1792 formally to propose the declaration of war (**114**).

Henceforth the war was to dominate the Revolution and the king's gloomiest predictions were to be exceeded. The war certainly embarrassed the king and indeed made the position of the monarchy untenable. The king's negative and self-righteous attitude towards the constitution, exemplified in document **92**, bad enough in a climate of revolutionary fervour, was quite unacceptable at a time of national crisis, whilst the queen was suspected of criminal intelligence with her Austrian relatives: documents **115** and **116** give Marie-Antoinette's celebrated betrayal of the French war plans. Whether Louis was aware of her action is not known, but her note to Fersen, her Swedish admirer, who had organized the escape from Paris (**117**) reveals a fundamental division, *in extremis*, between the royal couple. In the face of an imminent popular rising in Paris against the monarchy, the constitutional monarchists planned to get the king out of Paris to Compiègne, where they would have effected a troop junction. The king favoured this project; the queen did not, because it would involve wholehearted acceptance of the constitution and renouncing help from the foreign powers. In the event the king remained in Paris where the Girondin leaders, who had done so much to undermine the throne, attempted to save it.

Exasperated by their further presentation of embarrassing legislation, the king had dismissed his Girondin ministers on 12 June, and the advice they transmit to him for the salvation of the monarchy (**118** and **119**) is, in sum, to re-appoint them. Their argument that the king cannot regain his authority by force is exactly the same as the king had employed with his brothers, whilst the king acidly replies 'that they had only to thank the so-called "patriot" ministers for the declaration of war'. The most telling criticism is Vergniaud's:[3] 'The king has been cruelly deceived if he has been led to believe that not to deviate from the line of constitutional rectitude is to do all that he should.'

The King ignored the Girondins' advice but it is highly unlikely that it would have prevented the popular and highly organized insurrection which swept away the monarchy on 10 August (**120** and **121**).

104   Louis XVI to Charles IV of Spain, 12 October 1789

I owe it to myself, I owe it to my children, I owe it to my family and all my house to prevent the regal dignity which a long succession of centuries has confirmed in my dynasty from being degraded in my hands . . .

I have chosen Your Majesty, as head of the second branch, to place in your hands this solemn protestation against my enforced sanction of all that has been done contrary to the royal authority since 15 July of this year and, at the same time, [my intention] to carry out the promises which I made by my declaration of the previous 23 June.

> Published in A. Mousset, *Un témoin
> inconnu de la Révolution: Le comte
> de Fernan Nunez* (1924), p. 228

---

3 Pierre Victurnien Vergniaud, 1753–93, deputy for the department of the Gironde to the Legislative Assembly and the National Convention, the greatest of the Girondin orators. See also document **122**.

105   The king to the baron de Breteuil, 20 November 1790

Monsieur le baron de Breteuil, knowing the full extent of your zeal and fidelity, and wishing to give you a new mark of my confidence, I have chosen to confide the interests of my crown to you. Since circumstances do not permit me to give you my instructions on such and such a matter and to have a continuous correspondence with you, I am sending you this present to serve as plenipotential powers and authorization *vis-à-vis* the various powers with whom you may have to treat on my behalf. You know my intentions and I leave it to your discretion to make such use of it as you think necessary for the good of my service. I approve of everything that you do to achieve my aim, which is the restoration of my legitimate authority and the happiness of my peoples. Upon which, Monsieur le baron, I pray God that He keep you in His holy protection.

Annales historiques de la révolution
française [AHRF] (1962), p. 40

106   Louis XVI's objectives in the 'flight to Varennes': the account of the duc de Choiseul

Choiseul, who provided troop detachments along the route to Montmédy, read this memoir to the king, who corrected it in one place:

Few people had a clearer idea than the king of the situation in which France found herself; he was persuaded that the ills of his kingdom were so glaring that they would correct themselves. He dreaded the horrors of civil war; he was convinced that a foreign war would be useless. From his knowledge of the plans of the various cabinets [of Europe] he believed that the interests of each power would take precedence over the general interest of Europe. He thought that Frenchmen armed against France [the *émigrés*] would become the object of every hatred and feed discord. He believed that only he could erect a barrier against all the misfortunes which must result from these various predicaments; he was profoundly convinced of it.

He felt that the disabused part of the National Assembly would find in him a powerful help and a dike against the popular current. It was even the only way of guaranteeing, by his free and authentic consent, the sacrifices which he had always wanted to make and which came from the heart. He found himself the arbiter of the interests of the foreign powers, he would stipulate for everyone. He would oblige all parties to bend before the general will. He would have accepted reasonable proposals coming from Paris and he would have imposed obedience on Coblenz. All these principles were presented in the solemn declaration he left behind on his departure. . . .

He had chosen a point on the frontier, with no fear that his motive would be misunderstood; he wanted the fear of seeing him cross it – and the consequent fear of civil war – to become a powerful brake on treachery and stupidity. He was resolved, once the legitimate rights of the royal authority had been restored, and the constitution, freely discussed, should have been sanctioned by him, to proceed to Compiègne, to stay there for a long time, and thus gain respect for this fundamental law of the state, far from the impediments and disturbances of Paris, and to remain there until the constitution was fully operational. . . .

Apart from the danger of the actual journey, there was scarcely any doubt that such a wise plan, one so worthy of this virtuous prince, would have been successful. For, if his arrest threw France into an abyss of misfortune, the developments which took place during his three-day absence proved incontrovertibly that his calculations were not faulty. As soon as his departure was known, all the wise men of the Assembly, not troubling about the speeches from popular orators, agitators and their partisans, nor even a momentary outburst of anger from the people, took immediate steps to profit from the event to give a better turn to affairs. Commissioners were nominated from the constitutional committee to go to the king with proposals. Members of all the parties were to be in this deputation. M. de Cazalès was of the number and M. de Gouvernet, who was acceptable to everyone, was chosen to precede it. He was to leave at 10 p.m. to announce the arrival of commissioners to the king at Montmédy. The relay-horses had been ordered and he was about to step into his carriage when, at 9 p.m., it was learned that the king had been stopped. Here I call to witness all the enlightened men in the National Assembly, excepting only the party which wanted to establish a republic: all were devastated, all saw the dawn of public order and tranquillity evaporate.

> Duc de Choiseul, *Relation du départ de Louis XVI de 20 juin 1791* (1822), pp. 34–5

107   Marie-Antoinette to Mercy-Argenteau, 3 February 1791

Marie-Antoinette's letter to her mentor, the former Austrian ambassador, outlining her thoughts on a royal manifesto should be compared with the declaration Louis actually drafted (**108**). Louis's declaration is not simply based on the principles the queen outlines here. Louis does not mention pardons let alone punishments; the declaration of 23 June [the *séance royale*] is mentioned but is not central; also Louis scrupulously avoids the temptation to exploit the religious schism created by the Assembly's ecclesiastical legislation.

The king is busy now collecting together all the material for the manifesto which he must necessarily issue as soon as we are out of Paris. It will be necessary first to explain his flight, pardon the people which has only been led astray, flatter it with expressions of love; except from the pardon the revolutionary leaders [*chefs des factieux*], the city of Paris unless it returns to the old dispensation, and everyone who has not laid down his arms by a certain date; restore the *parlements* as ordinary law courts without their ever being able to meddle with administration and finance. Finally, we have decided to take as a basis for the constitution the declaration of 23 June, as necessarily modified by circumstances and events. Religion will be one of the great points to bring to the fore. We are now grappling together with the very difficult choice of the ministers we will want to appoint [*personnel que nous voudrons appeler près de nous*] when we are free. I thought it would be preferable to place one man at the head of affairs, as M. de Maurepas [*de facto* prime minister 1774–81] was formerly. In this way the king would avoid working with each minister separately and affairs would proceed with less fluctuation. Let me know what you think of this idea. The man is not easy to find as the harder I look the more disadvantages I find in them all.

Lettres de Marie-Antoinette, vol. II,
pp. 218–19

108   The king's declaration on leaving Paris, 20 June 1791

As long as the king could hope to see order and prosperity restored to the kingdom by the measures employed by the Assembly and by his residence near that Assembly in the capital, he counted as naught any personal sacrifices. Had this hope been fulfilled, he would not even have argued the nullity attaching to all his proceedings since the month of October 1789 on account of his total lack of freedom. But now, considering that the sole recompense for so many sacrifices is to behold the destruction of the monarchy, authority flouted, the sanctity of property violated, the safety of the citizen everywhere endangered, crime go unpunished, and total anarchy trample on the laws without the semblance of authority given him by the new constitution being sufficient to cure any of the ills afflicting the kingdom, the king, having solemnly protested against all acts emanating from him during his captivity, believes it right to lay before the eyes of Frenchmen and of the whole world the record of his conduct and that of the form of government which has been introduced into the kingdom.

Witness that His Majesty, in the month of July 1789, to remove all grounds of mistrust, sent away the troops which he had only summoned to him after the sparks of revolt had already manifested themselves in Paris and even in the regiment of his guards. The king, armed with a clear conscience and pure intentions, was not afraid to go alone among the citizens of the capital.

In the month of October of the same year the king, who had long been aware of the rising which the men of faction were seeking to instigate on the 5th, was given sufficient warning to be able to withdraw wherever he pleased. But he feared that such a proceeding would be exploited to kindle civil war and he preferred to make personal sacrifices and – what was more heart-rending – to expose the lives of those most dear to him. Everyone knows what happened on the night of 5–6 October and how it has gone unpunished for nearly two years. God alone prevented the perpetration of even greater crimes and saved the French nation from permanent dishonour [Marie-Antoinette narrowly escaped death].

The king, yielding to the wish expressed by the army of Parisians, installed himself and his family in the Palace of the Tuileries. The kings had not resided there regularly for over a hundred years, except during the minority of Louis XV. Nothing was ready to receive the king and the disposition of the rooms is far from affording the comfort to which His Majesty was accustomed in the other royal residences and which any private individual with a competence may enjoy. Despite the duress which had been exerted and the inconveniences of all kinds which followed the king's change of abode, His Majesty, faithful to his policy of personal sacrifice for the sake of peace, thought it right on the morrow of his arrival in Paris to reassure the provinces concerning his residence in the capital and to invite the National Assembly to join him by coming to the same city to continue its work.

But an even more painful sacrifice was reserved to His Majesty: he must needs send away his bodyguard who had just given him a striking token of their fidelity during the fatal morning of the 6th. Two of them had perished for their loyalty to the king and his family and several others had been grievously wounded whilst strictly executing the king's orders not to fire on a crowd which had been led astray. The men of faction showed great ingenuity indeed in painting so darkly such loyal troops who had just crowned the fine conduct they had always maintained. But they were not aiming so much at the bodyguard as at the king himself: they wanted to isolate him entirely by depriving him of the services of his bodyguard, whom they had not succeeded in corrupting as they had the regiment of French guards – the paragon of the army – but a short time previously.

It was the soldiers of that same regiment, a force now paid by the city of Paris, and the volunteer National Guards of the said city who were entrusted with the safety of the king. These troops are entirely under the orders of the municipality of Paris from whom the commander-in-chief holds his authority. With such a guard, the king has seen himself become a prisoner in his own territories; for how otherwise can one describe the condition of a king whose authority over his guard is restricted to ceremonial matters, who does not make any appointments and who is obliged to see himself surrounded by several people whom he realizes are ill disposed towards himself and his family? The king does not bring up these facts in order to blame the Parisian National Guard and its paid troops but to make known the full truth – and in so doing he is happy to do justice to the zeal for order and the attachment to his person which these troops have in general shown him when left to themselves and not led astray by the shouts and lies of the men of faction.

However, the more the king made sacrifices for the good of his peoples, the more the men of faction have worked to devalue the cost and paint the monarchy in the most false and lurid colours.

The convocation of the Estates-General, the granting of double representation to the deputies of the Third Estate, the pains the king took to smooth away all the difficulties which could have delayed the meeting of the Estates-General and those which arose after their opening, all the king's economies in his personal expenditure, all the powers which he surrendered to his peoples in the *séance* of 23 June; finally the union of the orders, effected by the expressed will of the king (a measure which the king then considered indispensable to the functioning of the Estates-General): all his painstaking solicitude, all his generosity, all his devotion to his people, all have been depreciated and distorted.

When the Estates-General, having styled themselves the National Assembly, began to occupy themselves with the constitution of the kingdom, remember the memoranda which the men of faction contrived to have sent in from several provinces and the agitation in Paris tending to make the deputies renege on one of the main clauses in all their *cahiers providing that legislation would be carried out in conjunction with the king.* In contempt of this clause, the Assembly has denied the king any say in the constitution by refusing him the right to grant or withhold his assent to the articles which it regards as constitutional, by reserving for itself the right to place such articles in that category as it sees fit and, as regards those deemed purely legislative, by restricting the royal prerogative to the right of a suspensive veto for two parliaments – a purely illusory right as is proved only too well by so many examples.

What remains to the king but the vain shadow of royalty? He has been given 25 million francs for the expenses of the civil list; but all of this must be consumed by the maintenance of a household of sufficient splendour to do honour to the dignity of the crown of France and by the burdens subsequently imposed on this fund – even after its size had been determined.

He has been left a life-interest in a few crown lands, with several restrictions on their enjoyment. These lands are but a tiny fraction of those possessed by the kings from time immemorial and of the patrimonies which His Majesty's ancestors added to the crown lands. It can be said without fear of contradiction that if all these properties were added together they would bring in far more than the monies allocated for the maintenance of the king and his family, which in that case would cost the people nothing.

Something which it grieves the king to mention is the careful distinction which has been made in the arrangements for the treasury and other matters between services to the king personally and those to the state, as if they were not in fact inseparable and services rendered to the king's person were not also rendered to the state.

Let us now examine the various branches of government.

Justice

The king plays no part in the legislative process: he merely has the right of a suspensive veto for two parliaments over matters which are not deemed to belong to the constitution and that of asking the National Assembly to look into such and such a matter without having the right formally to initiate legislation. Justice is administered in the king's name, the judges' letters of institution are drawn up by him: but that is a mere formality and the king is able only to nominate the *commissaires du roi,* a newly created post with only a portion of the powers of the former *procureurs généraux* and intended merely to ensure that the forms have been observed – the role of the state has devolved entirely to another judicial officer. These *commissaires* are appointed for life and cannot be dismissed whilst the judges' commissions are to last only for six years. By one of its latest decrees the Assembly has just deprived the king of one of the finest and most universal prerogatives of monarchy: that of mercy and commutation of punishment. However perfect the laws, they cannot foresee every case: it will then be the juries who will have the real right of pardon by a personal application of the spirit of the law, despite appearances to the contrary. Moreover, how far does this provision not diminish the royal majesty in the eyes of the peoples who for so long have been accustomed to turn to the king in need and in trouble and see in him the father of all who can relieve their distress!

Internal administration

This is entirely in the hands of the departments, districts and municipalities – a proliferation of jurisdictions, often overlapping, which impedes the running of the machine. All these bodies are elected by the people and do not, according to the decrees, take orders from the government except for implementing laws or individual orders deriving from them. On the one hand they have no rewards to expect from the government and on the other the means provided by the decrees for punishing and correcting their faults are so complicated in form that it would take very exceptional circumstances to be able to use them: this reduces to very little the surveillance which the ministers are supposed to have over them. These bodies, moreover, have acquired little weight and consideration. The Societies of the Friends of the Constitution [Jacobin Clubs] – which will be dealt with later – which have no responsibility are in fact much stronger than they and consequently the force of the government is nullified. Since their institution we have seen several examples of their not having dared, however good their intentions of maintaining order, employ the means given them by the law for fear of a populace responding to ulterior pressures. The electoral bodies, although they have no individual executive power and are confined to electing, have a very real force because of their collective weight, their two-year duration, and the fear, natural to men and especially to men possessed of temporary power, of displeasing those who can advance or harm them.

Control of the military forces

According to the decrees, this is in the hands of the king. He has been declared supreme head of the army and navy; but the whole task of organizing these two arms has been carried out by the Assembly's committees without the king's participation; everything, down to the last disciplinary regulation, has been done by them and if the king is left with a third or a quarter of appointments, depending on the occasion, this right is rendered virtually illusory by the countless obstacles and objections which everyone permits himself to put in the way of the king's choice. You have seen him obliged to draw up a complete new list of staff officers for the army because the original list did not find favour with the clubs. His Majesty yielded thus because he did not want to expose honourable and brave soldiers, expose them to the violence which would surely have been used against them, witness only too many lamentable examples in the past. The clubs and the administrative bodies interfere with the internal discipline of the troops which lies completely outside the competence even of the latter, who merely have the right to call on the public force when they think there is occasion to employ it. They have abused this right sometimes even to thwart government arrangements for the distribution of the troops, so that several times the soldiers have found themselves in the wrong location. To the clubs alone must be attributed the spirit of revolt against the officers and military discipline which is taking hold in many regiments and which, if not effectively checked, will be the destruction of the army. What becomes of an army when it no longer has either commanders or discipline? Instead of being the force and safeguard of the state, it becomes to it a terror and a scourge. When the scales have fallen from their eyes, how the French soldiers will blush at their conduct and look with horror at those who have perverted the fine morale which was the rule in the French army and navy! Fatal provisions those which encouraged the soldiers and sailors to frequent the clubs! The king has always considered that the law should be the same for everyone: officers who are in the wrong should be punished but they and other ranks should be punished according to the provisions of the laws and regulations. Every door should be open to encourage advancement by merit; all the comfort which can be given to the soldier is just and necessary but there can be no army without officers and discipline and this there will never be as long as soldiers think that they have a right to judge the conduct of their superiors.

Foreign affairs

The nomination of ambassadors to foreign courts has been reserved to the king as has the conduct of negotiations. But the king's freedom of choice here is just as non-existent as with army officers – witness the latest appointment. The right of revision and confirmation of treaties which is reserved to the National Assembly and the appointment of a diplomatic committee completely destroy the second provision. The right of declaring war would only be an illusory one because a king who neither is nor desires to be a despot would have to be insane just to go and attack another kingdom against the wishes of his nation, which would not in any case grant him any funds with which to prosecute it. However, the right of concluding peace is of a totally different kind. The king, who is but one with the whole nation, who can have no separate interest, knows its rights, knows its needs and resources and consequently has no fear of contracting those engagements which seem to him best calculated to assure its prosperity and peace. But, with treaties having to undergo revision and confirmation by the National Assembly, no foreign power will be willing to contract engagements which could be broken by others than those with whom it was negotiating; in which case all the powers would be concentrated in this Assembly. Moreover, however much discretion was employed in negotiations, could one confide them to an Assembly whose deliberations are necessarily public?

Finances

The king declared, well before the convocation of the Estates-General, that he recognized the right of national assemblies to grant taxation and that he no longer wanted to tax his peoples without their consent. All the *cahiers* of the deputies to the Estates-General were agreed that the restoration of the finances should be placed at the top of the list of matters for deliberation by that Assembly; some *cahiers* had restricted these deliberations by stipulating that certain [financial] matters had to be decided first. The king removed the difficulties to which these restrictions could have led, obviating them himself and granting, in the *séance* of 23 June, all that could have been desired. On 4 February 1790 the king himself urged the Assembly to deal effectively with so important a matter: it only got round to dealing with the matter later and in a way that cannot be considered perfect. There is still no reliable statement of revenue and expenditure, and to bridge the deficit the Assembly has made do with hypothetical calculations. The Assembly lost no time in destroying taxes which, admittedly, were a heavy burden on the population but which nevertheless provided an assured income; it replaced them virtually by a single tax which may be very difficult to collect in full. The ordinary revenues are at present far in arrears and the extraordinary sum of the first 1,200,000,000 of *assignats* is almost spent. The expenditure of the war department and that of the navy instead of decreasing have increased, without including the necessary expenditure occasioned by the mobilizations in the course of the last year. . . . The king, who had not feared to take the lead in publishing the financial accounts of his administration, and who had expressed the wish that publication of accounts should be instituted as a rule of government, has been made, if that were possible, even more of a stranger to the finance department than to the others, and the prejudices, jealousies and recriminations against the government have been even more widespread on this matter. The administration of funds, collection of taxation, allocation of money to the various government departments, rewards for services performed, all have been removed from the king's inspection: he is merely left with a few empty appointments, not even with the distribution of a few alms for the relief of the poor. The king understands the problems of this department and if it had been possible for the machinery of government to proceed without his direct surveillance over the administration of the finances, then His Majesty would only have regretted no longer being able to play his part in establishing a stable order, which might lead to a reduction in taxation (something which His Majesty is well known to have ardently desired and which he could have effected but for the expenses of the American war), and no longer being able to distribute alms for the relief of the poor.

Finally, according to the decrees, the king has been declared supreme head of the administration of the kingdom: other, subsequent decrees have regulated the organization of the ministry in such a way that the king – whom this ought most closely to concern – can nevertheless change nothing without new decisions by the Assembly. The policy of the leaders of the dominant faction has been so effective in directing mistrust against all government officials that today it has become practically impossible to fill the places in the administration. No government can function or endure without a reciprocal confidence between the government and the governed and the latest regulations proposed to the National Assembly concerning the punishments to be imposed on ministers or agents of the executive power deemed to have acted treacherously or to have exceeded the limits of their competence are calculated to give rise to all sorts of anxiety – these penal provisions extend even to junior officials, which destroys all subordination, as the junior should never judge the orders of his superior who is responsible for what he orders. These regulations, by the multiplicity of precautions and the kinds of crime specified, tend only to inspire mistrust instead of the confidence that would have been so desirable.

This form of government, so vicious in itself, has become even more so for the following reasons:

1 The Assembly, by means of its committees, constantly oversteps the limits which it has itself prescribed. It meddles with matters relating exclusively to the internal administration of the kingdom and to the administration of justice and thus combines all the powers. . . .

2 In nearly all the cities and even in several country towns and villages associations have been founded with the name of *société des amis de la constitution* [Jacobin Clubs]: in defiance of the laws, they do not permit the existence of any other clubs that are not affiliated to themselves, thus forming an immense corporation more dangerous than any of those which existed previously [e.g. the *parlements* who, according to their *théorie des classes*, regarded themselves as one body, the rights of each to be defended by all]. Without authorization, nay in contempt of all the laws, they deliberate on all aspects of government, correspond with each other on all subjects, make and receive denunciations, and post up their resolutions. They have assumed such a preponderance that all the administrative and judicial bodies, without excepting the National Assembly itself, nearly always obey their orders.

The king does not think it would be possible to govern so large and important a kingdom as France by the means established by the National Assembly such as they exist at present. His Majesty, in giving his assent, which he knew well he could not refuse, to all decrees without distinction was motivated by the desire to avoid all discussion which experience had taught him to be pointless, to say the least. In addition he feared lest people think that he wanted to delay or abort the work of the National Assembly, in the success of which the nation took so lively an interest. He placed his confidence in the wise men of that Assembly who would recognize that it is easier to destroy a form of government than to reconstruct one on totally different principles. They had several times recognized the necessity, when speaking about the intended revision of the decrees, of imparting that force of action and coercion which every government needs. They also recognized the need to give this government and the laws which ought to assure everyone's prosperity and place in society enough consideration to induce all those citizens to return to the kingdom who had been compelled to expatriate themselves, out of discontent in some cases and in the majority fear for life and property.

However, the nearer the Assembly approached to the end of its labours, the more the wise men were seen to lose their influence together with a daily increase of clauses which could only make government difficult, even impossible, and inspire distrust and contempt for it: the other regulations, instead of shedding a salutary balm on the wounds that were still bleeding in several provinces, only increased anxiety and soured discontent. The mentality of the clubs dominated and pervaded everything: the thousands of calumnious and incendiary papers and pamphlets which circulated every day merely echoed the clubs and pushed the public in the direction they wanted to lead it. The National Assembly never dared check this licence, far removed from true liberty; it has lost its influence and even the force it would have needed to retrace its steps and change what it thought should be corrected. It can be seen from the dominant mentality in the clubs and the way in which they are seizing control of the new primary assemblies what can be expected of them and if one can detect any disposition on their part to go back on anything, it is in order to destroy the remains of the monarchy and set up a metaphysical and doctrinaire form of government which would not work.

Frenchmen, is that what you wanted when you sent your representatives to the National Assembly? Did you want anarchy and the despotism of the clubs to replace the monarchical form of government under which the nation has prospered for fourteen hundred years? Did you want to see your king heaped with insults and deprived of his liberty whilst he was exclusively occupied with establishing yours? . . .

Paris, 20 June 1791
Louis

The king forbids his ministers to sign any order in his name until they have received further orders from him; he enjoins the keeper of the seal of state to send it to him as soon as he requires it.

AP, vol. XXVII, pp. 378–83

109　Mme. Roland's account of the massacre of the Champ de Mars (from a letter to Bancal des Issarts of 18 July 1791)

The Girondin group, of which Mme. Roland was a leading light, tended to adopt a republican stance after Varennes, whilst Robespierre cryptically observed that to declare a republic at that stage would be 'aristocratic'.

Death and mourning are within our walls; tyranny sits on a blood-stained throne, with its iron sceptre outstretched; and there is no longer liberty in Paris except for National Guards wanting to cut their brothers' throats. Citizens had proceeded to the Champ de Mars with the peaceable intention of hearing and signing a petition demanding the nomination of deputies to the next legislature; the municipality had been previously informed according to the rules; all were without arms or sticks; women carrying or leading their children comprised a large portion of this assembly held under open skies, around the altar of the fatherland, in a place open on all sides, in the confidence of the most sacred rights and most legitimate intentions. Two men were found hiding in the base [of the altar], having got in by lifting up the planks: they were busy making holes here and there in the place where the altar rises under the feet of the spectators. They were spotted, seized and taken to the neighbouring municipality; they had brandy and spirits on them; they refused to reveal their intentions and a group of angry men seized and hanged them. A cannon was brought up; three municipal officers arrived and found calm restored; they heard the petition, agreed it was sensible, said that they would have signed it had they not been functionaries and that they were going to have the cannon withdrawn, which was done. All this took place before three o'clock.

In the afternoon the crowd was swelled by a large number of people who had directed their stroll towards the Champ de Mars. Suddenly a new artillery battery arrived, ten cannon being placed in front of the Ecole Militaire. A corps of National Guards arrived and in their midst the red flag; the citizens, seated and signing on the altar, were not summoned; the three summonses prescribed by the law were neglected; the first volley, which should have been blank, was loaded; another five or six followed, the cavalry ran over people in flight, the sabre reaching those whom the cannon balls had spared and thus was this peaceful and trusting assembly of honest men put to rout. The alarm-drum had been beaten throughout Paris to spread fear and give the impression of a rising. Units of guards were everywhere, all bristling with bayonets; the Jacobins were surrounded and a small door, covered by soldiers, left as the only exit; the Palais Royal was full of armed men, their arms at the ready, presenting the bayonet to the smallest group: the children's battalion was put to the same use and youth prostituted by being made to play with the lives of citizens. Some chevaliers de Saint-Louis and other aristocratic denizens of the parade applauded. ... The conspirators, for such one must now qualify the dominant faction in the National Assembly, meeting at the Feuillants, are going to write – or have already written – to all the affiliated societies to detach them from the Jacobins and make them join them. ...

> *Lettres de Madame Roland*, ed. C. Perroud (2 vols., 1900–2), vol. II, pp. 335–6

110   From Louis XVI's secret memorandum to his brothers concerning his acceptance of the constitution, 25 September 1791

[He begins:] You have doubtless been informed that I have accepted the constitution and you will know the reasons which I gave to the Assembly; but they will not suffice for you. I want, therefore, to let you know all my reasons. [Then he continues by saying:] The condition of France is such that she is perhaps approaching a total disintegration which will only be accelerated if violent remedies are applied to all the ills which overwhelm her. The solution is to end partisan divisions and to restore the authority of the government. But for this there are only two means: force or reconciliation.

[He first considers force.] This can only be employed by foreign armies – the *émigrés* by themselves are capable only of exercising a suicidal revenge – and this means recourse to war. The *émigrés* flatter themselves that the rebels will capitulate immediately before such immense forces, thus avoiding war. But the leaders of the Revolution, those who control the levers of power both in Paris and the provinces, are committed up to the hilt to the Revolution. They will use the National Guards and other armed citizens; and they will begin by massacring those who are called aristocrats.

War will therefore be inevitable because it is in the interests of all those in authority to fight; it will be terrible because it will be motivated by violence and despair. Can a king contemplate all these misfortunes with equanimity and call them down on his people? I know that kings have always prided themselves on regaining by force that which people have sought to snatch from them, that to fear in such circumstances the horrors of war is called weakness. But I confess that such reproaches affect me less than the sufferings of my people and my heart rebels at the thought of the horrors which I should have caused. I know how much the nobility and clergy have suffered from the Revolution. . . . I too have suffered; but I feel myself equal to suffering still more rather than making my people share my misfortunes.

[So there would be no capitulation but a bitter war. Probably the foreign armies and the elite of the nobility would defeat] National Guards and regiments without officers. But these foreign troops could not settle in the kingdom and, when they were no longer there, how would one govern if insubordination began anew? I know that my *émigré* subjects flatter themselves that there has been a great changeabout in people's attitudes. I thought myself for a long time that this was happening but now I am undeceived. The nation likes the constitution because the word recalls to the lower portion of the people only the independence in which it has lived for the last two years and to the class above [the bourgeoisie] equality. The lower portion of the people see only that they are reckoned with; the bourgeoisie sees nothing above them. Vanity is satisfied. This new possession has made them forget everything else. The losses they experience seem to them to be coming to an end. The completion of the constitution was all that stood between them and perfect happiness; to delay it was in their eyes the greatest crime because all good things were to come with it: time will teach them how mistaken they were. But their error is nonetheless profound. . . . One can never govern a people against its inclinations. This maxim is as true at Constantinople as in a republic; the present inclinations of this nation are for the Rights of Man, however senseless they are.

[And even setting aside these considerations, how would one govern by means of the aristocracy?] Is the aristocracy which you say would be the support and refuge of the monarchy even united amongst itself? Does it not have its parties and differences of opinion? Would those who are called aristocrats in Paris be so called elsewhere? If well-informed people are to be believed there are as many parties on this side as on the other. One wants the old order; another the Estates-General; and yet another an English-style government. What real strength could the government derive from these different parties, which would be even more divided amongst themselves if they came to win and several of which would rather treat with the Jacobins than with another faction of the aristocracy?

I have carefully weighed the matter and concluded that war presents no other advantages but horrors and a continuance of discord. I have therefore thought that this idea should be set aside and that I should try once more the sole means remaining to me, namely the junction of my will to the principles of the constitution. I realize all the difficulties of governing a large nation in this way – indeed I will say that I realize it is impossible. But the obstacles that I would have put in the way [by refusing to accept the constitution] would have brought about the war I sought to avoid and would have prevented the people from properly assessing the constitution because it would only have seen my constant opposition. By my adopting its principles and executing them in good faith, they will come to know the cause of their misfortunes; public opinion will change; and since, without this change, I could only expect new convulsions I . . . [considered] that I would be proceeding towards a better order by my acceptance than by my refusal.

> Vienna State Archives, Familien Acten 88, dossier 3, fos. 108–25, published by P. and P. Girault de Coursac, *Louis XVI a la parole* (1989), pp. 263–72

111 Conversation between Louis XVI and Bertrand de Molleville concerning the constitution at the time of the latter's appointment as minister for the marine, October 1791

After some general observations upon the present difficult and perplexed state of public affairs, the king said to me, 'Well, have you any further objections?'

'No, Sire', answered I. 'The desire of obeying and pleasing Your Majesty, is the only sentiment I feel. But that I may know whether it will be in my power to serve you with utility, I hope Your Majesty will have the condescension to inform me of your sentiments respecting the new constitution and the conduct you expect from your ministers regarding it.'

'That is but just', said the king. 'This, then, is what I think. I am far from regarding the constitution as a *chef d'oeuvre*. I believe there are great faults in it; and that if I had been allowed to state my observations upon it, some advantageous alterations might have been adopted. But of this there is no question at present; I have sworn to maintain it such as it is, and I am determined, as I ought, to be strictly faithful to my oath; for it is my opinion that an exact execution of the constitution is the best means of making it thoroughly known to the nation, who will then perceive the changes proper to be made. I have not, and I cannot have, another plan than this. I certainly shall not recede from it; and I wish my ministers to conform to the same.'

> A. F. Bertrand de Molleville, *Mém-oires secrètes pour servir à l'histoire de la dernière année du règne de Louis XVI, roi de France* (3 vols., 1797), vol. I, p. 210

112   Louis XVI to Breteuil, 14 December 1791

Opinion is divided on whether this document is genuine.

The cruel law against the *émigrés* forced me to make use of the veto; the necessity of this has been recognized by a large part of the nation. But the men of faction, never for a moment losing sight of their aim of trying to put me in an embarrassing position, have returned to the charge from another flank. They have passed the detestable law on refractory priests. . . . The absurd law on *émigrés* was a two-edged sword: if I sanctioned it I should have dishonoured myself by seeming to approve its cruel dispositions. . . . They would also have exploited this sanction by saying that I only gave it to demonstrate thereby that I was not free; and from that follows the whole gamut of accusation you can easily imagine. The policy which I have laid down for myself, that of acting as freely as I can within the limits laid down by the constitution prescribed [my use of the veto]. . . .

It will be the same with the decree on the priests. But in using only the resources of the constitution I shall undoubtedly be obliged to lend myself to all the measures of justice and obvious necessity indicated by circumstances to back up the policy which I have adopted of creating for myself a force out of the favour of the people, who, for the most part, still want the constitution and fear a counter-revolution which is all too obviously the aim of the *émigrés*. From this it follows that the people regard them as the greatest enemies and that the surest way of de-popularizing the king is to present him as being in league with and favouring the plans of the *émigrés*.

> *Louis XVI, Marie-Antoinette et Mme. Elizabeth, lettres et documents inédits* (ed. F. Feuillet de Conches (6 vols., 1864–9), vol. IV, pp. 296–7

113   War-mongering: from two speeches by Brissot to the Legislative Assembly

(a) 29 December 1791

France wants peace but does not fear war. . . . War is necessary to France for her honour, external security, internal tranquillity, to restore our finances and public credit, to put an end to terror, treason and anarchy. . . . This war is a public benefit.

(b) 30 December 1791

Either we will win and restore public credit and our prosperity or we will be beaten and the traitors will finally be convicted and punished. I have only one fear; it is that we won't be betrayed. We need great treasons, our salvation lies there, because there are still strong doses of poison in France and strong emetics are needed to expel them.

Robespierre, *Oeuvres*, vol. VII,
p. 74

114   Declaration of war on Austria, 20 April 1791

For various reasons most politicians over a wide spectrum favoured war. Two exceptions were Louis XVI, who feared the strain that would be imposed on French society, and Robespierre, who feared a dramatic increase in the power of the executive and eventual military dictatorship. Both were to be proved right.

The National Assembly, deliberating at the formal request of the king, considering that the court of Vienna, in contempt of the treaties [of alliance, dating from the 1750s], has continued to afford open protection to French rebels, that it has instigated and formed a concert with several European powers against the independence and security of the French nation;

That Francis I, king of Hungary and Bohemia, has by his notes of 18 March and 7 April last refused to renounce this concert;

That despite the proposal made to him in the note of 11 March 1792 that both nations should reduce the troops on their frontiers to their peacetime effectives, he has continued and augmented his warlike preparations;

That he has formally infringed the sovereignty of the French nation by declaring his intention of supporting the claims of the German princes with possessions in France (to whom the French nation has consistently offered compensation [for their loss of feudal dues]);

That he has sought to divide French citizens and arm them against each other by offering the malcontents a support in the concert of powers;

Considering, finally, that this refusal to reply to the last despatches of the king of the French leaves him with no further hope of obtaining the redress of these various grievances by an amicable negotiation and is tantamount to a declaration of war, decrees that this is a matter of urgency.

The National Assembly declares that the French nation, faithful to the principles enshrined in the constitution 'not to undertake any war with a view to making conquests, and never to direct its forces against the liberty of any people', is only taking up arms in defence of its liberty and independence; that the war it is obliged to conduct is not a war of nation against nation but the just defence of a free people against the aggression of a king;

That the French will never confuse their brothers with their real enemies; that they will neglect nothing to alleviate the scourge of war, to spare and preserve property and to visit' all the suffering inseparable from war on those alone who conspire against her liberty;

That the French nation adopts in advance all foreigners who, abjuring the cause of her enemies, come to range themselves under her banners and devote their efforts to the defence of her liberty; that it will even facilitate their establishment with all the means at its disposal.

Deliberating at the formal request of the king, and having decreed that this is a matter of urgency, decrees war against the king of Hungary and Bohemia.

AP, vol. XLII, pp. 217–18

115   Marie-Antoinette to Mercy, 26 March 1792

M. Dumouriez [the foreign secretary], no longer having any doubts that the powers have agreed to march troops, plans a pre-emptive strike in Savoy and another via Liège. It is La Fayette's army which is to serve in this latter attack. That was the decision taken by the council yesterday; it is as well to know this plan to be on one's guard and take all the appropriate measures.

Lettres de Marie-Antoinette, vol. II,
pp. 391–2

116   Marie-Antoinette to Fersen, 5 June 1792

Luckner's army has been ordered to attack immediately; he is against this but the ministry wants it. The troops are lacking in everything and are in the greatest disorder.

Lettres de Marie-Antoinette, vol. II,
p. 399

117   Marie-Antoinette to Fersen, 11 July 1792

The Const.[itutionalists] in conjunction with La Fayette and Luckner want to conduct the king to Compiègne the day after the Federation. For this purpose the two generals are going to arrive here. The king is disposed to lend himself to this project; the queen is against it. The outcome of this great venture, which I am far from approving, is still in doubt.

Lettres de Marie-Antoinette, vol. II,
p. 415

118   The Girondins and the king: memorandum dictated by Gensonné[4] to the court painter Boze and transmitted to the king by his *valet de chambre*, Thierry; the memorandum was also signed by Vergniaud and Guadet

... What success can the foreign powers hope to achieve even if their intervention managed to increase the king's powers and establish a new form of government? Is it not clear that the men who dreamed up this congress have indeed sacrificed the monarch's interests to their own prejudices and personal interest; and that the success of these manoeuvres would invest powers, which only the nation can delegate and its confidence sustain, with a quality of usurpation. How could one have failed to realize that the presence of the force which would bring about this change would long be necessary to preserve it and that thereby a seed of contention and discord would be planted in the kingdom which could scarcely be eradicated in centuries? ...

[The best way the king could regain the nation's confidence] would be the most solemn declaration that in no case would the king accept an increase in powers which was not freely granted by the French people, without recourse to the intervention of any foreign power, and freely debated in a constitutional manner.

Indeed, it should be observed on this head that several members of the National Assembly know that such a declaration was suggested to the king when he proposed war against the king of Hungary and that he did not see fit to issue it. ...

[Other ways the king could improve his position would be:]

1 Why does the king not choose his ministers from those most strongly pronounced in favour of the Revolution? Why, when things are most critical, is he surrounded only by men who are unknown or suspect?

4 Armand Gensonné, 1758–93, lawyer, deputy for the department of the Gironde to the Legislative Assembly and the National Convention.

Would one act otherwise if one were deliberately trying to increase distrust or provoke the people to insurrection?

His choice of ministers has always been one of the most important functions of the power entrusted to the king. It is the barometer by which public opinion has always judged the dispositions of the court and it can well be imagined what the effect of these choices must be which, even at the best of times, would have caused howls of protest.

A really patriotic ministry, then, would be one of the great instruments which the king could employ to regain confidence. But one would be mightily deceived in thinking that it could easily be regained by an isolated measure of this kind. Only through time and sustained effort can one hope to efface impressions which have been too deeply etched to be entirely wiped out overnight.

2 At a time when all the means of defence should be employed, when France has not arms enough for all her defenders, why has the king not offered the guns and horses of his guard?

3 Why does the king not ask of his own accord for a law subjecting the civil list to accounting procedures capable of reassuring the nation that it is not being diverted from its legitimate purpose and being put to other uses?

4 One of the best ways of reassuring the people about the personal dispositions of the king would be for him to take the initiative in asking for a law concerning the education of the *prince royal*, thereby hastening the time when the care of this young prince is entrusted to a governor who enjoys the nation's confidence.

5 There is further complaint that the decree disbanding the general staff of the National Guard has not received the royal assent. These repeated refusals to sanction legislative provisions for which the public are clamouring and the urgency of which is beyond dispute throw into question the constitutionality of the veto when applied to emergency legislation and are hardly calculated to dispel alarm and discontent.

6 It would be very useful if the king were to relieve M. Lafayette of his army command. It is, to say the least, evident that he can no longer usefully serve the country in that capacity.

We shall conclude this brief survey with a general observation which is that nothing which is capable of averting suspicion or re-kindling confidence can or should be neglected. The constitution will be saved if the king courageously adopts this resolution and firmly perseveres in it.

[The King's response can be judged by the following letter to Boze from Thierry:]

I have just been taken to task for the second time for having taken possession of the letter which, out of zeal, I resolved to transmit. However, the king has permitted me to reply as follows:

1 That he was far from being inclined to put no thought into the choice of his ministers.
2 That they had only to thank the so-called 'patriot' ministers for the declaration of war.
3 That he had tried everything at the time to prevent the coalition of the powers and that at the moment he had only the resources of official diplomacy to make the armies withdraw from our frontiers.
4 That since he had accepted it, he had most scrupulously observed the provisions of the constitution but that now many other people were working against it.

[To this last point, Vergniaud replied in a subsequent memorandum:] The king has been cruelly deceived if he has been led to believe that not to deviate from the line of constitutional rectitude is to do all that he should. Merely not to infringe the constitution is nothing. His oaths also impose on him the duty to defend it: he would be betraying it no less by a policy of inactivity than by explicit collusion with the coalition powers. Those two crimes would be equal in the eyes of the nation; it would judge them with the same severity.

AHRF (1931), pp. 198–201, 207

119 Further contacts between the Girondins and the court: extract from the memoirs of Dejoly, the last keeper of the seals of the monarchy

Belonging to no party or faction, with no other aim but to do good, wanting to do so and thinking I could succeed, I had approached the *procureur-général-syndic* of the department [Roederer]. He was friends with the principal members of the Commission of Twelve, he was close to the mayor of Paris[5] and he had always shown the best intentions towards myself.

I had confided my plans to him and M. Roederer had gone along with them. He had consulted M. Vergniaud and M. Vergniaud had approved our plan, the one I had proposed in council.[6] The reception it had received made me try again. I sent M. Vergniaud a request to submit his idea to me in writing and he agreed ... His letter went as follows. [This letter is missing from Dejoly's papers which contain, however, a précis of it as follows:]

Letter from Vergniaud to the minister Dejoly in the form of advice on the conduct which the king should observe to keep his constitutional crown; it

5 Jérôme Pétion, 1756–94, lawyer, deputy to the Estates-General, mayor of Paris (November 1791), deputy to the National Convention. See also 108.
6 The main point was to strengthen the council by including, though without official position, men who might prove more popular than the existing ministers.

talks of a new order which will arise rapidly out of despair, despite the efforts of the constituted authorities and the operation of the law; people do not ask whether things will be any better but they want to change the present order which is bad. The king's situation demands painful sacrifices of him to reassure the nation. He terms the people sovereign judge. The king must summon four members of the Constituent Assembly to his council. They must be recommended by their talent and their love of liberty. They would not have any title, they would give advice and their services would be free. The *procureur-général* of the department of Paris and the mayor should be added. He ended by saying that his letter is too long since it will be useless and gives an abbreviated signature.

[The précis of the king's reply is as follows:] Draft reply to M. Vergniaud in the king's hand. This reply would not satisfy either a friend of liberty or a man of ambition. It is dry and negative.

AHRF (1946), pp. 353–4

120 The king abandons the Tuileries on 10 August: Dejoly's account

M. Roederer represented [to the National Guard] the full extent of the danger; he urged them to remain firm at their post. He exhorted them not to attack their fellow citizens, their brothers, whilst they remained passive; but he envisaged the moment when they would be attacked. He reminded them of the principles of a legitimate defence; he read out the provisions of the law of [3] May 1791 relative to the public force.

The guard remained silent and the gunners unloaded their cannons. What more could the department [of Paris] do? They joined the king's ministers and all, with one accord, begged him to save himself and his family by taking refuge in the National Assembly. 'Only there, Sire', said M. Roederer, 'in the midst of the representatives of the people, can Your Majesty, the queen and the royal family be safe. Come, let us fly, another quarter of an hour and it will be beyond our control.'

The king hesitated; the queen displayed the utmost displeasure.

'What', she said, 'are we alone? Can no one act?' 'Yes, Ma'am, alone, action is of no avail, resistance impossible.' One of the members of the department, M. Gerdret, tried to speak, insisting on the prompt execution of the plan proposed. 'Be silent, Monsieur', said the queen, 'be silent; you are the last person who should be speaking here. When you have done the damage it is pointless to pretend you want to repair it.'

M. Gerdret kept his mouth shut; the queen repeated her observations; the king was silent. As no one was speaking it was left to me to give the king his last ministerial advice; I had the firmness to say: 'Let us go and not debate. Honour requires it and the good of the state: let us go to the National Assembly – it is high time.'

'Let us go', the king said, raising his right hand, 'let us go and since it is necessary let us give this further, last proof of our dedication.'

The queen was swept along, turning first to the king and then to her son, the king to no one. 'M. Roederer, Gentlemen', said the queen, 'you will answer for the safety of the king's person and that of my son.' 'Ma'am', said M. Roederer, 'we promise to die at your side – that is all we can answer for.'

AHRF (1946), pp. 377–8

121 An idealized view of the *journée* of 10 August: Robespierre's account in *Le Defenseur du peuple*

The solemn manner in which [the people of Paris] proceeded towards this great action was as sublime as were its motives and its objectives.The sections of Paris, in permanent session since the proclamation of the *patrie en danger* [on 11 July] . . . had themselves publicly rehearsed the motives and indicated the moment for this courageous undertaking. They planned it with a unity which only the friends of liberty can display. It was not a purposeless riot [*émeute*] stirred up by a few firebrands; it was not a conspiracy shrouded in mystery; deliberations were in the open, in the presence of the nation; the day and the plan of the insurrection were indicated by wall posters. It was the entire people which exercised its rights.

Robespierre, *Oeuvres*, vol. IV, pp. 352–3

PART

THE NATIONAL
CONVENTION

|1|

Girondins and Montagnards

Although they had tried to prevent it, the insurrection of 10 August delivered power into the hands of the Girondins. They returned to the ministry where their exercise of power was no longer trammelled by the existence of a king. In addition they now dominated the Legislative Assembly, many of whose right-wing deputies withdrew. Nevertheless, their power did not extend to the city of Paris. The revolution of 10 August had been accomplished, in their despite, by the Paris sections (electoral wards) directed by the provisional Commune which now rivalled the authority both of the ministry, known as the Provisional Executive Council, and of the discredited Legislative Assembly during its last weeks before the meeting of the new constituent body, the National Convention, which replaced it on 21 September. Moreover the Commune at this period was dominated by men like Robespierre, Marat and Billaud-Varenne, Jacobins whose differences with the Girondins had first become apparent over the declaration of war which Robespierre and Billaud-Varenne had opposed.

The Girondins were not a party in the modern (or even contemporary English) sense. In particular they did not vote as a bloc on the great issues of the day, notably on the fate of the king, whose trial began in December. This point was made by Vergniaud during his own trial (**122**), when he had to answer the charge that he 'belonged to a faction'. Why was this a crime? Simply because all sides accepted Rousseau's assertion (**129**) that 'partial associations' caused the general will to 'err', to be 'less general' because formed of a smaller number of units. So party was equated with faction and faction with conspiracy, another charge Vergniaud had to answer.

The Girondins were felt to be particularly susceptible to this charge, since they were famous for their political dinner parties and the cult of friendship, as Brissot's letter to Mme. Roland shows (**123**). It is also quite open in its advocacy of patronage: 'I enclose, for your husband . . . a list of patriots to employ because one should always have such a list in front of one.' Robespierre has them in mind in document **127** when he asserts that 'the general will does not form in shadowy cabals nor around ministerial tables'. And in document **128** he is 'deeply shocked at the idea that he was no more than a party boss'. Yet that is precisely what he was. Brissot's 'list of patriots to employ' was matched by Robespierre's more famous list of 'patriots with more or less talent' (**176**); they both claimed that their men were the patriots, their adversary's the conspirators. And the 24 Montagnard deputies returned to the Convention for Paris voted as a bloc in a way the Girondins could not hope to emulate. Indeed the republican factions, as J. W. Croker put it in 1835, applied to the others 'exactly the same vocabulary of reproach':[1] in document **130** the Girondin, Louvet, accused the Montagnards of the same involvement in conspiracies and foreign plots that was deployed against his friends. The concept of the general will precluded that of the loyal opposition and led to a spurious and impossible quest for unanimity.

Were there, nevertheless, real differences even if they could not be expressed? There had been genuine and bitter policy differences between the Girondins and Robespierre over entering the war. Yet paradoxically Robespierre, who had been reluctant to enter the war, was able to accuse his adversaries of not taking the necessary steps to prosecute it successfully. The Girondins had been earlier on the republican scene, were ideological republicans in a way Robespierre had not been, yet they had been reluctant to admit that the war meant that the king would have to go. They entered it precisely to make his position untenable (**113**) but then tried to help him maintain his grip. The prosecution of the war, in the declaration of which the quarrel between Montagnards and Girondins originated, deepened the rupture. For the basic issue which divided the two factions was: shall normal procedures, the rule of law, constitutional government, freedom of the press, economic liberalism, social rank (things which both groups favoured) be temporarily abandoned in order to win the war? The Girondins, who had started the war, thought not; the Montagnards, who had opposed it, were prepared to make the sacrifice.

The quarrel between the two factions became hopelessly envenomed during the period of interregnum between 10 August and the meeting of the Convention, a period which is sometimes called the 'first Terror' and which was dominated by the September massacres when between the 2nd and the 5th of that month hysterical mobs broke into the prisons and massacred over 1,000 political and common-law prisoners. The massacres are still a matter of controversy in French historiography because unless they can be explained away they would seem to leave an indelible stain on the Revolution, the founding act of the modern French state. I follow J. W. Croker in seeing them as part of Robespierre's electoral tactics: the terror they created enabled his faction to take all 24 Parisian seats in the Convention. He also aimed, through the Paris Commune which he dominated, to have the leading Girondins arrested, which would have been the equivalent of a death warrant. This is the accusation made by Mme. Roland, the wife of the Girondin minister of the interior, but Robespierre comes close to admitting it in a throwaway line in the notes he prepared for the trial of Danton[2] (**126**).

1 J. W. Croker, *Essays on the Early Period of the French Revolution* (1857), p. 405.
2 George Jacques Danton, 1759–94, lawyer, minister of justice, August–September 1792, *conventionnel*, member of the 'first' Committee of Public Safety April–July 1793, executed 5 April 1794

Danton, as minister of justice, countermanded the arrest warrants (though Mme. Roland felt no gratitude) and Robespierre accuses him of thwarting his plans 'to crush Brissot's conspiracy'.

If Robespierre could have liquidated the 20 or so Girondin leaders, the ones who had had seats in the Legislative Assembly, his path in the Convention would have been smoother. As it was, despite his clean electoral sweep of Paris, his opponents beat him in the country and had a substantial majority in parliament. This may be a rather Anglo-Saxon way of putting it. For his part, Robespierre disputed that there was a majority and a minority. This was not just Rousseau again – 'the majority is [simply] that of good citizens' **(127)** – it also to an extent corresponded with reality. As A. Patrick has shown, although there was deep distrust of Paris, on matters of general defence and administration the Girondins were regarded as obstructionists and the Montagnards tended to staff the key parliamentary committees.[3] Also with time the Girondins' position deteriorated, the turning point being the king's trial.

In the trial Robespierre advanced a concept which was to have a powerful influence on the development of the Terror – that normal legal right to a fair trial can be waived either in dealing with an enemy or in a state of revolution **(131)**. At first, Robespierre only denies these rights to Louis, as being, in Saint-Just's phrase, 'outside the sovereign', but within nine months the 'law of suspects' will apply them not just to anyone who is deemed to be an enemy of the Revolution but to those who are merely 'neutral' and the 'state of revolution' will be deemed to be a continuous one.

The king was guillotined on 21 January 1793 and those deputies who had voted for a reprieve were totally excluded from the leading committees of the Convention, those of General Security (police) and Public Safety (instituted on 5 April) and from missions to the departments. These missions were designed to prepare the provinces for a coup against the Girondins along the lines indicated in Robespierre's speech of 8 May **(133)**. But these representatives-on-mission were tactless and their efforts counterproductive; their absence also temporarily restored to the Girondins their majority in the Convention. Document **137** shows that the great commercial city of Bordeaux was on a knife-edge.

Robespierre's undated memorandum **(136)** presents the *journées* of 31 May–2 June (when the Convention was surrounded by Hanriot's troops and 22 leading Girondin deputies were expelled) as a pre-emptive strike (document **135** shows that even in Paris there were some anti-Montagnard sections which had to be restrained during the *journées*) or even as a defensive reaction: although the expulsion and arrest of these provincial deputies exacerbated the situation in the provinces, the revolt of most departmental authorities against the Paris-dominated Convention predated 31 May. Thus Marseilles fell to anti-Jacobin forces on 28 April and Lyon on 29 May. Toulon was the last city of importance to fall (on 12 July).

Robespierre's memorandum has become famous for its opening line, 'There must be one will', and for another: 'The internal dangers come from the bourgeois; to defeat the bourgeois, it is necessary to rally the people';

3 A. Patrick, *The Men of the First French Republic* (1972), *passim.*

but both these assertions need interpretation. When Courtois published Robespierre's papers in 1795, he dated the memorandum to the summer of 1794 in order to present it as a blueprint for dictatorship.[4] The memorandum in fact dates to the previous summer, but is still a blueprint for dictatorship, though not of one man – rather for a Jacobin dictatorship. The words 'republic' or 'republican' occur ten times in the memorandum and taken literally make Robespierre's argument anodyne to the point of tautology – '[the will] must be either republican or royalist'. But substitute the word 'Jacobin' for 'republican' and the memorandum acquires a certain cogency.

Similarly the word 'bourgeoisie' in the context quoted above seems to imply a Marxian class war, unlikely in the summer of 1793. By 'bourgeoisie', however, Robespierre understands *'haute bourgeoisie'* and what he is denouncing is a tendency which he more explicitly denounces elsewhere for 'the aristocracy to reconstitute itself' out of the *haute bourgeoisie* and the remnants of the feudal aristocracy, an amalgam which in fact emerged after his fall and in the nineteenth century was called 'the notables'.

Before the rising of 31 May the fiery Girondin Isnard had threatened that if the provincial deputies were harmed, Paris would be obliterated – 'people would search along the banks of the Seine for traces of the city' (**134**). Paris is still standing but the majority of departmental authorities refused to recognize the authority of the rump Convention. Some of the Girondin deputies who had broken their house arrest withdrew to Normandy, set up their banner at Caen and invited the other departments to send troops (**138**). For the first time in the Revolution civil war seemed likely and this at a time when the war was going badly and there was a serious royalist rising in the Vendée. That a full-scale civil war did not develop was partly due to the fact that many men of military age were at the front and there were not enough left to fight at home. Also parliamentary immunity or moderate republican-ism were ideals of limited appeal: as Pétion notes, most well-to-do Normans were royalists. Thus the rising in Normandy fizzled out.

Where the struggle was fiercest, the palsied hands of the Girondin deputies were absent and local rather than national issues predominated, or rather just one local issue: resentment at the bullying and gerrymandering tactics of the local Jacobin Clubs. The worst rebellions occurred in the cities of the Midi, and in particular Toulon (which opened its gates to the English) and Lyon, the second city of France, which held out against the forces of the Convention until 9 October. Robespierre's entry to the Committee of Public Safety on 27 July marked a harsher policy towards the revolts. A com-promise settlement, which Danton and the 'first' Committee of Public Safety had sought, was firmly rejected (**139**). Once the city had fallen it was re-named Ville-Affranchie (Freedtown), orders were given for its public build-ings to be demolished, and mass executions were instituted (the *mitraillades*). Documents **140** and **141** show the blood-lust of the Jacobins on the spot. One of them, Collot d'Herbois, a member of the Committee of Public Safety, also advocated what we would call 'ethnic cleansing' –

dispersing 100,000 working men and their families over the face of France (though this option was rejected).

Collot thought that the *lyonnais* were racially deficient in patriotism, whilst Couthon, in a bizarre application of Montesquieu's climatic theories, thought that the local fogs made them stupid. Accordingly Collot told Robespierre that even those inhabitants who had not joined the rebellion could not be relied on for administration. His solution was to send in Jacobins from Paris but that posed a double problem, first because the Jacobins were a tiny minority and were mostly needed to staff the Parisian bureaucracy so few could be spared. Second, the locals who were passed over became resentful and they had a direct line to Robespierre. Achard, their leader, who was to work for the impeachment of Collot's colleague Fouché (**189**), sends fraternal greetings not only to Robespierre, but to Duplay, his host, and to Nicolas, his printer (**140**).

The Girondin deputies had been incompetent, irresponsible and intemperate; they had wrecked the monarchy and sought to save the king; but they had tried to uphold the rule of law whilst, in the Convention, debate had been free – if possible, too free. The deputy Thibaudeau, who passed as a Montagnard, considered that 31 May marked the beginning of the Terror and that thereafter 'the National Convention was itself no more than a nominal parliament, a passive instrument of the Terror' (**142**).

122 Vergniaud's notes for his defence before the Revolutionary Tribunal

I belonged to a faction. There was a conspiracy.

I knew B[rissot] at the Jacobins. The others unknown to each other: how in coalition?

Diversity of our opinions on various issues.

Appeal to the people – Death – Reprieve – Primary Assemblies.[5] . . . Their crime, and my consolation, that of being my friends.

If the blood of a Girondin is required, let mine suffice.

They will be able to make amends by their talents and their services . . . besides, they are fathers, husbands.

As for me, schooled in adversity. . . . My death will make no one unhappy.

H. Wallon, *Histoire du tribunal révolutionnaire de Paris* (8 vols., 1880–2), vol. I, pp. 480–1

5 All concerned with the trial of the king in which the Girondins were notoriously divided.

123 Brissot to Mme. Roland (sometime after 10 August 1792)

Jean-Pierre Brissot, 1754–93, journalist, deputy to the Legislative Assembly and National Convention, was one of the leading Girondins, and gave his name to that party who tended to be referred to by contemporaries as Brissotins rather than Girondins.

... I must forego the pleasure of dining with our friends on Thursday because we always have a dinner arranged for that day and I hope that friend Roland will be kind enough to come. M. Clavière is coming and either he or myself will receive M. Roland at four o'clock at the latest. I shall be free on Saturday and at Mme. Roland's service.

I enclose, for your husband and for Lanthenas, a list of patriots to employ because one should always have such a list in front of one. Regards to our friends.

J.-P. Brissot, *Correspondance et papiers*, ed. C. Perroud (1912), p. 293

124 Mme. Roland to Bancal des Issarts, 2 September 1792

I wrote to you at Clermont before learning that you had gone to Riom; I told you that more than 80,000 Prussians had entered France and that Longwy had been basely delivered to them. They are advancing rapidly, Verdun is under siege and cannot hold out long; their plan is to advance on Paris and they are in a position to do so. I shall not tell you of all the measures we are taking; our lack of sleep and superhuman exertions make no impression: it is impossible in a few hours to repair the damage done by four years of treason. The enemy has had a head start on us and we can only save ourselves by a kind of miracle which we must induce by hope. Send us men ready armed such as of old sprang from the earth and let them rush here with giant steps. What makes me despair is the cowardice of the municipalities; Clermont [en Argonne] has just given a devastating example. Our mad Commune hampers everything; it scraps with the Legislative and upsets all the plans of the executive. If this continues we are bound to expire soon and even more likely at the hands of the people of Paris than at those of the Prussians.

Even as I write the alarm cannon is fired, the drums beat out the call to arms, the tocsin is tolled and everyone rushes to his section. On what orders? No one has given any. But the Commune has said that this evening the people must assemble in the Champ de Mars and that 50,000 men must leave Paris tomorrow without considering that we cannot even dispatch 200 without arranging billets and provisions for them. Nevertheless, frenzied detachments of the people rush here demanding arms and think themselves betrayed because the minister is not at home at the moment they please to visit him.

The Assembly passes decrees smacking of fear; the mob proceeds to the Abbaye prison and massacres 15 people; it talks of going to all the prisons. The executive power has summoned all the officials of the sections to reason with them, to enlighten them if possible and to lay before them all the evils of anarchy to which they would necessarily be abandoned if the Executive Council withdrew because of the way the sections were thwarting those who were entrusted with co-ordinating action. All the horses have been seized and since this, as all the others, is a 'popular' operation, many have been lost through sloppy organization. The barriers have been closed again; they had at last been opened yesterday as their closure delays all operations because even the couriers of the executive power are often held at the Commune despite passports from the ministers. Adieu. My spirit feels inaccessible to fear and I could easily endure the marches and countermarches of a regular defence; my worthy friend [M. Roland] is as active and more firm than ever. But who could not be saddened by the confusion worse confounded by the agitators?

Adieu; in a few more days the fate of the capital will be much clearer. Perhaps it would be wise to evacuate the government but it is already too late even for that. Washington did well to translate the Congress and it was not out of fear.

Lettres de Madame Roland, vol. I,
pp. 432–4

125   Mme. Roland to Bancal, 5 September 1792

Robespierre and Marat have a knife at our throats; they are striving to stir up the people and turn them against the National Assembly and the [Executive] Council. . . . They have a small army paid from the proceeds of what they found or stole from the Palace and elsewhere or what Danton, the clandestine leader of this band, gives them. Would you believe that they have issued a warrant for the arrest of Roland and Brissot as being suspected of having secret dealings with Brunswick and that they only held back out of a kind of fear? They then confined themselves to placing their papers under seal but during their inquisitorial search through Brissot's papers they were ashamed to find only material refuting their claims. They dared not affix the seals nor proceed to the houses of Roland and Guadet, contenting themselves with carrying off the letters in English which they had not been able to understand. If they had used their arrest warrant, these two excellent citizens would have been taken to the Abbaye and butchered with the others. We are not safe, and unless the departments send a guard for the Assembly and the Council, you will lose both.

So work rapidly to send us this guard – on the pretext of the external enemies against whom those Parisians who can bear arms are being sent – so that the whole of France may participate in saving two powers which belong to and are dear to it.

Don't lose a moment if you want to find them still there; adieu.

Lettres de Madame Roland, vol. I,
pp. 434–5

126   Robespierre's notes for the accusation of Danton, 1794

Danton imperiously rejected all my proposals to crush the conspiracy and to prevent Brissot from resuming his conspiracy on the pretext that it was necessary to concentrate exclusively on fighting the war.

A. Mathiez, *Etudes sur Robespierre*
(1957), pp. 136–7

127   Robespierre on faction: from a speech in the Convention, 28 December 1792

Already, to perpetuate discord and to make themselves masters of debates, people have seen fit to divide the assembly into a majority and a minority – a new way of outraging and reducing to silence those who are designated by the latter term. I do not recognize either a majority or a minority here. The majority is that of the good citizens; the majority is not permanent since it does not pertain to any party; it is recreated after every free vote, because it belongs to the public good and to eternal reason; and when the assembly recognizes its error, as sometimes happens, the minority then becomes the majority. The general will does not form in shadowy cabals nor around ministerial tables. The minority has an eternal right every-where, that of proclaiming truth or what it regards as such.

Virtue was always in a minority on earth. Otherwise it would not be peopled by tyrants and slaves.

Robespierre, *Oeuvres*, vol. IX,
p. 198

128   Garat on Robespierre's view of parties

In the course of this work, I spoke continually of the various parties, of their origins and their mentality. 'One party', replied Robespierre, 'pre-supposes a correlative; when there is one, there must be two of them at least. So where have you seen parties here? There have never been any;

there is the Convention and a few conspirators.' He found the idea that he was no more than a party chief deeply shocking. . . .

P. J. B. Buchez and P. C. Roux, *Histoire parlementaire de la Révolution française* (40 vols., 1834–8), vol. XVIII, p. 440

129 Rousseau on faction: from the chapter 'Whether the general will can err' in *Du contrat social*

If when the people deliberates . . . there are intrigues [*brigues*], partial associations at the expense of the main one, the will of each of these associations becomes general in relation to its own members and in particular in relation to the state: one can say then that there are no longer as many voters as men but only as many as there are parties. The differences become less numerous and give a result which is less general.

J. J. Rousseau, *Du contrat social*, ed. C. E. Vaughan (1918), p. 24

130 Louvet on the Girondins

Jean-Baptiste Louvet, 1760–97, journalist, deputy to the National Convention, intemperately accused Robespierre of aspiring to dictatorship and was proscribed, together with his Girondin colleagues. After the failure of the Normandy rising he went into hiding and returned to the Convention in the Thermidorian period where, surprisingly, he advocated terrorist measures. His memoirs betray distinct signs of mental imbalance.

It is in general time to make this observation, that among the victims of 31 May were numbered many men distinguished by rare talents, capable of conducting a moral regeneration, of increasing the prosperity of a republic at peace and of deserving well of the fatherland both for their private life and their public virtues; but that there was not one of them who was used to the clash of faction or fitted to execute those vigorous blows by which one can prostrate conspirators. There was not one of them who was equipped to detect the hand of the enemy, to take in at a glance the vast network of a conspiracy or, if they had at least recognized one, who wished to fight it by methods other than those of moral principles and eloquent discourse. I except Salle, Buzot and Barbaroux who from the outset were well aware of the Orléans faction and who joined forces with me to combat it on every occasion. But their penetration did not go very far: here was only Salle whom I could ever persuade that Austria and England had their principal agents in the Jacobins; and I remember that Guadet, Pétion and even Barbaroux were still protesting in the Gironde, six months after the rising of 31 May, when I said that assuredly Marat and his band were in the pay of the foreign powers. Sometimes, in moments of indignation, Guadet certainly said that it was true but in a sort of metaphorical sense and indeed he would never have wished to base his conduct in the Assembly on what he called this hypothesis. Oh! friends you were too honourable to believe in such crimes; and I never tired of repeating to you that sooner or later you would fall victim to them.

J. Louvet, *Mémoires*, ed. F. A. Aulard
(1889), pp. 62–3

131 Robespierre's first speech to the Convention on the king's trial, 3 December 1792

Citizens, beware lest you are deceived by false notions; you are confusing the rules of civil and positive law with the principles of natural law; you are confusing the relations of citizens with each other with the relations of nations with an enemy who is conspiring against it; you are also confusing the situation of a people in the midst of a revolution with that of a people with an established system; a nation which is punishing a public functionary, whilst maintaining the form of government, with one which is destroying the government itself. . . .

When a nation has been forced to have recourse to the right of insurrection, it returns to the state of nature as regards the tyrant. By what title could he invoke the social contract, he who has destroyed it? The nation may still keep the social contract if it so judges, for that which concerns relations of citizens with each other. However the effect of tyranny and insurrection is to break it entirely in relation to the tyrant; to place them in a state of mutual war. Tribunals and judicial procedures are made for members of the city. It is palpably absurd to suppose that the constitution could preside over this new order of things; it would be to suppose that it had survived itself. . . .

There is another difficulty: what sentence shall we impose on Louis? . . . Personally, I detest the large number of death penalties provided for in your laws. I demanded the abolition of the death penalty in the assembly which you still call 'constituent', and it is through no fault of my own that the fundamental principles of reason seemed like moral and political heresies. But if you never thought to invoke them in favour of so many unfortunates whose crimes are less their own than those of the government, how perverse to remember them solely to plead the cause of the greatest criminal of them all. You ask for an exception to the death penalty on behalf of the one man who could legitimate it! Yes the death penalty in general is a crime, and for this reason alone that, according to the indestructible principles of natural justice, it may only be justified where it is required by the safety of the individual or of the body politic. Now public safety never demands it for ordinary crimes because society can always prevent them by other means and prevent the criminal from harming it. But a king dethroned in the middle of a Revolution which is far from being consolidated by laws; a king whose very name brings down the scourge of war on the troubled nation; neither prison nor exile can render his existence indifferent to the public good; and this cruel exception to the ordinary laws which justice admits can only be imputed to the nature of his crimes. I pronounce this fatal truth with regret. . . . But Louis must die that the *patrie* may live.

Robespierre, *Oeuvres*, vol. IX,
pp. 121–30

132 Robespierre on the food riots of 24 and 25 February 1793: speech in the Jacobins, 25 February

When the people arises, should it not have an objective worthy of itself? Should it concern itself with miserable comestibles? It has not profited from the riots because the sugar-loaves have been picked up by the valets of the aristocrats; and supposing it did so profit, what disadvantages would not accrue in return for this modest advantage? Our adversaries want to frighten anyone who has any property; they want to demonstrate that our system of liberty and equality is subversive of law and order.

The people should arise not to collect sugar but to fell brigands.

Robespierre, *Oeuvres*, vol. IX,
p. 275

133 Speech of Robespierre to the Jacobins on 8 May 1793

I demand:

1 That the sections raise an army sufficient to form the nucleus of an *armée révolutionnaire* to carry along all the *sans-culottes* of the departments to exterminate the rebels.
2 That an army of *sans-culottes* be raised in Paris to contain the aristocracy.
3 That all the dangerous intriguers, all the aristocrats should be placed under arrest; that the *sans-culottes* should be paid by the state and subsidized by the rich and that this measure should apply throughout the republic.

Robespierre, *Oeuvres*, vol. IX,
p. 492

134   A stormy debate in the Convention, 25 May 1793

Danton: I demand for the deputation from the Commune of Paris the same silence as for that from Marseilles.

The spokesman: . . . We have come to denounce before you the outrage perpetrated against Hébert, deputy *procureur* of the Commune, by the Commission of Twelve. (Loud murmurs from the right wing.) He has been snatched from the midst of the General Council and conveyed to the dungeons of the Abbaye. The General Council will defend innocence to the death. It demands that you restore to his functions a magistrate respected alike for his civic virtues and his sagacity. (Murmurs.) We demand that he be judged promptly. For honest men arbitrary arrests are civic crowns. (Applause from part of the Assembly and from the gallery.)

The president [Isnard]: The Convention, which has drawn up a Declaration of the Rights of Man, will not suffer a man to remain in prison if he is not guilty. Be assured that you will obtain swift justice but hearken to the truths I am going to tell you: France has entrusted Paris with the safekeeping of the representatives of the nation; Paris must respect this trust; the Parisian authorities must deploy all their power to guarantee this respect. If ever the Convention were to suffer outrage, if ever through one of those insurrections which since 10 March have constantly recurred and of which the municipal authorities have never warned the Convention . . . (Loud murmurs on the extreme left. Applause from the opposite side. Several voices on the left: 'That is not a reply!')

Fabre d'Eglantine: Permission to speak against you, President.

The president: If, as a result of one of these constantly recurring insurrections, the National Convention were to suffer attack, I declare to you in the name of all France . . . (Cries of 'No! No!' on the extreme left. The rest of the Assembly rose together. All the members shout: 'Yes, say in the name of France!')

The president: I declare in the name of all France: Paris will be annihilated.

Marat: Leave the Chair, President . . . you dishonour the Assembly . . . you are protecting the 'statesmen'. . . .

The president: Soon people would search along the banks of the Seine for traces of the city . . .

Buchez and Roux, *Histoire parlementaire*, vol. XXVII, pp. 224–5

135   The mechanics of insurrection: a note from the Evêché Committee, 2 June 1793

To prevent dangerous sections from deploying their cannons against the friends of the *patrie*, we must write to the commander-in-chief [Hanriot] to order the suspect sections to proceed to such and such a post with their cannons, etc. for the public safety, and there, surrounded by the other armed citizens of reliable sections, we will be safe from danger.

P. Saint-Claire Deville, *La commune de l'an II* (1946), p. 91, n. 1

136   Undated memorandum of Robespierre, June 1793

There must be one will.

It must be either republican or royalist.

For it to be republican, there must be republican ministers, republican newspapers, republican deputies, a republican government.

Whilst the body politic suffers from revolutionary sickness and a divided will, the foreign war is [necessarily] a mortal illness.

The internal dangers come from the bourgeois; to defeat the bourgeois, it is necessary to rally the people. Everything was ready to place the people under the yoke of the bourgeoisie and send the defenders of the republic to the scaffold. They have triumphed at Marseilles, at Bordeaux and at Lyon; they would have triumphed at Paris but for the present insurrection. The present insurrection must continue until the measures necessary to save the republic have been taken. The people must make an alliance with the Convention and the Convention must make use of the people.

The insurrection must spread by degrees along the same lines; the *sans-culottes* must be paid and remain in the towns [rather than being sent to the front].

They must be found arms, incited [*colérer*] and enlightened.

Republican enthusiasm must be exalted by all means possible.

If the [proscribed] deputies are merely sent home, the republicans are lost; the deputies will continue to mislead the departments, and their replacements will be no better.

[General] Custine: to be watched by new and trustworthy commissioners.

Foreign affairs: alliance with the smaller powers; but impossible until we have a single national will.

Papiers inédits trouvés chez Robespierre, Saint-Just, Payan, etc. (3 vols., 1828), vol. II, pp. 15–16

137   General Biron to Cambon on the state of Bordeaux, 31 May

Cultivate Bordeaux, keep someone there who inspires confidence, who can calm the *bordelais* and assure them that you don't want to disturb their rest and you will keep this city loyal. The mood there is one of obstinacy rather than hot-headedness. They struck me as quite determined not to interfere with Parisian affairs but even more determined to preserve their liberty, property and opulence. Their confidence in their deputies appears very great and widespread. No one wants to adopt a violent course of action but if a policy of severity were adopted towards Bordeaux there would be a great explosion. They would ask for help from anyone who could provide it and it would not be refused them [Biron is referring to England] . . . They do not want a king but a rich and tranquil republic. 1 will let you know everything I learn and I shall try to be well informed by people who, like me, want the republic one and indivisible. At this moment Bordeaux is not our smallest danger. With good sense we can keep it and draw immense resources from it; to act imprudently could have disastrous and incalculable consequences.

H. Wallon, *La Révolution du 31 mai
et la Fédéralisme en 1793* . . . (2 vols.,
1886), vol. II, pp. 452–3

138 Extracts from Pétion's account of the Federalist rising in Normandy

What greatly struck me was that these societies [i.e. the political clubs known as *sociétés populaires*] were always deserted, that there were 20 women to one man and that the women displayed much more energy and patriotism than the men. What was no less striking was that I did not see any of the young bourgeoisie of the town in the clubs. They were composed of artisans, men whose aspect suggested poverty.

Subsequently I learned that the political complexion of these little gentlemen was decidedly aristocratic. Nor did we receive any visits from any of those people termed *comme il faut* before the Revolution.

It was easy to see that the political disposition of the bulk of the citizens was bad. Caen was evidently of a royalist bent.

This insight provides the key to an enigma we sought to unravel. Those of our colleagues who had arrived first had been given a very warm welcome in several prosperous households among the *haute bourgeoisie*. Even the nobility seemed pleased to see them. They were in the belief that the proscribed deputies were royalists who disdained that portion of the people who were known by the coarse and low term *sans-culottes*. As these calumnies and stupidities were repeated every day in the newspapers, as the Mountain cultivated a 'popular' image, it was hardly surprising that miles from the scene of action these false judgements should have been made. But when all these gentry saw that the proscribed deputies detested the monarchy and sincerely desired the republic, they kept their distance and cold-shouldered them. They had a hearty dislike of the Mountain, but they did not like republicans any better. . . .

We were awaiting the arrival of the departmental forces. We were given to hope that those departments of Normandy who had not yet declared themselves were about to do so. Seine-Inférieure was the most important; if it had come out in our favour so would the others who were wavering. Rouen would have furnished a sizeable contingent. The National Guards were well armed and trained. Rouen maintained an equivocal conduct and in the event we were lucky to secure her neutrality. . . .

Orne, which had shown itself favourable at first, subsequently retracted its adhesion.

Thus, of the five departments carved out of the former province of Normandy, only two, Eure and Calvados, entered the union. Indeed, one could reduce these two departments to two towns, Evreux and Caen, because, with the exception of Vire, none of the other places in these departments provided men.

Eure and Calvados fielded no more than 800 men. Brittany raised more troops and exerted itself more: Ille-et-Villaine sent 500 men, Finistère nearly 600, including 50 cavalry; Morbihan sent 200; Mayenne about the same. . . .

Such was the army which was so noised abroad that it was said to consist of 60,000 men, the army which caused all Paris to tremble. Admittedly an experienced general [Wimphen] was seen at its head who had covered himself with glory during the defence of Thionville; admittedly this general had announced that he would march on Paris at the head of 40,000 men – and admittedly he had a general staff organized as for a great army. . . .

Exerting ourselves to the limit and using every resource, we could not assemble more than four or five thousand men. These forces may seem very small; they were, however, more than enough for our objectives. If we had advanced as far as Paris with these forces we should have struck fear into the hearts of the scoundrels, and the good citizens, who outnumbered them but were feeble and cowardly and who were only waiting for a rallying point to revive, would rapturously have joined this embryonic army and counter-anarchy would have been achieved in Paris.

It would not even have been necessary to wait for the Midi in order to bring about this beneficent revolution; it would have happened inevitably.

What greatly injured the success of this enterprise was that people had a very false idea of the right *modus operandi*. Throughout, they thought that it was a matter of conducting a regular siege, of fighting the whole of Paris: consequently they exerted every fibre to raise huge armies. Nothing was more absurd. If two or three thousand men had been at the gates of Paris eight days after the rising of 2 June, the anarchists would have been overthrown. They profited from all the respites they were given and used them to divide and corrupt.

The departments, having delayed sending forces for so long, could have employed another no less powerful weapon – that of inertia: if they had refused to implement legislation, the reign of rogues would have been at an end and a new Convention would have had to be nominated. The punishment of the traitors would have followed inevitably from such a course of action.

But let us return to the little army of Bretons and Normans. We had it file past at Evreux; a battalion from Caen and that of Ille-et-Villaine were already there; they had joined the National Guard of Evreux and some 150 or 200 dragoons from La Manche. Morbihan and Mayenne were arriving, with Finistère behind them.

At this juncture Wimphen sent on ahead Puisaye, his camp marshal and friend. Did Puisaye have orders from Wimphen? Did he want to attempt the operation on his own initiative or cause it to miscarry? That I do not know, but he decided to act with just the troops who had then reached Evreux. He occupied the advantageous position of Pacy, which is 12 miles from Evreux. In Paris it was announced that 20,000 men had taken Pacy despite a stout resistance by its inhabitants. Let it be said that there was no resistance and that the inhabitants were in no position to offer any; that Pacy is a straggling village and that 60 men were enough to take it; also that Puisaye, instead of 20,000 men had sent 200. . . .

[The Mountain] proclaimed that this army intended to starve Paris to death and that it was holding up grain being sent to provision the city, whereas in fact it had not held up a single bag and was itself short of provisions; and it had been announced at the bar of the Convention that Paris had enough for six months.

Paris, despite these declamations, these predictions of civil war, did not rush to arms. On the contrary, those sections who were not groaning under the yoke of the Maratistes sent deputies to Evreux to tighten the bonds of union and fraternity which existed between all the sincere friends of the republic. The position, then, was extremely favourable. It was clear that the ring-leaders were not able to send out of Paris a force capable of resisting the one that was advancing.

Puisaye, at this moment, without waiting for the battalions which were on the march, risked an attack on Vernon. Vernon was the town where the few forces the Maratistes were able to scrape together were to be found. He marched on Vernon. About three miles off he halted his troops. He abandoned them to themselves, to drink, eat, disperse; he placed no lookout for the enemy; the gunners left their cannons, placing them side by side along a wall.

An enemy column appeared when least expected; no one was at his post, people ran off in disorder and this was made worse by a few loose shots. But for the presence of mind of one gunner who checked the march of this column by firing off three or four very accurate volleys, our men would have fallen on top of each other and the enemy, though inferior in strength, would have had a complete and easy victory.

Our men had time to form themselves into some sort of battle order. The cavalry advanced for a few minutes, then retreated with a precipitation which somewhat disconcerted the infantry and made confusion worse confounded. The enemy fired off three volleys of grapeshot. They pointed the cannon so high in the air that no one was hit but that was all the men of Caen needed to take flight and abandon their cannons.

The men of Ille-et-Villaine remained in good order and reclaimed the cannon whose traces had been cut, replacing them with their handkerchiefs. At the sound of a few cannon volleys and rifle shots the enemy column likewise took flight, so that no one remained in possession of the field because both sides panicked and both sides ran away.

The consequences of the battle were more fatal than the battle itself since no one had been killed or captured.

Mémoires inédites de Pétion,
ed. C. A. Dauban (1866), pp.
147–55

139   Robespierre rejects compromise

Garat, minister of the interior, sought to win back the departments that had revolted by offering fresh municipal elections, particularly in Lyon, but was reprimanded by Robespierre, who joined the Committee of Public Safety on 27 July.

I see. You propose that we should dismiss a patriot Commune; it is against all true principles; the revolutionary government is here to maintain them and not to annihilate them.

G. D. J. Garat, *Mémoires* (1862),
p. 248

140   The punishment of Lyon: Achard, *agent national* of Lyon to Gravier, juror in the Revolutionary Tribunal at Paris, 17 frimaire year II (7 December 1793)

More heads, and every day they fall! What exquisite pleasure you would have experienced the day before yesterday if you had seen this national justice being exercised on 209 scoundrels. What majesty! Such an imposing tone! It is all so edifying. So many great villains bit the dust today in the arena of the Breteaux! What a cement for the republic! Yesterday and today some poor devils were publicly found innocent: they were embraced and cheered to the rafters. What a sentiment for a people which still believes that we are bloodthirsty brigands. Billematz has paid the price of his treachery; an infinity of others you know . . . have done as much. The president and the public prosecutor of the department of Puy-de-Dome have followed them. What a spectacle worthy of liberty! Five hundred have already gone that way; doubtless twice as many again will follow and so it goes on.

Fraternal greetings.

Regards to Robespierre, Duplay and Nicolas.

Papiers inédits, vol. II, p. 233

141 Administering the Terror: Collot d'Herbois to Robespierre, Ville-Affranchie [Lyon], 3 frimaire year II (23 November 1793)

Those fears for the suffering *patrie* which determined me to come here at your suggestion were not misplaced. ...There's no food, no official bodies working; the orders of the CSP [Committee of Public Safety] misunderstood. . . . The *armée révolutionnaire* arrives tomorrow at long last and I will be able to accomplish great things. I can't wait for all the conspirators to be liquidated; the impatience of the *patrie* and of the sovereign people which composes it thrills through all my fibres and my heart. It is necessary that Lyon should really no longer exist and that the inscription ['Lyon n'est plus'] which you proposed should become reality. . . . It is necessary to disperse, to evacuate 100,000 working individuals. . . . by placing them among free men they will adopt their sentiments, which they would never do if they remained together. You are too much the philosopher not to realize this. . . .

We have created two new tribunals to judge the traitors . . . Several times twenty criminals have paid the price due for their crimes on the same day. That is still slow for the justice of an entire people which should strike all its enemies with lightning at once but we are occupied with forging the lightning. . . . [His predecessors had been too indulgent towards the rebel city, the loyal natives useless.] I do justice to my colleagues but they were exhausted by the external siege and the internal siege we had to begin required new forces. I think I have poured out my whole heart and mind to you, my friend; you will realize that what is needed here is men for all the posts and they are numerous. I am very satisfied with the Jacobins who came [from Paris]; the majority form a revolutionary commission which we have set up; it is the only body that works. I would also have liked some brothers for administrative work. We need similar qualities and I have designated two or three people who have not come. They should address themselves to you or to Billaud-Varenne before leaving, with the approval of the [Jacobin] society. They have been described as capable and of good will by the Jacobins who are here. We also need a prosecutor for the tribunal which will be established here for a long time. I was given the name of Saintexe; I scarcely know him or several others recommended, because my missions and my constant occupations have left me unsure, being often absent from the [Jacobin] society. Correct my choices if they are no good, but in that case send others. If I could have asked for some of our old friends I would have done it but they are required at Paris, being nearly all functionaries. And yet if they don't come, all the details will fall on us and crush us. . . .

Look after your health, it is precious to republicans and to your devoted friend.

Papiers inédits, vol. I, pp. 318–22

142 Thibaudeau on the extinction of parliamentary life after the fall of the Girondins

Antoine-Claire Thibaudeau, 1765–1854, lawyer, *conventionnel*, was an unobtrusive Montagnard who played an important role in the Thermidorian period and was later made a count by Napoleon.

Anyone who spoke of order was branded as a royalist; anyone who talked of laws was derided as a statesman [a term of abuse applied to the Girondins] – an honourable title becoming injurious and grounds for proscription. It began with mutual abuse and accusations – and ended in proscription. The Gironde was the furthest bourne between light and darkness. When it had been overthrown, we fell into chaos.

This revolution had been accomplished in Paris on 10 August when authority fell into the hands of the demagogues; the rising of 31 May gave them power all over France . . . ever we advanced because we dared not go back, seeing no other way out. For Camille Desmoulins and Danton – the one famous for the audacity of his ideas and the spice of his pamphlets and the other for his athletic frame and popular eloquence – perished for having spoken of moderation, and Robespierre, when he was attacked by men more concerned with their own safety than that of France, was planning to shift the crimes of the Terror on to them.

It was the opposition of the internal and external enemies of the Revolution which gradually brought about the Terror. This opposition provoked an exaggerated patriotism. It began, in the superior classes, with heated and violent speeches and ended, in the lower orders, with physical atrocities. When the Third Estate had overthrown the privileged classes, it assumed in the eyes of the people the place of the aristocracy; and when the people had fought the defenders of its rights, it sought within itself obscure victims with whom to feed the Terror. . . .

Just as, in normal times, people seek to shine, so, in this time of calamity, people sought to humble themselves in order to be forgotten or to coarsen themselves so that their superiority might be pardoned. People concealed not only their birth and wealth but all the still more legitimate advantages offered by nature or education. Everyone diminished himself to pass beneath the popular level. Everyone was confounded in the people. People forswore dress, manners, elegance, cleanliness, everyday luxuries, politeness and decorum so as not to arouse the envy of those to whom these things were alien.

The National Convention was itself no more than a nominal parliament, a passive instrument of the Terror. From the ruins of its independence arose that monstrous dictatorship which grew to such fame under the name of the Committee of Public Safety. The Terror isolated and stupefied the deputies just as it did ordinary citizens. On entering the Assembly each member, full of distrust, watched his words and actions lest a crime be made out of them. And indeed everything mattered: where you sat, a gesture, a look, a murmur or a smile. Everyone flocked to the summit of the Mountain, as that was regarded as the highest degree of republicanism; the right wing was deserted after the Girondins had been snatched from its midst. Those who had sat there with them and had too much conscience or shame to turn themselves into Montagnards took refuge in the Plain which was always ready to receive those who sought their safety in its complaisance or self-effacement. Those who were even more pusillanimous did not settle anywhere and changed place several times during the session, trusting thereby to deceive the spy and, by flying several flags, avoid quarrelling with anyone. The most prudent of all went one better: in the fear of dishonouring, or rather of compromising themselves, they never sat down at all and remained at the foot of the tribune, away from the benches, and on big issues, when they found it repugnant to vote for a proposal and dangerous to vote against, they slipped furtively out of the chamber.

The majority of the Convention was no more terrorist than the majority of the nation. It did not order the *noyades* of Nantes or the *mitraillades* of Lyon. But being unable or afraid openly to criticize that which they inwardly disliked, they maintained a dull silence. The sessions, once so long and stormy, were for the most part calm and unimpassioned and lasted only an hour or two. They could only use the shadow of liberty remaining to them on matters of slight importance and on weighty matters they waited for the initiative to come from the Committee of Public Safety and quietly followed its lead. Its members, its reporter, were awaited like heads of state and the depositories of the sovereign power; as they made their way towards the debating chamber they were preceded by a handful of base courtiers who seemed to announce the masters of the world. People tried to divine from their faces whether they brought a decree of proscription or news of a victory. The reporter mounted the tribune amidst the most profound silence and when he had spoken, if anyone spoke after him it was merely to re-emphasize what he had said and his proposals were always adopted, tacitly rather than by a proper vote. When he announced, shall we say, the triumph of the armies, his insolent mien seemed to say: 'it is not you, nor the people, nor the army who have triumphed, it is the Committee of Public Safety'. It had in fact taken possession of all the powers, of legislation and government, thought and action. It had ended by taking over proscriptions from the Committee of General Security which was soon reduced to the odious function of collating evidence.

A. C. Thibaudeau, *Mémoires sur la Convention et le Directoire*, ed. Berville and Barrière (2 vols., 1824), vol. I, pp. 36, 46–9

2

The constitution of 1793 and its Enragé critics

The function of the National Convention was to provide France with a republican constitution but before 31 May the lack of a consensus had made this impossible (the 'Girondin' constitution drafted by Condorcet had been rejected in February). With the removal of the Girondin leaders and the imprisonment of the 73 deputies who had protested at their expulsion, work on a 'Jacobin' constitution proceeded fast – too fast thought many, Garat writing (**161**) of a constitution 'drawn up by five or six young men in five or six days'. It was adopted by the Convention on 25 June and ratified by the people in a referendum.

The constitution of 1793 (**143**) is often regarded as the most democratic ever to have been devised. It is, in the sense that it most nearly approaches the Greek or Rousseauesque ideal of direct democracy which holds that the people cannot be represented. Obviously 28 million Frenchmen could not fit into the Champ de Mars as the citizens of a Greek city state had into the agora, but the constitution makes provision for a referendum on every law. Moreover, to emphasize the deputies' temporary – there are to be annual elections – and fiduciary character they are termed not representatives but mandatories, a key word in the radical thought of the period denoting direct democracy.

The constitution of 1793 is consistent with much of Enragé thinking: Jacques Roux had given a clear exposition of the principles of direct democracy at the time of the elections to the National Convention (**145**): 'the people, jealous of its sovereignty, expressly reserved the inalienable right to sanction all the decrees emanating from it and completely to withdraw its mandate from those members who betray its trust'. Moreover the *journée* of 31 May is sanctified by the articles in the Declaration of Rights which abolish parliamentary immunity (article 31) and assert the 'right and duty of insurrection' (article 35). Nevertheless, the Enragés were dissatisfied with the constitution because it did not embody the economic demands of the *sans-culottes*[1] (though article 21 of the Declaration of Rights stipulated the right to

---

1 Literally, without knee breeches, i.e. wearing the trousers of the ordinary man and, by extension, that section of society in its political aspect. In practice this means the urban lower-middle class and those who identified with them, since the very poor had no leisure for political activity and the peasant had different political and economic priorities.

work or to public assistance). Duret, in the Cordelier Club (**146**), even called for another insurrection, though his colleagues contented themselves with sending a 12-man deputation headed by Jacques Roux to present a petition to the Convention.

This lengthy 'manifesto' of the Enragés (**147**) is an important document because Roux, more than any other revolutionary leader, is able to articulate the hopes and fears of the *sans-culottes* without distortion or ulterior motive. He demands, in sum, the suspension of free trade which was a canon of orthodoxy, an achievement of the Revolution of 1789, but which, particularly in wartime, bore more heavily on the poor than the regulatory regime of the old monarchy. The equality that had been sought and obtained by the men of 1789 had been equality of opportunity, equality before the law, not absolute equality such as nineteenth-century socialists were to demand. Roux moves towards the latter when he proclaims: 'Equality is but a vain phantom when the rich exercise the power of life and death over their fellows through monopolies.' He asks for a 'maximum' to be put on the price of essentials and as a necessary concomitant (otherwise no one would sell except on the black market) the death penalty for hoarders, and that these provisions should be embodied in the constitution.

The reaction of the Montagnard deputies to the Enragé demands was to denounce and imprison their leaders – document **148** contains Robespierre's denunciation of them in the Jacobins – but to adopt many of their measures (e.g. laws of the maximum – **159** – and the death penalty for hoarding were decreed), either to satisfy their most reliable, if demanding, supporters, or because a regime of price controls and rationing would channel resources into the war effort.

143   The constitution of 1793

Declaration of Rights

1 The aim of society is the public good.

4 The law is the free and solemn expression of the general will; it is the same for all whether it punish or protect: it may only prescribe what is just and useful to society; it may only forbid that which is harmful.

9 The law must protect public and private freedoms against the oppression of those who govern.

11 Every act exerted against an individual otherwise than as provided for by law is arbitrary and tyrannical; the man against whom such violence is threatened has the right of forcible resistance.

17 A man may not be prevented from bestowing his labours on any form of employment, whether agricultural or commercial.

18 Every man may engage his services and his time but he may neither sell himself nor be sold. He does not have an alienable property in himself. The law does not recognize domestic service: all that can exist is a contract for the payment of services rendered between the man who works and the man who employs him.

19 No one can be deprived of the smallest portion of his property without his consent except when required by public necessity, legally expressed, and on condition of the prior payment of fair compensation.

21 Public assistance is a sacred debt. Society owes a living to unfortunate citizens either by providing them with work or by giving those unable to work the means of subsistence.

25 Sovereignty resides in the people. It is one and indivisible, imprescriptible and inalienable.

31 The crimes of the people's mandatories should never rest unpunished. No one has the right to claim a greater inviolability than the other citizens.

33 The right of resistance to oppression follows from the other rights of man.

34 Society is oppressed when one of its members is and vice versa.

35 When the government violates the rights of the people, insurrection is the most sacred of rights and the most imprescriptible of duties for each and every section of the people.

Constitutional Act

THE REPUBLIC
1 The French Republic is one and indivisible.

DISTRIBUTION OF THE PEOPLE
2 The French people is divided, for the exercise of its sovereignty, into primary assemblies of the cantons.
3 For matters of administration and justice it is divided into departments, districts and municipalities.

THE STATUS OF CITIZENS
4 The following categories are allowed to exercise the rights of a citizen of France:

Every man born and domiciled in France over 25 years of age.
Every foreigner over 25 who has lived in France for a year and:

(i) works for a living OR
(ii) has bought property OR
(iii) has married a Frenchwoman OR
(iv) has adopted a child OR
(v) who maintains an old man.

Finally every foreigner who is judged by the legislative body to have deserved well of humanity.

SOVEREIGNTY OF THE PEOPLE
7 The sovereign people is the totality of French citizens.

8 It nominates its deputies directly.

9 It delegates to electors the choice of officials, public assessors, criminal and appeal judges.

10 It deliberates on laws.

PRIMARY ASSEMBLIES

11 Primary assemblies consist of citizens domiciled for over six months in each canton.

12 They comprise not less than 200 and not more than 600 citizens called upon to vote.

15 No one may appear bearing arms.

16 Elections are conducted by ballot or *viva voce*, as each voter chooses.

18 Tellers record the vote of citizens who cannot write but prefer to vote by ballot.

19 Votes on laws may only be expressed in the form 'yes' or 'no'.

REPRESENTATION OF THE PEOPLE

32 The French people assembles every year on 1 May for elections.

34 An extraordinary meeting of a primary assembly takes place at the request of one-fifth of the citizens with a right to vote.

35 In this case it is convoked by the municipality of the place where it normally meets.

36 These extraordinary assemblies only deliberate if over half the citizens with a right to vote are present.

ELECTORAL ASSEMBLIES

37 The citizens in a primary assembly nominate one elector for every 200 citizens (present or absent). . . .

THE LEGISLATIVE BODY

40 The session of the legislative body is for one year.

41 It meets on 1 July.

42 Over half the deputies must be present to constitute a quorum.

ORGANIZATION OF THE SITTINGS OF THE LEGISLATIVE BODY

45 The sittings of the National Assembly are in public.

50 Fifty members have the right to demand a roll call.

51 The Assembly has the right to censure the conduct of its own members.

THE FUNCTIONS OF THE LEGISLATIVE BODY

53 The legislative body proposes laws and passes decrees.

54 Included under the general heading 'laws' are the enactments of the legislative body concerning: civil and criminal legislation; the general administration of the ordinary revenue and expenditure of the republic;

... the declaration of war; public instruction; public honours to the memory of great men.

55 Included under the specific heading 'decrees' are the acts of the legislative body concerning: the army and naval establishments ... the measures of general safety ... unforeseen extraordinary expenditure ... the trial of those accused of plotting against the general security of the republic ...

LEGISLATION

56 Proposed legislation is preceded by a report.

57 Discussion may not begin nor the law be provisionally drafted until a fortnight after the report.

58 The projected law is printed and sent to all the communes of the republic with the title: Proposed Law.

59 If, 40 days after sending out the proposed law, a tenth of the primary assemblies in each of a majority of departments has not objected, the project is accepted and becomes a law.

60 If there is objection, the legislative body convokes the primary assemblies.

THE EXECUTIVE COUNCIL

62 There is an Executive Council composed of 24 members.

63 The electoral assembly of each department nominates one candidate. The legislative body chooses the members of the Council from the consolidated list.

65 The Council is charged with the direction and surveillance of the general administration. It can only act in execution of the laws and decrees of the legislative body.

NATIONAL CONVENTIONS

115 If a tenth of the primary assemblies, regularly convoked, in each of a majority of departments asks for a revision of the Constitutional Act or changes in some of its provisions, the legislative body is required to convoke all the primary assemblies of the republic to determine whether there shall be a National Convention.

116 The National Convention is formed in the same way as the legislative body and subsumes its powers.

117 As regards the constitution, it only deals with those matters which have led to its convocation. ...

GUARANTEE OF RIGHTS

122 The constitution guarantees all Frenchmen equality, liberty, safety, the rights of property, the inviolability of the national debt, freedom of worship, a common education, public assistance, unlimited freedom

of the press, the right of petition, the right to assemble in popular societies and the enjoyment of all the rights of man.

123 The French republic honours loyalty, courage, old age, filial piety and misfortune. It places the constitution under the aegis of all the virtues.

124 The Declaration of Rights and the Constitutional Act shall be engraved on tablets within the legislative body and in public places.

144   Hérault de Séchelles and Barère discuss the constitution after dinner, autumn 1793

Marie-Jean Hérault de Séchelles, 1759–94, was the principal draughtsman of the constitution of 1793. He held important positions both at the end of the *ancien régime* and in the Revolution, being *avocat général* in the Parlement and later a member of the Committee of Public Safety. His doubts about his own constitution are noteworthy.

Hérault de Séchelles resumed: 'Nature will be the god of Frenchmen as the universe is her temple.' Barère: 'Equality, that is the social contract of peoples.' Hérault de Séchelles: 'The Ancients could only institute liberty by placing slavery side by side with it.' I [Vilate] said: 'In France we have eliminated even domestic service.' Hérault de Séchelles: 'But hasn't Condorcet's constitutional imbroglio forced us into issuing nothing but a popular impromptu? Our political decalogue worries me. Will the people's sanction of laws proposed by the legislative body be effective in such a vast empire? . . . Will democracy be contained within its limits?' Barère: 'The 24-man executive power could well become the stepping-stone for a leader as is seen today in various guises in Venice, Holland, Switzerland, America and England.' There was also question of the *gouvernement révolutionnaire* the inauguration of which was under discussion [see below, III(3)]. Hérault de Séchelles mused: 'Can a nation, as Raynal said, only regenerate itself by a bloodbath?' Barère: 'What is the present generation compared with the aeons to come?'

> J. Vilate, *Causes secrètes de la révolution du 9 au 10 thermidor an II*, ed. Berville and Barrière (1825), pp. 235–6

145   Speech of Jacques Roux to the Gravilliers section, 19 September 1792

Jacques Roux, 1752–94, priest, Enragé leader, member of the Commune, killed himself in prison.

Citizens . . . in the midst of all these dangers, in the midst of these violent commotions, it is characteristic of a free people, of a sovereign people but one which exercises its sovereignty without pride, it is, I say, characteristic of such a people to suspend the exercise of its rights and consonant with its generosity to say to each of its members chosen to represent it and carry out its wishes for this period: 'Of course we have the imprescriptible and eternal right to examine your ability, your motives and your entire life. At this time especially, when by well-directed laws you should seal the happiness of a regenerated empire, it would be our duty to regulate your conduct; but the fatherland is in danger and for the moment we are not objecting to the choice that has been made of you to save it. Hasten then to fly to the sanctuary of the laws where our confidence has just placed you but never forget that if the fatherland, which is observing you, sees you, in contempt of your oaths, depart from the line of conduct it has prescribed for you, you will be declared infamous and subjected to the rigour of the laws.'

The General Assembly, after consultation, unanimously decreed that the members elected to the National Convention would not, for the moment, be subjected to the *examen épuratoire* but that the people, jealous of its sovereignty, expressly reserved the inalienable right to sanction all the decrees emanating from it and completely to withdraw its mandate from those members who betray their trust. It also decreed that 12 commissioners should be chosen from among their number to communicate the General Assembly's wishes both to the electoral college and to the other 48 sections.

Jacques Roux, *Scripta et acta*, ed. W.
Markov (1969), pp. 388–9

146   Session of the Cordelier Club, 22 June 1793

Note Varlet's speech at the end which reflects the disquiet of the skilled workman, beginning to be threatened by an incipient Industrial Revolution, and his demand to find a safe haven in the burgeoning state bureaucracy spawned by the war.

Jacques Roux complained bitterly that the Commune had rejected his motion that all speculators should be punished with death. 'If this article is not in the Constitution', he said, 'we can say to the Mountain: "you have done nothing for the *sans-culottes* because they are not fighting for the rich but for liberty. If the leeches of this good people are always allowed to drink its blood drop by drop with the blessing of the law, then liberty resembles a pretty woman with one eye." I invite the Cordelier Club to present this petition to the Convention themselves tomorrow and to make sure that this principle is enshrined before they vote thanks to the Sacred Mountain. Let all the people surround the Convention and cry with one voice: "We worship liberty but we do not want to die of hunger; extirpate speculation and we will have nothing further to ask."'

Jacques Roux's proposal was adopted and 12 commissioners nominated to present this petition, including Varlet, Roussillion, Leclerc and Duret. But the latter refused to be one of the deputation and said angrily: 'I am indignant that people talk of petitions when we need to arm ourselves with cannons and daggers. . . . Therefore let us rise up and if the risings of 31 May were merely written in water let this new insurrection be written in the annals of history in letters of blood; we need another 10 August and for the heads of the criminals to fall.' (Long and rousing cheers.) . . .

Varlet was given leave to speak and spoke warmly, saying: 'I have studied the people for four years, I have mingled in their gatherings. The *sans-culottes* of Paris, Lyon, Marseilles and Bordeaux are the same: they alone constitute the people. We must therefore establish a line of demarcation between, on the one hand, the shop-keeper and the aristocrat and on the other the artisan; we must disarm the two former categories. The people of Paris, in the name of all the departments, must give a mandate to the Convention tomorrow; within 24 hours they must decree that all nobles will be dismissed from all the employments which belong to the *sans-culottes* alone. Tomorrow the people must triumph, tomorrow we must complete our work.' (Applause, motion carried.)

Roux, *Scripta et acta*, pp. 474–5

147   The 'manifesto' of the Enragés. Jacques Roux before the Convention, 25 June 1793

Delegates of the French people!

A hundred times have these sacred precincts resounded with the crimes of the egoists and knaves; you have always promised us to strike the bloodsuckers of the people. The Constitutional Act is about to be presented to the sovereign [Rousseauesque jargon for the people] for its sanction, and does it proscribe speculation? No. Have you declared the death penalty for hoarders? No. Have you determined in what consists freedom of commerce? Have you forbidden the sale of the metallic currency? No. Very well, we declare before you that you have not done everything for the welfare of the people.

Liberty is but a vain phantom when one class of men can starve the other with impunity. Equality is but a vain phantom when the rich exercise the power of life and death over their fellows through monopolies. The republic is but a vain phantom when the Counter-Revolution is accomplished daily through the price of provisions which three-quarters of the citizens cannot pay without shedding tears. However . . . it is only by putting foodstuffs within the reach of the *sans-culottes* that you will attach them to the Revolution and rally them around the constitutional laws.

You have not hesitated to strike dead those who should dare propose a king, and you have done well; you have just outlawed the counter-revolutionaries who reddened the scaffold with the blood of patriots at Marseilles, and you have done well. You would have deserved still better of the fatherland if you had put a price on the heads of the fugitive Capets and the deputies who have deserted their posts; if you had expelled the nobles and those who were appointed by the court from our armies; if you had taken hostage the wives and children of *émigrés* and conspirators; if you had retained the pensions of the former privileged orders for the cost of the war and confiscated for the benefit of volunteers and widows the treasure acquired since the Revolution by bankers and hoarders; if you had expelled from the Convention the deputies who voted for the appeal to the people; if you had handed over to the revolutionary tribunals the municipal officers who have stirred up federalism; if you had struck with the sword of justice the ministers and members of the Executive Council who have allowed the germ of Counter-Revolution to develop in the Vendée; if finally you had placed under arrest those who have signed anti-civic petitions. . . . Now are hoarders and speculators not just as guilty and more so? Are they not, like them, veritable national assassins?

Hitherto, the big merchants who are by principle the abettors of crime and by habit the accomplices of kings, have abused the freedom of commerce to oppress the people. They have falsely interpreted the clause in the Declaration of the Rights of Man which lays down that one is allowed to do everything which is not forbidden by law. All right, pass a constitutional decree stating that speculation, the sale of the metallic currency and hoarding are harmful to society. The people, who knows its true friends, the people, who has suffered for so long, will see that you pity its lot and that you want seriously to cure its ills. When it has a clear and precise law in the Constitutional Act against speculation and hoarding, it will see that you are more affected by the cause of the poor than of the rich; it will see that bankers, munitioners and monopolists do not sit among you; it will see in short that you do not want the Counter-Revolution.

You have, it is true, decreed a forced loan of 1,000 million francs payable by the rich. But unless you extirpate the tree of speculation, if you do not impose a national limit to the greed of the hoarder, then the very next day the stock-jobber [capitalists] and the merchant will recover this sum from the *sans-culottes* by means of monopolies and extortion: thus you will have hurt not the egoist but the *sans-culotte*. Before your decree, the grocer and the banker constantly squeezed the citizens; what vengeance will they not wreak today, when you lay them under contribution, what new tribute will they not levy on the blood and tears of the wretched?

In vain is it objected that the workman receives a wage proportionate to the increase in the price of provisions. In truth, there are some who are paid more for their work; but there are also a lot whose work is less well paid than before the Revolution. Moreover, all the citizens are not workmen; not all the workmen are employed and there are some with eight to ten children who cannot earn a living, and women in general do not earn more than 20 sous a day.

Deputies of the Mountain, had you but climbed from the third to the ninth floor of the houses of this revolutionary city you would have been touched by the tears and groans of a vast populace without bread and clothes, reduced to this state of distress and misfortune by speculation and hoarding because the laws have dealt cruelly with the poor, because they have only been made by the rich and for the rich.

Oh madness, oh shame of the seventeenth [*sic*] century! Who will be able to believe that the representatives of the French people, who have declared war on the tyrants abroad, were cowardly enough not to crush those at home? Under the Sartines and de Flesselles [responsible for the administration of Paris under Louis XV and Louis XVI], the government would not have allowed the price of essentials to be forced up to three times their value; what am I saying, they froze the price of arms and meat for the soldier!

But it is the war, it will be said, which is the cause of the high price of provisions. In that case, representatives of the people, why did you bring it about in the first place? Why, under the cruel Louis XIV, when the French had to repel the league of tyrants, did speculation not raise over this empire the standard of revolt, famine and devastation? And on this pretext, then, the merchant would be allowed to sell candles at six francs the pound, soap for six francs the pound and oil for six francs a pound. On the pretext of the war, then, the *sans-culotte* would pay 50 francs for a pair of shoes, 50 francs for a shirt and 50 francs for a poor hat. . . .

But it is the paper money, it is further objected, which is responsible for the high price of provisions. Ah! the *sans-culotte* is scarcely in a position to perceive that there is a lot in circulation . . . in any case the prodigious amount issued is proof that it passes current and is highly regarded. If the *assignat* has real backing, if it is based on the faith of the French nation, the quantity of national stock [in circulation] deprives it of none of its value. Because there is a lot of money in circulation, is that a reason to forget that one is a man, to commit robbery in the banking dens, to make oneself master of the life and property of the citizens, to employ all the methods of oppression suggested by avarice and party spirit, to stir up the people to revolt and force it, through shortage and the rack of need, to devour its own entrails?

But the assignats *are considerably devalued in commercial transactions.* . . . Why then do bankers, merchants and counter-revolutionaries stuff their coffers with them? Why are they so cruel as to reduce the wages of certain workmen without granting an indemnity to the rest? Why do they not offer a discount when they acquire national property? Does England, whose debt is perhaps 20 times the value of her territory and whose prosperity is solely due to her banknotes, pay as much proportionately for her produce as we do? Ah! the minister *Pith* [*sic*] is too clever to allow George's subjects to be oppressed in this way. And will not you, citizen representatives, you deputies of the Mountain, you who glory to be numbered among the *sans-culottes*, will not you, from the height of your immortal rock, crush the inextinguishable hydra of speculation?

But, it is added, we buy many goods from abroad and they will only accept payment in specie. That is false. Trade is nearly always conducted by exchanging goods for goods and notes for notes; often, indeed, notes are preferred to specie. The metallic coins circulating in Europe would not be sufficient to cover the hundred thousandth part of the notes in circulation. So it is as clear as the day that the speculators and bankers only discredit the *assignats* in order to sell their specie for more, to find an opportunity of creating monopolies with impunity and of dealing in the blood of patriots which they are burning to shed. . . .

Roux, Scripta et acta, pp. 140–6

148 Session of the Jacobin Club, 5 August 1793

Robespierre: . . . Two men, paid by the enemies of the people, two men denounced by Marat, have succeeded, or thought to succeed, that patriotic writer. It is because of their methods that the enemies of the state believed that they would break our defences again. The fury with which they distilled the venom of their calumny just at the moment when the *fédérés* were arriving in Paris from all parts of the country, and still further connections which could be established, demonstrate their complicity.

I must name them: the first [Jacques Roux] is a priest, known only by two dastardly actions, the first that of wanting to have the merchants murdered because, he said, they charged too much; the other, that of wanting to make the people reject the constitution on the pretext that it was defective.

The second is a young man who proves that corruption can enter a young heart. He has a seductive manner and talents, he is Leclerc, a former noble, the son of a noble.

Roux, Scripta et acta, pp. 533–4

|3|

Gouvernement révolutionnaire: *politics, Terror and bureaucracy*

The constitution of 1793 was never implemented. On 10 October Saint-Just told the Convention, cryptically, 'In the circumstances in which the Republic is placed, the constitution cannot be implemented: *on l'immolerait par elle-même'* (**151**); and, at his proposal, the Convention decreed that 'The provisional government of France is revolutionary for the duration of the war.' 'Revolutionary' government, in this technical sense, means emergency, discretionary government – a suspension of the rule of law. Probably the constitution of 1793 was never intended as more than a gesture to heal the divisions in the country caused by the *journée* of 31 May. The weak executive which it, in common with all the constitutions of the Revolution, established would have been unable to govern the country. But Saint-Just does not criticize this constitution but rather that of 1791 which was still operative. This constitution had been supplemented by a series of ad hoc 'revolutionary' laws since 10 August 1792 and these were finally rationalized and codified by the law of 14 frimaire[1] (**152**) which amounted to a veritable constitution of *gouvernement révolutionnaire*, if that is not a contradiction in terms.

The law of 14 frimaire aimed to end the anarchy caused by rival authorities with conflicting jurisdictions, each wielding exceptional powers which had sprung up after 10 August, and to concentrate power in the hands of the two most important committees of the Convention, the Committee of Public Safety, concerned with foreign policy and everything which came under the wide umbrella of 'public safety', and the Committee of General Security, concerned with police matters. Thus the law of 14 frimaire reduced the independent role of the Commune – by making the revolutionary committees of the sections report not to it but to the Committee of General Security – the Provisional Executive Council, the departmental authorities (which had mostly joined the Girondin or 'federalist' revolt and now saw the implementation of 'revolutionary' measures pass to the districts), and finally

---

1 On 7 October 1793 the Convention decreed that a republican calendar should replace the Gregorian one. Day 1, year I, was backdated to the declaration of the republic, 22 September 1792, and the names of the months were taken from the appropriate seasons. Thus 14 frimaire year II is 4 December 1793.

the members of the Convention who had been sent on various missions to the departments. Documents **153–5** deal with the implementation of the law of 14 frimaire. In document **153** a radical representative-on-mission is sceptical about the decree and in document **154** a country district is ignorant of its existence, whilst in document **155** an independent-minded representative is reprimanded by the Committee of Public Safety for flouting it.

The law of 14 frimaire describes the mechanism of *gouvernement révolutionnaire*, and its application to institutions ('constituted authorities'). The spirit of *gouvernement révolutionnaire* was the Terror, as experienced by individuals. Experience of the Terror could mean the gnawing fear graphically depicted by Thibaudeau (**142**) and Desmoulins (**163** and **165**) or it could simply mean oppression by a bloated bureaucracy employing 'more officials than the literate population of Europe' (**149**); the invasion of privacy involved in the government's insatiable demand for information (**156**) or the rigmarole Morellet had to go through to get a *certificat de civisme* from the 'revolutionary committee' of his section, a prerequisite for obtaining public employment or drawing a pension (**158**). Morellet presents his predicament humourously, as a world turned upside down: former ladies' hairdressers and butchers lording it over the former academician that he was – and enjoying every minute of it as such officials always do; another official (who turns out to be a married, unfrocked priest) reversing the rules of Chérin, the court genealogist, by insisting not on heraldic quarterings but ones based on the genealogy of revolutionary deportment.

By this stage the revolutionary authorities were concerned with categorizing everyone. As Saint-Just said in document **151**, 'you have to punish not only the traitors but even those who are neutral'. Such sentiments are embodied in the law of suspects of 17 September 1793 (**157**). But an equally pressing problem was to 'discover and inventory' 'patriots' to work the vast bureaucracy. This is Robespierre's intent in document **160b** but the task was difficult and increasingly so as the canons of orthodoxy narrowed with each succeeding purge to the point where one deputy correctly predicted 'that Robespierre's party will become extinct through lack of manpower'.[2]

One of the problems about understanding the mentality of the Jacobins is to know how far they were fooled by their own rhetoric. The rare occurrence of cynicism, even in their private letters, would suggest that they were taken in completely. That being so, the comments of Payan (**160a**), at the time a juror on the Revolutionary Tribunal, on the innocence of the duc d'Orléans, for whose death he had just voted, is refreshing if also chilling.

149 From a report by Robert Lindet concerning the *comités de surveillance*, 20 September 1794

This justification of *gouvernement révolutionnaire* when it was under attack during the Thermidorian period shows the scale of the operation, the

---

2 M. J. Michelet, *Histoire de la Révolution française*, ed. G. Walter (2 vols., 1952), vol. I, p. 95.

paranoia which inspired it and the impossibility of its complete implementation.

If one day it be asked why the National Convention organized a plan of surveillance demanding more officials than the literate population of Europe, Frenchmen will reply: 'this plan was wise and necessary; our enemies were so great in number and so widely disseminated and they had so many different guises and means of infiltrating public offices, popular societies and our very homes, that every citizen had to consider himself a sentinel at his post.' . . .

> P. Mautouchet (ed.), *Le Gouvernement révolutionnaire* (10 août 1792–4 brumaire an IV) (1912), pp. 130–1

150 Decree establishing the Committee of Public Safety, 6 April 1793

The Committee became the organizing force of *gouvernement révolutionnaire*. In order to preserve the separation of powers, the Committee supervised rather than replaced the ministers, but increasingly this distinction became a formality. The members were to be elected monthly to emphasize the Convention's authority over its Committee, but from July 1793 to July 1794 – the period of the 'great' Committee – the membership was substantially unaltered. However, when Robespierre quarrelled with his colleagues on the Committee, it was to the Convention he appealed and thereafter that body reasserted its independence.

1 A Committee of Public Safety will be nominated by roll call and consist of nine members [later increased to 12] of the National Convention.
2 This Committee will deliberate in secret. It will be charged with supervising and activating the administrative activity confided to the Provisional Executive Council whose resolutions it may even suspend provided it informs the Convention without delay.
3 In matters of urgency it is authorized to adopt measures for general defence, external and internal, and its resolutions – signed by the majority of its members present who may not be less than two-thirds of the total – will be executed without delay by the Provisional Executive Council. It may not under any circumstances issue arrest warrants or subpoenas except against agents of the Executive and that on condition of informing the Convention without delay.
4 The National Treasury will keep a sum of up to 100,000 francs at the disposal of the Committee of Public Safety for secret expenditure.
5 Each week it will present a general, written report on its operations and the situation of the republic.

6 It will keep minutes of all its deliberations.

7 The National Treasury will remain independent of the Committee and under the immediate surveillance of the Convention, as provided by the decrees.

Mautouchet, *Gouvernement révolutionnaire*, pp. 173–4

151 The declaration of *gouvernement révolutionnaire* preceded by extracts from Saint-Just's speech, 19 vendémiaire year II (10 October 1793)

You can hope for no prosperity as long as the last enemy of liberty breathes. You have to punish not only the traitors but even those who are neutral; you have to punish whoever is inactive in the republic and does nothing for it: because, since the French people has declared its will, everyone who is opposed to it is outside the sovereign body; and everyone who is outside the sovereign body is an enemy.

If conspiracies had not troubled this empire, if the *patrie* had not been a thousand times the victim of indulgent laws, it would be sweet to rule by maxims of peace and natural justice: these maxims are good among the friends of liberty; but between the people and its enemies, there is nothing in common except the sword. Those who cannot be governed by justice must be ruled with a rod of iron. . . .

In the circumstances in which the republic is placed, the constitution cannot be implemented; people would use it to destroy it. It would protect attempts against liberty, because it would lack the force necessary to repress them. The present government is also too encumbered. You are too far from all the plots; the sword of justice must stride everywhere rapidly and your arms must be present everywhere to prevent crime.

The Decree

THE GOVERNMENT

1 The provisional government of France is revolutionary for the duration of the war.

2 The Provisional Executive Council, the ministers, the generals and the constituted authorities are placed under the surveillance of the Committee of Public Safety which will report every week to the Convention.

3 All security measures should be taken by the Provisional Executive Council, with the Committee's authorization, which will report to the Convention.

4 Revolutionary laws must be executed rapidly. The government will correspond directly with the districts as regards measures of public safety.
5 Army commanders will be appointed by the National Convention at the recommendation of the Committee of Public Safety.
6 Since the inertia of the government is the cause of our reverses, there will be fixed time-limits for the execution of laws and measures of public safety. Non-observation of these time-limits will be punished as an attack on liberty.

Mautouchet, *Gouvernement révolutionnaire*, pp. 196–202

152   The law of 14 frimaire

Section II: Implementation of laws

1 The National Convention is the only centre of impulse on government.
2 All the constituted authorities and public functionaries are placed under the immediate supervision of the Committee of Public Safety for measures concerned with government and public safety, in conformity with the decree of 19 vendémiaire [10 October], and for everything relating to individuals and to general and internal police, this particular supervision belongs to the Convention's Committee of General Security, in accordance with the decree of 17 September last; these two committees are obliged to give an account of their operations to the National Convention at the end of each month. Each member of these two committees is personally responsible for the performance of this duty.
3 The execution of laws is divided into surveillance and application.
6 Surveillance over the execution of revolutionary laws and measures of government, general security and public safety in the departments is exclusively attributed to the districts, who are obliged to give a faithful account of their operations every ten days to the Committee of Public Safety for matters of government and public safety and to the Convention's Surveillance Committee for matters of general and internal police and for individuals.
8 The application of revolutionary laws and measures of government and general security is entrusted to the municipalities and to the surveillance (or revolutionary) committees, who are likewise obliged to give an account every ten days of the execution of these laws to the district of their area, to whom they are immediately subordinate.
9 Notwithstanding, in Paris, in order that police action should not encounter any obstacles, the revolutionary committees will continue to

correspond directly and without any intermediary with the Convention's Committee of General Security, in accordance with the decree of 17 September last.

11 It is expressly forbidden for any authority or public functionary to issue proclamations or to take measures which extend, limit or contradict the literal meaning of the law, on the pretext of interpreting or expanding it.

14 In place of the attorney-general of the district and the attorney of the Commune and his deputy, posts which are abolished by this decree, there will be *agents nationaux* specially entrusted with requiring and enforcing the execution of the law and also with denouncing negligence in such execution and infringements which may be committed. These *agents nationaux* are authorized to move from the seat of administration and travel round the area of their jurisdiction to exercise surveillance and to assure themselves more positively that the laws are being executed to the letter.

Section III: Competence of the constituted authorities

5 ... The hierarchy which placed the districts, municipalities or any other authority under the departments is abolished as regards revolutionary and military laws and measures of government, public safety and general security.

10 All the changes ordered by the present decree will be implemented within three days of its publication.

20 No armed force, tax or loan (whether forced or voluntary) may be levied except in virtue of a decree. The revolutionary taxes of the representatives of the people will not be collected until they have been approved by the Convention, unless it be in enemy or rebel territory.

Section IV: Reorganization and purging of constituted authorities

1 The Committee of Public Safety is authorized to take all the measures necessary to proceed with the reorganization of the constituted authorities provided for by this decree.

2 The representatives of the people in the departments are charged with assuring and accelerating the execution of this and also with achieving without delay a complete purge of the constituted authorities and of sending the National Convention a special report of these two operations before the end of next month.

Mautouchet, *Gouvernement révolutionnaire*, pp. 233–43

153   Javogues, representative-on-mission in Saône-et-Loire to Collot d'Herbois, 16 pluviôse year II (4 February 1794)

Collot d'Herbois was a member of the Committee of Public Safety and, with Billaud-Varenne, the most radical member of the Committee.

. . . The priests have done appalling damage in the department of Rhône-et-Loire. I find the Committee of Public Safety's proclamation [concerning freedom of worship] incomprehensible and calculated to retard the progress of the Revolution. Apparently Couthon has need of some sort of religion to sustain the rule of knaves and royalists who have taken refuge in his own department. The best way of sowing the seeds of religious wars is to talk about them. All the methods of coercion you employ against the chameleons who claim to be apostles of various sects will be evaded. It would be much simpler to shoot them.

I find equally incomprehensible the recent decrees concerning the *gouvernement révolutionnaire. Agents* [*nationaux*] with extensive powers have been established; if their choice falls into the hands of the aristocrats the patriots could well have their throats cut. To my mind the *agents nationaux* are nothing but dictators whose influence and authority could compromise the liberty and security of the republic.

Another absurdity which struck me just as forcibly is the obligation to send the decrees of each district to the Committee of Public Safety every ten days. To unravel this chaos it would take 5,000 clerks, each ignorant of what the others were doing. And what would be the result of the operation? All I know is that unless this monstrosity is destroyed we will no longer have 25 million free men but rather 500 and as many *agents nationaux* arbitrarily disposing of the lives and property of the citizens.

It has also grieved me to note that for some time you have been passing a lot of decrees and reviving the practice of taking meaningless oaths. I note in comparison that the Brissotins also had this mania for over-legislation. When people follow this path, they want to distract attention. Frequent legislation favours only large landowners, big merchants and all those who live off the people. . . .

I have been no less distressed to see that you have placed in your Committee of Public Safety a certain Prieur (de la Côte-d'Or), the nephew or relative of Guyton-Morveau, former *avocat général* in the Parlement de Dijon. The name of his department seems appropriate: he refuses grain to the poor.

F. A. Aulard, *Recueil des actes du Comité de salut public . . .* (21 vols., 1889–1933), vol. X, pp. 700–1

154 Bo, representative-on-mission in Cantal and Lot, to the Committee of Public Safety, 24 pluviôse year II (12 February 1794)

Here I am, citizen colleagues, at Saint-Flour which I reached this morning after spending a night in the snow. I owe you an account of my operations in the district of Murat where, as everywhere, I found the authorities weak rather than disloyal and the people ready to hearken to the truth. Everywhere I explain this to them patiently and gently and everywhere they recognize it and thank me. I assembled the *agents nationaux* of this district, as I did in the others, and I have replaced several. None of them had heard of the law of 14 frimaire. I expounded it to them and enjoined them, in their own interests, to imbibe its principles and to maintain a regular correspondence with the *agents nationaux* of the other districts; and I believe that they will do all that can be expected of almost illiterate peasants. When my work here is completed, I shall send you details.

Aulard, *Recueil*, vol. XI, pp. 107–8

155 The Committee of Public Safety to Roux-Fazillac, representative-on-mission in Corrèze and Puy-de-Dôme, 26 pluviôse year II (14 February 1794)

Citizen colleague, the Committee of Public Safety has discovered provisions in your proclamation of 10 frimaire which are in conflict with the law concerning the *gouvernement révolutionnaire*. Admittedly, before this law was passed it was not surprising that there should be a discrepancy which you would hardly have foreseen. But as soon as the new law became known to you, you will doubtless, in conformity with your known zeal, have lost no time in changing or modifying those provisions of your proclamation which hindered or conflicted with the execution of this law.

Article 1 [of your proclamation] provides that there will be only one surveillance committee in each district and attributes to it the power of levying extraordinary taxation on those who are rich and disaffected.

This provision is contrary to article 20, section III, of the law of 14 frimaire which stipulates that no tax or forced or voluntary loan can be raised except in virtue of a decree [of the Convention].

Article 9 of your proclamation gives the revolutionary committees powers of surveillance over industry, taxation and the sale of *émigré* lands.

These various functions are attributed to the departmental authorities (article 5, section III of this law) with overall supervision falling to the Executive Council (article 4, same section). Article 20, section III, also applies to article 21 of your proclamation which provides that expenditure arising from measures of public safety will be met out of the property of suspects. This provision presupposes the power of taxation which, as already said, requires a decree.

'The revolutionary committees will institute a salaried force in their respective districts entrusted with all measures necessary for the public safety.' This article is contrary to article 20, section III, which stipulates: 'No armed force may be raised except in virtue of a decree.'

These, citizen colleague, are the main provisions of your proclamation to which the Committee thought it right to draw your attention. You will doubtless have compared them with the law which provides (article 10, section III) that all changes required by the law shall be implemented within three days of its publication.

The Committee likes to think that you will have carried out this requirement and invites you to inform it whether this is the case.

Aulard, *Recueil*, vol. XI, pp. 148–9

156 Questionnaire sent by the Committee of Public Safety to the district authorities, together with the replies of the district of Le Mans, January 1794

The bureaucratic terror is exemplified by the questionnaire which the district of Le Mans had to send the Committee of Public Safety. To appreciate the irony of some of the replies it must be realized that Le Mans, in the Catholic west, was not in the vanguard of the Revolution and was, in fact, occupied by the rebels from the Vendée between 10 and 12 December. The authorities are loyal to the republic but they cannot use or even understand the wooden jargon employed by the Committee. To one question they reply: 'We do not know how to answer this question' and often replies are merely lifeless repetitions of the question in a non-interrogatory form. There is dignity and courage in many of these answers, particularly those to questions 6, 14, 15 and 26.

Q.1 Have the surveillance committees been established in accordance with the law?

A.1 Surveillance committees have been established in accordance with the law in the principal communes of the district.

Q.3 Has the law of 17 September (old style) on suspects been completely implemented.

A.3 We presume so.

Q.4 Have the particulars of arrests been duly sent to the district authorities as prescribed by the law on *gouvernement révolutionnaire*?

A.4 The particulars of arrests have not been sent to the district authorities. The surveillance committees will doubtless excuse themselves on the grounds that they were unaware of the contents of the recently promulgated law on *gouvernement révolutionnaire*, the printing of which was delayed by the arrival of the rebels who forced all the constituted authorities to abandon their post.

Q.6 Do you believe that there have been arrests prompted by private animus rather than the dictates of the law? If so, append to each report you will be sending us between now and the 30th of this month the grounds on which you base your opinion and, in order to direct towards the Committee of General Security all the rays of light which can help it to determine the legitimacy of these measures, do not fail to mention the occupation of the detained citizen, both before and after the Revolution, if the particulars omit this.

Append a list of the names of the members of the surveillance committees to your replies to the various questions asked.

A.6 We do not know how to answer this question.

Q.7 How many popular societies are there in your district and where are they situated?

A.7 There are seven popular societies for the district of Le Mans. They are situated at Le Mans, Coulans, Vallon, Savigné, La Bazoge, Ecommoy and Ballon.

Q.8 Do these societies, which should everywhere be the eye of the magistrate and the legislator, exercise the salutary right of censure?

A.8 They exercise the salutary right of censure, particularly at Le Mans.

Q.9 Are they affiliated to the Jacobin Club of Paris?

A.9 That of Le Mans is the only one which is.

Q.11 Have the laws on the division of the common land, the maximum, certificates of civism and residence and the burning of feudal charters been implemented?

A.11 The law on the division of the common land has not yet been implemented. This delay is due to the communes and the interested parties with whom the initiative lies, who have to send a report of the division to the district authorities.

The law of the maximum, except as applying to grain and bread, has encountered very great obstacles arising from differentials in tariffs: one district prices certain essential goods 30 per cent higher than its neighbouring district; the latter sees all its trade diverted and would find itself reduced to utter privation if it did not purchase – often at an exorbitant price – goods with which people have inundated the other district in the hopes of greater profits.

The law relative to certificates of civism and residence is being executed according to the intentions of the law.

The district administration has urged implementation of the law ordering feudal charters to be burned. Reports received from several communes confirm that this law has been implemented. The administration will conduct still further and most rigorous investigations in order to destroy the last remaining document recalling the memory of feudal and monarchical servitude.

Q.12 Have you observed in your National Guards that ardour and devotion which so eminently characterize the French people?

A.12 If we have not observed in our National Guards exactly that ardour and devotion which distinguish the French people we can, in general, give the assurance that they are devoted to their duty and perform it zealously and impartially.

Q. 13 Was the raising of the first batch of volunteers accompanied by that *élan* worthy of men who should be burning with the holy love of liberty?

A.13 Although the raising of the first batch of volunteers was not accompanied by that *élan* which characterizes true republicans, we are nonetheless sure that the majority is perfectly ready to support the cause of liberty.

Q.14 Does fanaticism still rule in any part of the district and if so who is responsible for this corruption of public morals?

A.14 Fanaticism does not rule in the district but a very large proportion of the citizens seems to be attached to the Catholic religion, though much less to its ministers whom they despise.

Q.15 Has the sublime movement of the people against superstition encountered any obstacles to its progress and what details can you give the Committee of General Security?

A.15 The sublime movement of the people against superstition has encountered great obstacles to its progress. We do not think that these obstacles have other causes than old habits which are hard to eradicate in the peasant, arising as they do from his ignorance.

Q.16 How is the sale of the movables and real estate of the *émigrés* proceeding?

A.16 The sale of the *émigrés'* movables is proceeding rapidly and most advantageously for the republic. That of their real estate has been delayed by the eruption of the rebels and the ensuing disorder. But the tenders which have been submitted and the great interest shown by a large number of citizens gives us reason to believe that this sale will be no less advantageous to the republic than that of the movables.

Q.18 Are there people in your area who have sought to discredit the *assignats*, the pledge of public finances, and thereby diminish our resources against the tyrants?

A.18 Everyone realizes that public and private finances depend on the credit of the *assignats*; no one will seek to discredit them.

Q.19 Have you any individuals who have been in correspondence with *émigrés*, refractory priests or other persons living in countries with whom the republic is at war?

A.19 We have no knowledge that any individual has been in correspondence with *émigrés*, refractory priests or other persons living in countries with whom the republic is at war, but the files to be forwarded to us may disclose some.

Q.20 Do letters arrive directly or are they intercepted and are there, in intercepted correspondence, any proofs or at least clues which could be used to grasp the threads of the recent plot to extinguish the liberty of the people?

These two points require clear and precise replies. . . .

A.20 We may be informed through the same channel.

Q.21 Has there been or is there any hoarding of grain, flour and other necessaries by the internal enemies with the intention either of starving the people and wearying it of liberty or of feeding the counter-revolutionary armies which the conspirators, in their wickedness, intended should roam through the departments?

A.21 We have not received any information or denunciation suggesting the existence of this kind of hoarding.

Q.25 Have you within your jurisdiction any traitors who have openly contested the national verdict on the events of 31 May and 2 June?

A.25 We do not know of any individual who has openly contested the national verdict on the events of 31 May and 2 June.

Q.26 Do there exist any of those false patriots who by the unnatural exaggeration of their principles seek to deceive the people, either in order to obtain places or to mislead the people about the constant and doughty friends of the Revolution and bring about the triumph of the cause of tyranny by means of deception?

A.26 We believe that there are some false patriots who wish to deceive the people by the exaggeration of their principles in order to obtain places. But since it is hard to judge intentions, we can only have suspicions here. Even assuming such exaggeration, we can be certain that it is not based on the desire to bring about the triumph of the cause of tyranny by means of deception. . . .

> Mautouchet, *Gouvernement révolu-
> tionnaire*, pp. 302–8

157 The law of suspects, 17 September 1793

Article 1. Immediately after the publication of the present decree, all the suspects in the republic who are still at liberty will be placed under arrest.

Article 2. Suspects are deemed to be:

1 Those who whether by their conduct, their liaisons, speech or writings have shown themselves to be adherents of tyranny, federalism, or enemies of liberty.

2 Those who cannot justify, in accordance with the law of the previous 21 March, their means of livelihood and the fulfilment of their civic duties.

3 Those who have been refused *certificats de civisme*.

4 Public functionaries suspended or dismissed from their jobs by the National Convention or by its commissioners and not reinstated, notably all those who have been or should have been dismissed in virtue of the law of the previous 14 August.

5 Those former nobles, including the husbands, wives, fathers, mothers, sons and daughters of *émigrés*, who have not constantly displayed their devotion to the Revolution.

6 Those who have emigrated in the period between 1 July 1789 and the publication of the law of 8 April 1792, even though they have returned to France within the time-limit stipulated by this law or previously.

Wallon, *Tribunal révolutionnaire,*
vol. I, p. 288

158 The abbé Morellet applies for a *certificat de civisme*

Morellet applied in vain to several officials of the Commune for his certificate. After the passing of the law of suspects he withdrew his application because refusal would render him suspect (clause 3). This, however, meant that he could not draw on his pension as a priest or as a member of the suppressed Académie française. Appearing before one Vialard, he showed him his patriotic writings over a 30-year period.

. . . I was about half way through my works when my man stopped me in my tracks by saying: 'nothing you can show me in that line is of the slightest relevance now. You have to prove your civic conduct during the *journées* of 10 August and 31 May, and all that doesn't prove it. Look, we are well aware that some men of letters had fairly good principles in the old days, before any of this; but none of them has put himself out subsequently, and all the academicians are the enemies of the republic. . . .

[Morellet explained that he had lost heavily in the Revolution and did not feel like celebrating.] 'Oh! so you have lost out, well we're all in the same boat. I too have lost my profession through the Revolution.' Showing an interest, I asked him what sort of a loss he had sustained and what had been his profession. He replied courageously: 'I was a ladies' hairdresser; and', he added, 'I have always liked inventions and I have presented the Academy of Sciences with some toupés of my own construction. . . .'

'Didn't you know Barentin?' he asked. 'Not in the least.' 'And the other ministers?' 'I knew some of them. I was closest to Turgot whom I have known since we were boys and whose society I sought until he died.' 'And more recent ministers?' 'I knew the archbishop of Sens [Brienne] well for I studied under him and saw him often.' 'Oh him, he served us well.'

'I don't know exactly what you mean by that but I can assure you that I have never approved the measures you probably blame him for and notably that plenary court which would have prevented the convocation of the Estates-General, and which I censured in company of all right-thinking men. As for the Estates-General, you can see from these three or four pamphlets that I wanted them to be convoked in the same manner as you would have yourself, that is to say with double representation for the Third and no distinction of orders in voting. . . .

[Vialard told Morellet to see his colleague Bernard at home in the working-class district of the Faubourg Saint-Antoine.] I found Citizen Bernard there, a man with an ignoble appearance . . . and with him his little wife, fairly young but very ugly and extremely dirty.

As I was getting down to business, a big young man arrived, obviously a friend of the house, and asked if he could have lunch. The little woman took a cheese and a bottle of wine from a cupboard and they sat down to eat whilst I tackled my official. One after the other I presented the evidence in my case. I refuted the imputation that I had written a work in favour of despotism . . . but, like Vialard, he adduced the frightening argument that I had not proved my civism on 10 August, 2 September or 31 May; and it will not escape the attention of the reader that in this respect he was more exigent in proofs of civism than his colleague Vialard, who had made no mention of 2 September. But Bernard, the new Chérin, demanding proofs of my revolutionary nobility, insisted on four quarters.

> *Mémoires de l'abbé Morellet sur le dix-huitième siècle et sur la Révolution*, ed. M. Lemontey (2 vols., 1821), vol. II, pp. 77–83

159   Decree on the *maximum général*, 29 September 1793

This 'prices and incomes policy', the result of popular pressure culminating in the *journée* of 5 September, is tougher on prices (1790 level plus 30 per cent) than wages (1790 level plus 50 per cent). The latter, moreover, was not enforced until the summer of 1794. Both levels were way below the levels of inflation and led to hoarding (which became a capital offence). Grain was covered by existing legislation.

The National Convention, after hearing the report of its Commission for the drafting of a law on fixing the maximum price for basic produce and merchandise, decrees:

1 The goods which the National Convention has judged to be ones of basic necessity and for which it has thought it should fix a maximum or highest price are as follows:

Fresh meat	Sugar
Salt meat and bacon	Honey
Butter	White paper
Olive oil	Leather
Livestock	Iron
Salt fish	Alloys
Wine	Lead
Brandy	Steel
Vinegar	Copper
Cider	Hemp
Beer	Flax
Firewood	Wool
Charcoal	Fabrics
Coal	Linen
Candles	Raw materials for industry
Lamp oil	Clogs
Salt	Shoes
Soda	Colza and rape-seed oil
Soap	Tobacco
Potash	

2 Of the objects listed above, the maximum price for grade one firewood, of charcoal and coal, is the same as in 1790 plus 5 per cent. . . . The maximum or highest price for plug tobacco is 20 sols a *livre* . . . that for smoking tobacco is 10 sols; that for a pound of salt is 2 sols; and a pound of soap is 25 sols.

3 The maximum price of all other produce or merchandise listed in article 1 will be, throughout the republic and until next September, the price of each in 1790, as stated in the market price lists or the price current in each department, plus a third, once all taxes whatsoever to which they were then subject have been deducted.

7 Anyone selling or buying the articles listed in article 1 at a price above that of the maximum decided and published in each department will pay . . . [a fine] double the value of the object sold to the man who has informed on him. They will be placed on the list of suspects and treated as such. Notwithstanding, the purchaser will not be subject to the above-mentioned penalty if he denounces the vendor's contravention of the law; and each merchant will be required to have a table on display in his shop listing the maximum or highest price of his goods.

8 The maximum or highest price of salaries, wages, labour and day-wages in each area will be fixed, from the publication of this law until next September, by the general councils of the communes, at 50 per cent higher than in 1790.

9 The municipal authorities can requisition the services and punish with three days' imprisonment, as the case may be, the workers, manufacturers, etc. who refuse to undertake their regular work without good reason.

17 For the duration of the war, all export of essential merchandise or produce is forbidden along all the frontiers . . . with the exception of salt.

Le maximum général, ed. P. Caron (1930), pp. 32–5

160   Two private reflections

(a) Claude Payan to his brother Joseph, 18 brumaire year II (8 November 1793)

Philippe [Egalité, former duc d'Orléans] had to die. He was a rogue; even if he was innocent, provided his death could have been useful, it was expedient that he should die. He was definitely not an accomplice of Brissot. He defended himself well on that one; no witnesses against him. Nevertheless we must spread it about that he was guilty to put a stop to these counter-revolutionary calumnies. Bailly and Roland will go the same way.

Papiers inédits, vol. II, p. 348

(b) Extracts from Robespierre's notebook, autumn 1793

Principal measure of public safety. It will be necessary to send through all the republic a small number of strong commissioners, armed with good instructions and above all good principles, to reduce public opinion to unity and to republicanism [i.e. Jacobinism] – the sole means of ending the Revolution to the profit of the people.[3]

These commissioners will above all concentrate on discovering and inventorying men who are worthy to serve the cause of liberty. To purge the surveillance committees, we must produce a list of all their members, their names, occupations and addresses. . . .

We must revise the list of the leaders of the counter-revolution in each locality. . . .

Overturn the decree of the municipality which bans the saying of mass and vespers. It does not have the right. It is a source of trouble. [The decree was overturned on 8 frimaire (28 November)].

Mathiez, *Etudes*, pp. 229–30

---

3 This private reflection suggests that at this stage Robespierre did intend one day to end the provisional or 'revolutionary' government by the application of the constitution.

|4|

The Hébertists and the
Dantonists

After the arrest of Jacques Roux and the eclipse of the Enragés in September, their political position was taken over by a group of more conventional politicians who already held some of the key positions in Paris
(controlling the Commune, the Cordelier Club and the war ministry) and
wanted, with *sans-culotte* support, to improve on this and in particular to
capture the ministry and free it from its subservience to the Committee of
Public Safety. They are usually called the Hébertists, after Hébert, the deputy
prosecutor of the Commune and author of the violent, radical journal *Le
Père Duchesne*. Other members included Chaumette, the *agent national* of
the Commune, Bouchotte, the minister for war (the war ministry was an
enormous source of employment and patronage), Vincent, secretary-general
of the war ministry and Ronsin, the commander-in-chief of the *armée
révolutionnaire*, an internal, civilian force set up as a result of popular
pressure in September 1793. Collot d'Herbois and Billaud-Varenne, the most
radical members of the Committee of Public Safety who had been elected to
it in September to placate the *sans-culottes*, supported the general position
of the Hébertists. Their policies were those of the Enragés with the important addition of de-Christianization – an attack not just on non-juring
priests but on Catholic worship as such.

   At the same time another group, whose strength lay in the Convention
itself and in the personal prestige of its members but which controlled none
of the levers of power except the foreign office, hardly a power-house in
time of war, argued that so far from there being a need to step up the Terror,
it could now be relaxed, as the war was going well and rebellion at home
was faltering. This group included Danton, who as minister of justice had
inspired France to repel the Prussian invasion of August–September 1792;
Fabre d'Eglantine, the author of the revolutionary calendar; Camille Desmoulins, the celebrated pamphleteer; and Bourdon de l'Oise, Delacroix and
Philippeaux, all deputies. This group was less closely knit than the Hébertists
and its aims were less clearly defined or at least less transparent. The
account by Garat, a former minister of the interior, of several conversations
with Danton (**161**), probably gets as close as one can to the latter's

objectives. Thus Danton perceived the intimate connection between the war and the Terror and was continuing the policy he had pursued as the dominant member of the 'first' Committee of Public Safety (April–July 1793), that of seeking an accommodation with the foreign powers as the pre-requisite for a relaxation of the Terror at home. (This policy had been abandoned when Danton and his friends left the Committee and were replaced by more radical deputies such as Robespierre.) To conduct a bold foreign policy and command the respect of the powers and also to repress anarchy at home, a strong government was needed and this could either be the Committee of Public Safety, officially declared the government,[1] and staffed with his friends, or come into being under a revised version of the constitution of 1793. In either case provisional government would end and the rule of law and free trade would be re-established. Public opinion would be prepared for such a change 'by means of journals such as those of Camille Desmoulins' (**163** and **165**).

Most of the struggle between the two groups took the form of the exaltation of their own and the vilification of their opponents' chosen instruments of power. Thus the Dantonists attacked the war ministry – Philippeaux attributing the reverses in the Vendée to its bureaucratic jobbery (**164**) – and, as early as August, tried to strengthen the Committee of Public Safety, though they were not uncritical of it as it stood (**161** and **165**). Bouchotte defended himself in a letter to Robespierre (**168**) which is reveal-ing as to the inner state of the Jacobins. He finds the twists and turns of revolutionary dogma as laid down by Robespierre baffling and time-consuming to follow; running the largest ministry, with 600 employees, he simply does not have the time to be *'au courant'*. He had stuffed the ministry full of patriots because he thought that was what was wanted, only to have them now described as ultra-revolutionaries and worse. The letter was not written in vain because Robespierre was to save Bouchotte, whom he had described as 'a good son of the *patrie'* from perishing in the holocaust of Hébertists, which included Vincent, the secretary-general of the war minis-try.

The Committee of Public Safety itself stood between and aloof from the two groups, though Robespierre, one of its most influential members, tended at first to support the Dantonists. He was in particular repelled by Hébert's de-Christianizing policy and thought it would discredit and alienate men from the Revolution: he himself proposed a decree guaranteeing freedom of worship. The Committee also allowed the Convention to set up a 'Committee of Clemency' on 20 December to investigate arrests made under the law of suspects of 17 September, the particular subject of attack in the famous no. 3 of Desmoulins' *Le Vieux Cordelier* (**163**). On the other hand, Collot d'Herbois, returning on 17 December from Lyon where he had been exacting a terrible vengeance on that rebellious city, signalled the dangers to which a policy of clemency would lead. Robespierre also became convinced that both factions, the 'ultras' and the 'citras', i.e. those who were too revolutionary and those who were not revolutionary enough, were

---

1 The Convention had hitherto shrunk from so formal a violation of the doctrine of the separation of powers.

complementary parts of a highly ramified foreign plot. Thus when the Hébertists were arrested on 12 March, after an abortive coup or *journée* launched in the Cordelier Club, Collot and Billaud were able to insist that the Dantonists also be arrested – they were executed on 5 April 1794.

For the *sans-culottes*, these struggles and their denouement were bewildering: how could Danton, the man of 1792, attack so obvious a patriot as Hébert? How could the Committee of Public Safety have both arrested? The natural result was cynicism and apathy. This bewilderment comes through strongly in the two police reports on the *état des esprits* (**166** and **167**), the first written at the height of the polemical debate between the ultras and the citras, the other shortly after the arrest of the former. Both reports tell the Committee of General Security what it wants to hear: of the blind faith of the people in the National Convention and its two committees. But in the first 'people are . . . pained to see the Jacobin Society . . . turning themselves into doctors of the Sorbonne, censuring writing and examining whether such and such a phrase is or is not heretical'; whilst the acquiescence, indeed joy, of the Cordelier Club in the arrest of its leaders – their 'regret that there is no more rigorous form of execution than the guillotine' – is, ironically, reminiscent of the mood of no. 3 of *Le Vieux Cordelier*. 'You had to show joy at the death of your friend or relative unless you wanted to risk death yourself.'

The 'insurrection' which the Cordelier Club had announced but not implemented on 4 March had not been a response to popular pressure – as the *journée* of 31 May had been – but rather a political manoeuvre by men who wanted to exploit the *sans-culottes* for ends they would not have understood (jobs in a strengthened ministry). Nevertheless, the popular movement was implicated in the fall of the Hébertists as surely as if they had been its natural leaders: not only was the Council of Ministers abolished and replaced by 12 commissioners (as the Dantonists had been demanding) but the role of the *sans-culottes* as an independent political force was ended and their remaining institutions (some 40 of their political clubs were dissolved) became integrated into the governmental bureaucracy.

161 Garat on Danton's plans

Joseph Dominique Garat, 1749–1833, a lawyer, historian and deputy to the Estates-General, was Danton's successor as minister of justice; then, from March to August 1793, minister of the interior. Though connected with the Girondins, he survived their fall.

When the fate reserved for the 22 [Girondin deputies expelled from the Convention] seemed inevitable, Danton, as it were, already heard his own death sentence in theirs. All the strength of this triumphant athlete of democracy gave way under the sense of its crimes and disorders: he could no longer talk of anything but the countryside; he was stifled and needed quiet in order to breathe. At Arcis-sur-Aube the presence of nature only calmed his soul by filling it with generous and magnanimous resolutions. Then he returned, bearing in his heart the conspiracy he had in part conceived in the silence of the fields and of his solitude.

All his friends participated.

I was not his friend and I was under such close surveillance as to throw suspicion on anyone I were to see often. But they were all well aware that I would be the friend of such a conspiracy and that I would lend it all the good offices left in my power.

It was at this time that I had several conversations with Danton. In these I learned to take confidence in all the better feelings which I had long suspected that he possessed. It was then that he talked to me, often with desperate candour, about the quarrels in the Convention, about everyone's mistakes and his own and the catastrophe they had brought about: 'Twenty times', he told me one day, 'twenty times I offered them [the Girondins] peace; they wouldn't have it; they refused to believe me so as to preserve the right to ruin me; it was they who forced us to throw ourselves into *sans-culotterie* – which devoured them, which will devour everyone, which will devour itself.'

The aims and method of Danton's plan of conspiracy, though they were fairly carefully concealed, were both very clear.

The aim was to restore the rule of law: justice for everyone and clemency for enemies; to recall to the bosom of the Convention all those members who had been removed, by granting them amnesty and requiring the same of them in return; to subject the constitution of 1793 – which was drawn up by five or six young men in five or six days and which should have been the masterpiece of the present state of human knowledge since it is to be the pattern for a democracy of 25 million men – subject it to the most thorough scrutiny by the representatives of France, by France as a whole and by Europe; to offer peace to the European powers whilst continuing to fight them; to raise commerce and industry, by unlimited free trade, from ruin, and the arts and sciences by munificent patronage; to abolish all the barriers dividing department from department and all inquisition-seeking to find in portfolios and on cards proof of a civic duty which can only be real in people free from all sense of inquisition; to consider good laws, a good government and the victories of our armies as the only cards capable of protecting the republic.

The plan of campaign in Danton's conspiracy was as follows: to induce a favourable change of climate among the public by means of journals such as those of Camille Desmoulins; to open up a channel of communication between the left wing and what remained of the right wing in the Convention, thus ending that division which had delivered them all up to the despotism of the two committees; to regard Collot, Saint-Just and Billaud alone as being irrevocably wedded to the policy of extermination; to try to detach Barère from them by appealing to such humanity as he was thought to possess and Robespierre by appealing to his known pride and attachment to liberty; steadily to augment the powers of the Committee of Public Safety so that, with nothing left to satisfy their personal ambition, they might at last do something for the good of the republic whilst if, on the contrary, they continued to make their new powers the instrument of new crimes, their power, become more odious by virtue of its very grandeur, would lead them to retribution through that insolence and effrontery which always mark the final excesses of tyranny; finally to pave the way, gradually or by a sudden impetuous movement, for the total or partial replacement of the members of the two committees so that the great, generous and truly patriotic sentiments which had united the conspirators might happily be brought into the government.

Such is what I was able to see or know concerning that conspiracy which led so many citizens to the scaffold; and if, in their intimate relations, men are vouchsafed some way of distinguishing sincerity from imposture, magnanimous intentions from petty and personal ones, then I would say that Danton's only ambition at this time was to make amends, by an immense and durable benefit to mankind, for the terrible, short-term evils he had inflicted on France; to put an end, under a democracy whose organization was inspired by elevated and mature wisdom, to the folly and disasters of *sans-culotterie*; to bring an end to the Revolution under a republican form of government powerful and imposing enough to perpetu-ate for ever the alliance between liberty and order; to secure the prosperity of his country; to give peace to Europe and to return to Arcis-sur-Aube, there to grow old in idleness on his farm in the midst of his children.

> *Mémoires de Garat*, in Buchez and
> Roux, *Histoire parlementaire*,
> vol. XVIII, pp. 451–3

162 Early tension between the ultras and the citras, from a session of the Jacobin Club of 5 August 1793

Vincent defended the minister of war against the accusations levelled against him on the subject of various appointments. He cited one – that of the former duc de Châtelet – made before his appointment.

He reproached Danton and Delacroix for trying to obtain a decree making the Committee of Public Safety a committee of government. He regarded it as infringing the sovereignty of the people, as contrary to the constitution and emanating from conspirators. After demonstrating that the Committee of Public Safety, accumulating all the powers, would itself become a monstrous power, Vincent desired that the society should con-sider ways of preventing such a decree from ever being passed.

Bourdon asserted that it was not the role of popular societies to nominate to employments but rather to scrutinize those who occupied them. He did not want the Jacobins to solicit such employments for themselves or for their friends but rather that they should reserve the right to put the minister's choice to the test of their examination.

Vincent maintained that the Jacobins should draw up lists of candidates whom they believed fit to occupy positions and present them to the minister.

Robespierre said that new men, one-day patriots, wanted to destroy the people's confidence in its oldest friends.

He gave as an example Danton, who was being calumnied; Danton against whom no one had the right to cast the slightest reproach; Danton whom no one had a right to discredit without proving that he possessed more energy, talents or patriotism.

'I am not trying to identify with him on this occasion in order to increase our combined strength, I merely cite him as an example.'

Roux, *Scripta et acta*, pp. 533–4

163   Extracts from no. 3 of Camille Desmoulins' *Le Vieux Cordelier*, 15 December 1793

Lucie Simplice Camille Benoit Desmoulins, 1762–94, lawyer, journalist, *conventionnel*, had been at school with Robespierre at the Collège Louis-le-Grand. The bulk of this issue of *Le Vieux Cordelier* consists of commentaries on Tacitus, the reader being left to draw parallels between the Rome of the Caesars and the French republic. Above all, it is an indictment of the law of suspects of 17 September 1793, which ordered imprisonment on suspicion of political crimes.

. . . Once words had become crimes against the state, from there it was only one step to turn into crimes mere looks, sadness, compassion, sighs, even silence.[2]

Soon the town of Nursia was accused of *lèse-majesté* or Counter-Revolution for having raised a monument to those of its inhabitants who had died in the siege of Modena, even though they had been fighting under Augustus himself, because Augustus was then fighting on the side of Brutus . . . The journalist Cremutius Cordus was guilty of Counter-Revolution for having called Brutus and Cassius the last of the Romans. One of Cassius' descendants was guilty of Counter-Revolution for having in his possession a portrait of his great-grandfather.[3] Mamercus Scaurus was guilty of Counter-Revolution for having written a tragedy in which there was a certain verse which was capable of two interpretations. Torquatus Silanus was guilty of Counter-Revolution for spending extravagantly[4] . . . It was a crime of Counter-Revolution to bewail the misfortunes of the times because that was to accuse the government . . . The mother of the consul Fusius

2 Desmoulins was blamed for weeping at the fate of the Girondins.
3 In France it was a crime punishable by two years' imprisonment to keep portraits of members of the royal family.
4 Desmoulins' friends Danton, Legendre and Fabre were taxed with this in the Jacobins.

Geminus was guilty of Counter-Revolution for having wept over the sad death of her son.[5]

You had to show joy at the death of your friend or relative unless you wanted to risk death yourself. Under Nero, several whose close ones he had put to death went to offer thanks to the gods; they lit up their houses. At the least you had to appear content, open, calm. People feared that their very fear would make them guilty.

Everything made the tyrant suspicious. If a citizen were popular, he was a rival to the Prince who could start a civil war: *Studia civium in se verteret et si multi idem audeant, bellum esse.* Suspect . . . If a man were of a sombre, melancholy disposition or neglected his personal appearance, what afflicted him was that public affairs were going well. *Hominum bonis publicis maestum.* Suspect . . . Finally, if one had acquired a military reputation one was all the more dangerous for that because of one's talent. With an incompetent general there was a chance. If he was a traitor he would be unable to deliver an entire army to the enemy. But if an officer of the merit of Corbulo or Agricola defected, no one would be saved. The best thing was to get rid of him – at the least, Sire, you must promptly remove him from the army. *Multa militari fama metum fecerat.*[6] Suspect.

You may imagine that it was much worse if you were the grandson or relative of Augustus: one day you might have pretensions to the throne: *nobilem et quod tunc spectaretur e caesarum posteris.* Suspect.

And none of these suspects got off with being sent to the Madelonettes, the Irlandais, or Sainte-Pélagie [all prisons], as with us. The prince sent them orders to summon their doctor or apothecary and to choose the manner of death they preferred within 24 hours. *Missus centurio qui maturaret eum.*

Thus it was impossible to have any qualities – unless they were put in the service of tyranny – without arousing the despot's jealousy and risking certain ruin.

It was a crime to hold high office – or to resign. . . . One man was struck down because of his name or that of one of his ancestors; another because of his fine house at Alba; Valerius Asiaticus because his gardens had pleased the empress; Statilius because his face had displeased her; and a host for reasons which could not be discovered. . . .

In a word, during these reigns the natural death of a famous man, or even one in office, was so rare that it was put in the papers as an event and commended by the historian to the remembrance of future centuries: 'During this consulate', says our annalist, 'there was a Pontiff, Piso, who died in his bed, which seemed like a prodigy.'

---

5 Pétion's parents wept at their son's death and were arrested.
6 Several generals were executed in 1793–4.

The death of so many innocent and respectable citizens seemed a lesser calamity than the insolence and scandalous fortunes of those who murdered and denounced them. Every day the sacred and inviolable delator made his triumphal entry into the palace of the dead and picked up some rich inheritance.[7] All these delators bedecked themselves with the finest names, having themselves called Cotta, Scipio, Regulus, Cassius Severus. . . . Such accusers, such judges! The tribunals, the protectors of life and property, had become slaughter houses where that which bore the name of punishment and confiscation was simply theft and assassination.

If there was no way of sending a man before the tribunal, recourse was had to assassination and poison. . . . When these half-measures did not suffice, the tyrant had recourse to a general proscription. . . .

> Camille Desmoulins, *Le Vieux Cordelier*, ed. H. Calvet (1926), pp. 67–90

164   Extracts from an open letter by Philippeaux on the war in the Vendée, 6 nivôse year II (26 December 1793)

Pierre Philippeaux, 1754–94, *conventionnel*, was executed with Danton. Recalled from a mission to the Vendée, he became obsessed with the mismanagement of the war on that front.

. . . The friends of the republic anxiously await the issue of this fearful struggle between crime and virtue. As stubborn in its efforts as its methods are perfidious, the league of tyrants dons any costume to achieve its atrocious ends. Recently it directed the operations of a conspiratorial faction which sought to plunge us into the ravages of federalism. Now that this faction is overthrown, it stirs up another which, under a different mask, seeks results no less detestable. Several of its agents are in the ministry of war, are office bearers in the Commune and are among the general staff of the *armée révolutionnaire*. I shall enable the reader to judge them by a simple exposition of facts, the least detail of which I defy the most brazen of them to have the nerve to challenge.

The war in the Vendée, so long a labyrinth of secrecy and deceit, by turns a source of hopes and fears, has mown down more than a hundred thousand patriots; it has deprived the people of more food, the national treasury of more money and our arsenals of more artillery than all the other wars put together. . . .

Whilst these things were going on Ronsin, who had filled his pockets with gold at Liège and lived in scandalous luxury as commissioner-

---

7 The decree of 26 July 1793 on hoarding provided (article XII) that the delator should receive one-third of the value of the confiscated goods. Hoarding was punishable by death.

paymaster, came to exercise his baleful influence on the western provinces. The minister had entrusted him with a sort of dictatorship over the war in the Vendée – together with considerable sums of money and blank *lettres de cachet* – which he directed with the title of minister-general. What did he do, together with Rossignol and the phalanx of general staffs, actors and whores with whom he associated? Instead of training our soldiers in tactics and military discipline, they offered them every example of dissolute living and pillage, turning them into an unruly rabble no less terrifying to the peaceful inhabitants than were the rebels themselves. The results were worthy consequences of this fatal system. The succession of defeats – Saumur, Vihiers, Coron, Doué, etc. – were the natural consequences. Forty or fifty thousand patriots regularly fled before a handful of rebels, abandoning rifles, ammunition, cannon, baggage: the only function of our army in this area was to attest to our shame. It is a fact that the generals in the Saumur region, whilst performing their successive feats of valour, have furnished the rebels with over 200 cannon. . . . A power [i.e. the war ministry] which was capable of causing all these disasters, which disposes of a thousand jobs and 300,000,000 francs a month, has cohorts of advocates and libellers at its command. If its pretensions went as far as to rival the Senate, if it even tried to violate and dissolve it, what will it not do against an ordinary representative of the nation? I was under no illusions as to the peril I ran in attacking a monster with such colossal resources.

Wallon, *Histoire du tribunal révolu-tionnaire*, vol. III, pp. 499–505

165 Camille Desmoulins on the Committee of Public Safety (from no. 7 of *Le Vieux Cordelier*, published posthumously)

. . . If such a power, and one of such long continuance as the Committee of Public Safety, were in other hands than his [Robespierre's] and those of people like Couthon and Lindet I would believe that the republic faced ruin.

As it is, however exempt they are from ambition, since they have been in possession of these two levers [the Committees of Public Safety and General Security] and through the sheer power of this governmental machine, can anyone cite me a single appointment or a single law proposed by the Committee which has experienced the slightest opposition, a single error that it has committed, or at least one that has been revealed in the Convention or in a newspaper? In such difficult times, at such a delicate juncture, when it would need all the prudence of a god to hold the helm, is not this total absence of criticism concerning the Committee's measures the strongest criticism of all in the eyes of republicans and the denial of freedom of speech? Were the Committee of Public Safety composed at one and the same time of a Nestor, an Aristides, a Pericles, a Sully, a Richelieu, a Colbert and a Louvois, it would still be criticized by a free people both as a consequence of freedom of speech and because a short-term view often reveals things that are missed in an examination of the longer-term consequences. Barère comes to the Convention in the name of the Committee of Public Safety to propose the abolition of our freedom of worship for the Catholic religion; peace or war; fire and the sword in the Vendée or the demolition of Lyon, Toulon and Marseilles: no one contradicts him, there is not the shadow of a discussion – even for the sake of form.

> Desmoulins, *Le Vieux Cordelier*, ed.
> H. Calvet, pp. 221–2

166   Police report, 18 nivôse year II (7 January 1794)

Rue Saint-Martin. In several bars the men as well as the women of the locality showed their satisfaction at the arrest of several butchers in this street who, not content at selling meat at 16 sous, gave a quarter of a pound short measure.

Philippeaux's letter, Camille Desmoulins' numbers, the placards, etc. of Rossignol, Ronsin, Vincent, Chaumette and Hébert are still the main topic of conversation in the bars. There was a great debate about them at the Café Brutus. Hébert had his supporters and Philippeaux his, as well as Camille; but when someone broke in to observe that they should be quiet and let the Convention decide, all debate ceased.

Rue de Saintonge, section of the Temple. A little news-hawker, his papers in his hand, was crying; 'Great denunciation of the minister of war who has given money to the Père Duchesne and allowed the wives of patriots to die of hunger.' Two men went up to him and said: 'You lie, you little devil, no doubt you're paid to slander the true patriots!' Then they gave him a kick up the backside and tore up his papers. The child began to cry but some people came up to him and asked him what was the matter and one of them gave him 15 sous with the words: 'There now, dry your eyes and be a good patriot.'

. . . The children who are being sent to the primary schools are not being brought up on superstition. Love for the virtues and for the republic is what is instilled into them by Citizen Rollin who lives in the Panthéon section and he has acquired a reputation in the neighbourhood.

Philippeaux's denunciation of the generals of the Army of the West has not been well received but people are satisfied with the decree referring the whole matter to the Committee of Public Safety.

Some citizens leaving the Convention seemed pleased with Bourdon's attack on the ministers, but others were strongly opposed to this opinion and said that all that was needed was to purge the government departments, particularly the war ministry. . . .

Since the introduction of the maximum, charcoal has become scarce. The merchants who previously gave good measure, now cut it fine, so fine that they are a few bushels short.

The price of poultry goes up every day – it has doubled in a fortnight. Eggs are so expensive that no one can touch them now.

The price of fresh pork has shot up and it is also in very short supply. Lard is 40 sous a pound and it looks like hog's grease; that which sells for 24 sous a pound is capable of poisoning the public – it is really lamp oil.

Bread is very plentiful in Paris, but that does not hold for the surrounding area where people have to pay 18 sous for a 4 lb loaf: thus they do their best, despite a strict watch, to take away as much as they can from Paris. . . .

The popular society of the Panthéon section has for some time suspended the issue of certificates of civism on various pretexts; consequently many citizens can neither draw their pensions nor continue in their functions. According to one *citoyenne* from this section a number of wretches are bathed in tears and cannot get any credit at all until they are provided with certificates.

'Hébert', several citizens said in a bar, 'is a patriot – but for money.'

Wood and wine are plentiful everywhere; there is plenty of fresh-cut wood. Many people take away two loads at a time when they often only need one. The *comités civils*, however, should only deliver one ticket at a time for a single load. It has been noted that the government departments use too much.

The sections intend to present a petition asking the Commune to implement the decree ordering an inventory of wealth. They are likewise due to present another asking that employees with a private income should give up their jobs to *sans-culottes*. . . .

The session of the Jacobins was not as interesting as expected. Philippeaux, unable to get a hearing during the previous session, took his denunciation to the Convention and Camille's biting reproaches of Hébert had no effect. However, no. 5 of *Le Vieux Cordelier* was read from the rostrum and Robespierre criticized the provocative tone of its author. Danton's judgement was less severe.

Fear of passing for a *feuillant*[8] or moderate has made significant inroads on the subscription list of *Le Vieux Cordelier*. Many have had their names removed from the list, contenting themselves with buying it from the street-vendors. . . .

Complaints against the *comités révolutionnaires* are always the topic of conversation and people are aggrieved to see that they decide what they like.

---

8 Constitutional monarchist; from the Feuillant Club which seceded from the Jacobins in 1791.

It is said that seats in the Jacobins are let out for as much as 10 francs. For the sake of its honour it is to be hoped that the club will take measures to prevent such a shameful commerce.

The two parties are still as much at each other's throats, and good citizens sadly prophesy that this unfortunate contest will cost the republic some of those in whom it had placed its confidence.

People are likewise pained to see the Jacobin Society – deviating from the aims of its founders and neglecting the great interests of the fatherland, instead of concerning itself solely with the task of reconciliation, of ending private feuds and reminding its members that their main task is to save the republic – entering into a fullscale polemical debate and its members turning themselves into doctors of the Sorbonne, censuring writings and examining whether such and such a phrase is or is not heretical. People demand more than ever that the Convention put an end to all these writings which uselessly prolong a debate that has already lasted too long and that may compromise the peace of the republic.

La Révolution française, vol. XXIII,
pp. 182–7

167   Police report on the session of the Cordelier Club of 26 ventôse year II (16 March 1794)

At the opening of the session a member demanded that Cordeliers who missed a session whilst the club was in continuous session should be expelled from the society. This motion was vigorously opposed and defeated .

On all sides people asked for correspondence to be read out, but none had arrived. A member who happened to have Saint-Just's latest report in his pocket mounted the rostrum and read it out. This occupied the society for an hour. Next it was announced that the caretaker had received letters addressed to Vincent. The society had them brought in and decided that a deputation should take them to the public prosecutor. . . . Since the society had only declared it was in permanent session because several of its members had been arrested and since no orator had spoken to the matter, it was decided that there would be sessions on the ordinary days only.

Session closed at 9.30.

Observations

The *habitués* of the gallery, those who occupy the front benches, said nothing. They no longer spoke of snatching those arrested from prison. The other people in the gallery said openly that the Père Duchesne and the others were knaves who deserved the guillotine. They rejoiced in anticipation of the moment when they would see them suffer. These demonstrations of joy are common to the whole people of Paris: in the markets, at the street corners, everywhere they say the same. This desire to see the conspirators punished proves how attached the people are to liberty. They regret that there is no more rigorous form of execution than the guillotine. They say that one should be invented to make them suffer longer. Condemnation is general. The day before yesterday several people took up their defence but yesterday they were afraid to presume them innocent.

28 ventôse [18 March]

During the session of the Cordelier Club on 24 ventôse when Prétot was plucked from the rostrum and expelled from the hall for saying that Hébert was a knave and when the news of the arrest of Vincent, Ronsin, Hébert and Momoro caused such trouble and excitement, it was resolved that every day of each *décade*,[9] except the fifth and the tenth, the society would be in session to consult as to ways of serving their incarcerated brethren in their imminent peril and to nominate deputies empowered to make representations to the public prosecutor in favour of their brethren, who were detained in the Conciergerie prison. In accordance with this resolution, the Cordelier Society assembled the day before yesterday, the 26th, but it was clear that the rats were leaving the sinking ship. People came late and the meeting was thinly attended. They say no one knew what to discuss, nothing was decided and before nine o'clock the session was closed and everyone retired. This proves the proverb: 'I will strike the shepherd and the flock shall be scattered.'

An underground rumour is circulating to the effect that the mayor, Pâche, and the *agent national*, Chaumette, have been put under house arrest or that they have been given guards to keep them under surveillance. I am not confirming anything about this rumour; I still do not know whether it has any foundation.

The arrest of Hérault de Séchelles and Simon, or rather their complicity with the conspirators, increases both the people's indignation against the knaves who sought to betray them and their confidence in the Committees of Public Safety and General Security and the Convention. In all the public places and in private there is nothing but praise for the latter and curses for the others. They ardently desire that all those who have taken part in this infernal conspiracy should be arrested and punished and they impatiently await the day when the sword of justice will cut off their heads. Among those to whom the voice of the people would especially draw the attention of the Committee of General Security as aristocratic or conspiratorial

9 The revolutionary calendar with ten-day weeks had been decreed on 5 October 1793.

suspects (I have to report this) is the minister of war and his department which is regarded as a breeding-ground of anti-patriotic sentiment.

Grivel

W. Markov and A. Soboul, *Die San-sculotten von Paris, Dokumente zur Geschichte ver Voksbewegung* (1957), no. 69

168 Bouchotte,[10] minister of war, to Robespierre, 4 frimaire year II (24 November 1793)

... I swear that there have been no quarrels arising out of *amour propre* or abuse of power in the seven months [I have been war minister]; however we live at a time where points of contact are continuous. ... I meddle with nothing: you should be sufficiently convinced of that. Absorbed as I am by a mound of paperwork out of all proportion [to my strength], I do not even take my wonted pleasure of following all the twists and turns of the Revolution and of being what is called *au courant*. There are ardent patriots at the war ministry; that is not surprising; I searched them out because they were lacking. People want me to tell them what to think: it is not my place, whether they are right or wrong. It is for the public alone to judge. Often indeed I am not *au fait* with what has been said; I do not have the time to read the newspapers at all systematically.

Papiers inédits, vol. II, p. 324

10 Jean-Baptiste-Noel Bouchotte, 1754–1830, general, minister of war 1793–4.

|5|

Robespierre's red summer

The elimination of the Hébertists and Dantonists left the Committees of Public Safety and General Security unchallenged. But soon conflicts developed within the committees themselves – in particular, Robespierre and his allies Saint-Just and Couthon (nicknamed 'the triumvirate') drifted apart from their colleagues. There was also friction between the two committees arising from some overlapping of functions, aggravated when the Committee of Public Safety established its own *bureau de police*, for a short while under Saint-Just and then from 9 floréal to 12 messidor (28 April–30 June) under Robespierre. This was the only regular 'nine to five' work Robespierre did in his life. Some of his directives are given in document **181**. They are a mixture of the sensible and the paranoid but all are essentially trivial (except the subject of the report) and it is likely that this minute police work kept his eye off the main political ball during the last months of his life.

Robespierre was in no sense a dictator but neither was he just another member of the Committee of Public Safety, for he had sources of power outside the Committee and indeed outside the Convention. The oldest was the Jacobins with its nationwide network of clubs, but by this stage it was less a dynamic political force than the largest source of employees in the bloated revolutionary bureaucracy. In this respect membership of the Jacobin Club was similar to membership of the Communist Party in the former Soviet Union.

This institutionalization of the Jacobins reflected a similar development of Robespierre's own political power. The fall of the Hébertists brought vast additions to Robespierre's powerbase but they were mostly of an institutional nature: the Commune which was staffed with his adherents, notably Payan, who became *agent national*, and Fleuriot-Lescot, who became mayor; and the 12 executive commissions which replaced the ministries on 12 germinal (1 April). These too mostly fell to Robespierrists, notably the 'Civil Commission' which was headed by a friend from Arras, Herman. Herman's commission was the main agent of execution for the police bureau and also directed the Revolutionary Tribunal, which had itself been staffed with Robespierre's nominees from September 1793. The final element in Robespierre's powerbase was the National Guard under Hanriot who, it was not forgotten, had directed operations against the Convention on 2 June 1793. But for Robespierre, Hanriot could easily have perished with the Hébertists, and Hanriot was to repay the debt on 9 thermidor.

Robespierre exercised his patronage through a system of personal recommendation. This was necessary because his personal acquaintance was not large. He believed that if the man who made the recommendation was a 'patriot' the man he recommended would be. Even better if the recommendation was made by an entire popular society (177). He went to considerable lengths to check the patriotism of the recommender and (on less happy occasions) the denouncer. To cope with his vast accession of patronage in the spring of 1794 he constructed a list of 116 'patriots with more or less talent' consisting of men known personally (often from the circle of his host the carpenter Maurice Duplay) and their recommendations. For Robespierre patriotism was the first requirement, with 'more or less talent' a poor second. A shorter list (176) contains the names of those destined for high office.

Robespierre and Saint-Just seem to have had definite ideas about what to do with this access of power beyond just enjoying the exercise of it and this may be the clue to their quarrels with their governmental colleagues. Committee men like Carnot (who was responsible for army organization), Prieur and Lindet were technocrats who wanted to concentrate on winning the war and directing the country to that end with a minimum of ideological baggage. When France moved on to a solid offensive after the battle of Fleurus on 26 June, Carnot raised his sights to incorporate natural frontiers and beyond; Robespierre detected a creeping militarization of national life, with armies staffed by professionals rather than enthusiastic volunteers, and the ever-present threat of a military dictatorship.

Whereas Carnot was not afflicted by doubts, Saint-Just was aware that the Revolution had lost its way and become 'frozen' (169 and 170). By 'frozen' he probably meant 'bureaucratized' – he specifically attacked his governmental colleagues for becoming bureaucrats – but there is also a sense that the Revolution had lost its soul. The progressive removal of the *sans-culottes* from politics (September 1793–March 1794) had had the blessing of all the members of the Committee but it is possible that Robespierre and Saint-Just were worried that by muzzling the shock troops of the Revolution its momentum could be lost, the torrent 'frozen'. Thus, to compensate the *sans-culottes* for their loss of political activity and keep their interest in the Revolution alive, Saint-Just sought to cater for their material needs by confiscating the property of suspects and giving the proceeds to needy patriots (the laws of ventôse – 172) whilst to minister to their spiritual needs, Robespierre instituted a state religion, as proposed by Rousseau (180). In fact the economic impact of the ventôse laws would not have been great, whilst the ordinary man would have preferred a more carnal religion than Robespierre's.

The extract on Saint-Just's economic ideas (171) shows that he saw the distribution of land not just as a political move – the creation of a class with a vested interest in the Jacobin Revolution – but as the only way out of an otherwise insoluble impasse based on a pessimistic reading of the laws of supply and demand. At the beginning of the Revolution, Saint-Just argued, there had been deflation since the court hoarded and the *émigrés* exported 'metal coinage'. No one wanted goods, everyone wanted coins. With the introduction of paper money (the *assignats*) the reverse happened and, to pay for the war, far more paper was issued than was covered by the confiscated church lands. This was compounded by the decline of imports resulting from the collapse of the livre. Too much money chased too few goods: result – inflation.

The introduction of price controls, the maximum (**159**), resulted in famine because no one would sell at these prices paid in a depreciating currency. In a perfect world price controls were excellent but at present they were inoperable because of human 'avarice'. Moreover the state could not afford to buy the produce of the land it had sold: because of inflation, in two years the new proprietors recovered the cost of their purchase. The only solution was for everyone, including the state, to have some land or raw materials and for taxes to be paid in kind, as Calonne had advocated in 1787.

The new land was to come from the enemies of the Revolution and in particular the nobility. As Barère said, they were presumed to be the enemies of the Revolution because they had already lost so much by it (**175b**). This presumptive guilt of an entire social category is reminiscent of the Nazis' treatment of the Jews (a similar proportion of French nobles – 3 per cent – perished in the Revolution as of French Jews in the Second World War).[1] There is a similar discussion of 'mixed marriages' (**174**). The germ of the doctrine lies in Saint-Just's assertion during the trial of Louis XVI that 'kings cannot reign innocently'. The proscription led to a caricature in reverse of the *ancien régime*'s qualifications for noble status (**173**, supplementary articles; **158**).

Under Saint-Just's law of 27 germinal (16 April) (**173**) nobles had to report daily to the authorities and were forbidden to reside in Paris or militarily sensitive areas – Robespierre moves to a wide definition of the latter in document **181d**. Barère's account of 'the Parisian bourgeois who was determined to be banished from Paris as a noble' (**175b**) provides a comic interlude but one with a point, for when Saint-Just's law was repealed during the thermidorian reaction (**199**) a deputy insisted that the police passes authorizing certain nobles to remain in Paris (**173**, article 10) should be destroyed because they 'conferred patents of nobility'. Apparently the desire to be considered a nobleman could run deeper than the fear of death and explains if it does not justify the ferocity of Saint-Just's legislation. Further evidence of inveterate respect for the nobility is provided by Barère's reaction to Saint-Just's proposal that, by a symbolic inversion of the practice under the *ancien régime*, the nobility should perform enforced labour or *corvée* on the roads (**175a**). Barère, whose mother was a noblewoman who married a *roturier*, attacks the proposal on the somewhat curious ground that it 'would offend our sense of decency' because 'nobility may have been

1 P. Higgonet, *Class Ideology and the Rights of Nobles during the French Revolution* (1981), p. 217.

abolished by political laws but nobles still retained a natural rank in the opinion of the bulk of the people'.

Such thinking only served to confirm Robespierre and Saint-Just's belief that the present generation, the product of the *ancien régime*, was incorrigible and had to be restrained by the Terror until a new generation had grown up under the auspices of a national republican education[2] and the republican institutions on which Saint-Just laid such stress but which, despite the setting up of a commission on the subject (**173**, article 25), were never established. And Payan chastised Robespierre for having 'only centralized physical, material government', whereas what was needed was the centralization of 'public opinion, that is to say moral government' (**188**). Only when such measures had brought men once more into harmony with nature would the need for Terror and even strong government disappear.

Meanwhile Frenchmen had to live with the paradox that the Terror seemed to increase as the military situation, which had been the official excuse for it, improved. Excuses for a state of continuous revolution were provided by plays on words, Robespierre arguing that the Terror could not end till every *moral* enemy had been destroyed and Payan invoking a second front, the home front (**188**). The charter for the grand terror was the law of 22 prairial (10 June 1794) (**184**), which was particularly associated with Couthon, who presented it, and Robespierre, who railroaded it through the Convention (**185**). This law deprived the accused of counsel and witnesses and in June and July the Revolutionary Tribunal in Paris sent some 1,500 people to the guillotine, many of them on the most far-fetched charges that have ever been devised, such as that of planning 'to tear out [the] hearts [of the entire revolutionary establishment], broil and eat them' (**187**). The prototype for the prairial law had been the Orange Commission set up the previous month and the brainchild of Payan who in document **183** lectures one of its judges on the principles of revolutionary justice and the distinction between ordinary tribunals and those which he is not ashamed to call 'political tribunals'. With the latter, what we would call 'due legal process' is inappropriate.

The close affinity between the Orange Commission and the prairial tribunal tends to invalidate Lefebvre's celebrated argument that the latter was set up to pander to the hysteria generated in the government by the assassination attempts on Collot and Robespierre on 5 prairial.[3] When the government, instead of checking popular blood lust, becomes itself infected with the disease, a holocaust was inevitable. That the attempts did induce governmental hysteria is evident from the letter recalling Saint-Just (**182**) but inauguration of the Orange Commission predated them.

The prairial law marked the beginning of the end of the terrorist regime, and this for several reasons. The Committee of General Security (which had not been consulted) took umbrage; sensing an imminent crisis they cynically wooed the right wing of the Convention by visiting the 73 imprisoned Girondin backbenchers, whom Robespierre had preserved alive for just such a contingency since the previous autumn (**192**). The colleagues of the

2 Legislative provision had been made for this on 6 January 1794.
3 G. Lefebvre, 'A propos de la loi du 22 prairial', *AHRF*, p. 253.

'triumvirate' in the Committee of Public Safety who had been consulted about the general provisions of the law but probably not about the attempt to remove parliamentary immunity by implication (repealing all previous legislation on the subject) became restless and, at least according to their later accounts, saw Robespierre revealed as a dictator for the first time.

That is how he must have seemed to the parliamentarians who stood to lose their immunity – precious at a time when life was cheap – as they saw Robespierre for the first time as a dictator behaving dictatorially, threatening to keep the deputies in detention like naughty schoolboys, 'if need be till 9.0 p.m.', until they had passed the law. The effect of Couthon's denial was effectively to make immunity stronger than ever. Moreover, during the debate on the law, deputies for the first time started questioning the wooden language of the year II, the clichés and trite paradoxes which camouflaged the loss of basic human rights in the name of liberty (186). Once that happened the spell was broken.

The prairial law had another consequence which was at first concealed. On the 23rd Robespierre quarrelled violently with his colleagues over his attempt to send a number of deputies to the scaffold. In a rage he withdrew to the police bureau and ceased to take part in the general measures of the Committee. Then on 12 messidor (30 June) he withdrew altogether, again secretly, dividing his time between his lodgings and the Jacobin Club which he had so far neglected that his enemy, Fouché, had been elected president on 18 prairial. It suited both Robespierre and his governmental colleagues to keep his secession secret because they were all too aware that if Robespierre fell the whole edifice might come crashing down. Even the Parisians were suffering from *nausée de la guillotine* (which had to be removed to the outskirts of the city).

Events moved rapidly now in an almost cinematic, fragmented way. Every alcove hid a separate conspiracy. The Robespierrists themselves pursued different agendas: Saint-Just sought compromise with the Committee until the eleventh hour, inducing it to implement his social programme; Payan pressed Robespierre to attack and lose no time about it (188). Document 193 suggests that he and Fleuriot-Lescot were planning to turn the festival for the pantheonization of two young Robespierrist martyrs, Barra and Viala, when the Convention was to have been surrounded by *invalides* on 10 thermidor, into a purge of Robespierre's enemies. As in the previous revolutionary *journées* Robespierre's involvement was probably not so great that it could not conveniently be denied in case of failure. Another group of Robespierrists, the Lyon faction known as the 'friends of Chalier' were seeking to bring to trial Fouché, who had denied them a share in patronage after the reconquest of Lyon (189). Robespierre, who detested Fouché for his atheism, was probably closest of all to this group, many of whom had their lodgings in adjacent houses to his. Robespierre himself denounced Fouché as the 'conspirator-in-chief' in the Jacobins and two letters of Fouché's (190) suggest that he was not far wrong in this assessment.

In addition, other deputies who feared they were about to be denounced by Robespierre – friends of Danton such as Bourdon de l'Oise and Thuriot, or ultra-terrorist proconsuls who had been recalled from bloody and/or lucrative missions in the provinces, such as Tallien – planned a pre-emptive strike. Document **191** shows that Tallien, Bourdon and Thuriot were being watched by the police, though it is not known whether the report was destined for Robespierre's police bureau or the Committee of General Security.

Robespierre ignited all this combustible material when, on 8 thermidor, he returned to the Convention after an absence of nearly two months. Most of his two-hour speech was vague and allusive, but the conclusion (**194**) is crystal clear: Robespierre wanted to purge the Committee of General Security and subordinate it to a purged Committee of Public Safety. The issue on the 8th was inconclusive, but on the 9th Robespierre, Saint-Just, Couthon, Augustin Robespierre and Lebas were arrested. The rest of the story is given in document **198**. The Robespierrists at the Commune assembled enough troops from the Paris sections – more than they asked for – to overawe the Convention, but the civilian response was so poor that they lacked the legitimacy to move against the venerated National Assembly. The reason for the poor response may have been, as Soboul suggests, that the government had knocked the stuffing out of the popular movement but document **195** suggests that the *sans-culottes* had become so bureaucratized – they were mostly salaried officials – that they had acquired a hierarchical mentality, so that, as they put it, 'under a *gouvernement révolutionnaire* they needed to be guided in their actions, lest they fall into the traps constantly being set for them by the enemies of the republic'.

Finally document **196** shows just how isolated and self-deluded the Robespierrists had become. Couthon proposes to issue a proclamation to the armies 'in the name of the Convention': they (just five deputies) are the *real* Convention. Robespierre then goes one better and says that the proclamation should be 'in the name of the French people'. By the time he uttered these words the Robespierrist troops on the place de Grève had melted into the warm thermidorian night and there could have been scarcely more than 100 people in the Hôtel de Ville, many of these locked in from the inside. But as Rousseau had said (**197**), it was quality not quantity which counted when determining the general will, whereas in a true democracy the reverse is usually the case. Minutes later it was all over, as the password was betrayed and troops loyal to the *real* Convention poured in.

169   Fragment from Saint-Just's notebook

The misfortunes of the country have tinged the whole empire with a sombre and religious hue. Meditation is necessary in these painful circumstances. It should be characteristic of all the friends of the republic.

Saint-Just, Oeuvres complètes, ed.
Ch. Vellay (2 vols., 1908), vol. II,
p. 537

170   Two sections from Saint-Just's *Fragments sur les institutions républicaines*, summer 1794

We must examine the system of collective government, such as municipalities, administrations, surveillance committees, etc. and see whether handing the functions of these bodies to a single magistrate would not be the secret of consolidating the Revolution.

> Saint-Just, *Oeuvres complètes*, vol. II,
> p. 502

The Revolution is frozen; all the principles are enfeebled; all that remains are *bonnets rouges* worn by intriguers.

The operation of the Terror has blunted the sense of crime, as strong liquors blunt the palate.

> Saint-Just, *Oeuvres complètes*, vol. II,
> p. 508

171   Saint-Just's economics: from his *Fragments sur les institutions républicaines*

Never has the need for precise definitions been greater than today, especially on financial questions. For, since the Revolution began, all economic theory has been seen through a prism.

I am going, therefore, to attempt to chart the progress of economic errors which have reached us whether from pressing needs or from foreign influences and what has been their effect on morals.

In 1789 money was scarce, whether through the fault of the court, which was conspiring, or through the fault of rich individuals who were planning to emigrate. . . .

There was a revolution in the economy no less astonishing than the one which took place in government; but less attention was paid to it. Money was scarce, so were goods; everyone wanted to keep what he had in safety. This mistrust and avarice destroyed all social relationships to the point that, for a moment, society no longer existed. Money was no longer seen.

The avarice and mistrust which produced this social isolation then, by a bizarre turn of human nature, brought everyone together again. I refer to that period when paper money replaced the metal coinage which had disappeared.

Everyone fearing to keep the new notes and be caught out by a sudden repudiation, passed them on into circulation with alacrity. Suddenly commercial activity exploded, a trend which was accentuated by the eagerness of those who had been compensated [for loss of *ancien régime* offices] to convert their money into goods.

Since commercial activity depended solely on mistrust and the collapse of credit; since we ceased to import and the foreign exchange market turned against us, the immense quantity of notes we had issued, which increased daily, could only be spent on produce within France. Good were hoarded and exported for large sums; they were consumed; they became rare and notes accumulated and depreciated more and more.

Since everyone possessed lots of paper money they worked correspondingly less and morals were sapped by idleness. Wages increased as fewer people wanted to work. . . . The tax-take did not increase and the republic, involved in universal war, was obliged to increase the money supply to cope with enormous expenses.

The sale of church lands and taxation constituted the only circulation of money; but 30 millions came in a month and notes were issued to the tune of three or four hundred. So the *assignat* depreciated every month; . . . Then the state which was selling land found it could not afford to buy the produce from it.

A man who had bought an *arpent* of land from the state for 600 livres, sold the state its [annual] produce for 300 livres, instead of for 30 livres, at 5 per cent. This ingratitude towards the *patrie*, which forced the state to buy the produce more dearly than it had sold the land, forced it to employ penal laws [against hoarding].

The foreign powers have led us from shock to shock to these extremities. They suggested the remedy. The first suggestion of price control came from abroad, brought by the baron de Batz: it was a plan to cause famine. It is generally accepted in Europe today that they counted on famine to rouse popular anger, on popular anger to destroy the Convention, and on the dissolution of the Convention to dismember France.

See what history teaches us about the effects of price controls. When the Emperor Julian introduced price controls at Antioch, he caused a terrible famine. Why? Not because the law on price controls was bad but because men were avaricious. And the same avarice and corruption causes everyone to buy without restraint when prices are regulated and be unwilling to sell. . . .

The circulation of produce is necessary when everyone does not have a property and raw materials. Produce does not circulate where there are price controls. If you impose price controls without reforming morals, the consequence is avarice. To reform morals we must begin by satisfying men's needs and their interests. We must give some land to everyone.

We must, by the same token, have a public domain and public revenues paid in kind.

Saint-Just, *Oeuvres complètes*, vol. II,
pp. 510–14

172   The ventôse decrees, 3 March 1794

Saint-Just read out a proposed decree which the Convention adopted as follows:

The National Convention, having heard a combined report of the Committees of Public Safety and General Security, decrees:

1 All the communes of the republic will draw up a list of needy patriots including their names, ages, occupations and the numbers and ages of their children. The district authorities will send their lists to the Committee of Public Safety as soon as possible.
2 When the Committee of Public Safety has received these lists it will draw up a report on the means of indemnifying all the destitute with the property of the enemies of the Revolution on the basis of a schedule provided by the Committee of General Security which will also be published.
3 Consequently the Committee of General Security will give precise instructions to all the surveillance committees in the republic that, within a period fixed for each district according to its remoteness, they shall provide it with the names and conduct of all those detained since 1 May 1789; and likewise of all those subsequently detained.
4 The Committee of General Security will append a directive to the present decree to facilitate its execution.

The Convention adopted this decree amidst applause.

AP, vol. LXXXVI, pp. 23–4

173   The law of 27 germinal, *sur la police générale*

1 Those accused of conspiracy anywhere in the republic shall be brought before the Revolutionary Tribunal in Paris.
6 No ex-noble or enemy national may live in Paris or any fortress or naval town. Any noble or foreigner in the above category found there at the end of ten days will be automatically outlawed.
7 Workers employed in the arms factories in Paris, foreigners who have married French patriots and noble women who have married non-noble citizens, are not covered by the previous article.
10 The Committee of Public Safety is likewise authorized specially to requisition the services of those former noblemen or foreigners whom it thinks can be of use to the republic.
11 The surveillance committees will issue passports. Individuals receiving

them are to state their place of banishment. This will be indicated on the order.

12 The surveillance committees will keep a register of all the passports they issue and send a daily extract of this register to the Committees of Public Safety and General Security.

13 The former nobles and foreigners are obliged, on arrival, to show their passport to the municipal authorities of the place of banishment. They will equally be obliged to present themselves every day before the said municipal authorities.

14 Municipal authorities are obliged to send to the Committees of Public Safety and General Security without delay a list of all the former nobles and foreigners living in their *arrondissement* and of all those banished there.

15 Former nobles and foreigners may not be admitted to popular societies or surveillance committees nor communal nor sectional assemblies.

16 Generals who are not on active service there are forbidden to live in Paris or fortress or naval towns.

21 Representatives-on-mission will make use of the constituted authorities and may not delegate powers.

22 Only the *commission des subsistances* and representatives-on-mission with the armies may requisition and then only with the express authorization of the Committee of Public Safety.

23 In future anyone convicted of complaining about the Revolution who lives off unearned income and is neither over 60 nor an invalid will be deported to Guyana. Matters of this kind will be judged by popular commissions.

25 The National Convention will nominate two three-man commissions from its members. One will be charged with reducing to a complete and succinct code all the laws which have been passed to date, suppressing those which have become confused. The other commission will be charged with drafting a body of civil institutions fit to preserve the morals and spirit of liberty. These commissions will report back within a month.

Supplementary articles decreed the following day:

2 Those who, without being nobles according to the notions and regulations of the *ancien régime*, have usurped or bought titles or privileges of nobility and those who have pleaded or fabricated false titles in order to be given nobility are classified as nobles and included in the same law.

Mautouchet, *Gouvernement*
révolutionnaire,
pp. 291–4

174 Decree of the Committee of Public Safety, 2 floréal (21 April 1794)

Citizens are flocking to the committee to seek clarification of the law of 27 germinal, *sur la police générale*: widows of former nobles but without children and born *roturières*; wives of former nobles divorced before the present law; citizens who have styled themselves *écuyer* whilst exercising offices which conferred personal nobility: all want to know whether they fall within the provisions of the law.

The Committee's reply is 'no', for since there is clearly no mention of these categories in the law they are *ipso facto* exempt.

> Buchez and Roux, *Histoire parlementaire*, vol. XXXII, pp. 327–38

175 Extracts from the memoirs of Barère

Bertrand Barère de Vieuzac, 1755–1841, lawyer, deputy to the Estates-General, *conventionnel*, and *rapporteur* of the Committee of Public Safety, was the great trimmer of the Revolution.

(a) Saint-Just proposes to make the nobles perform labour on the main roads

One evening about this time Saint-Just came to the Committee and coolly proposed a strange way of terminating the Revolution's struggle against noble suspects and detainees. Here is what he said: 'For a thousand years the nobility has oppressed the French people with feudal exactions and persecutions of all kinds. Feudalism and nobility no longer exist; you need the roads of the frontier departments repairing to facilitate the passage of artillery and supply convoys to our armies; order that the noble detainees do enforced maintenance work (*corvée*) on the main roads.'

. . . When Saint-Just had finished, a wave of silent indignation swept over all of us, followed by a unanimous call for the rejection of the proposal. I felt that I had to testify on behalf of our national character by telling Saint-Just and the Committee that such a form of punishment for detainees, even if prescribed by law, would offend our sense of decency; that the nobility may indeed have been abolished by political laws but that nobles still retained a natural rank in the opinion of the bulk of the people, a difference due to their education, and that this prevented us in Paris as Marius had in Rome.

(b) The Parisian bourgeois who was determined to be banished from Paris as a noble

Whilst these severe measures were being taken against nobles, my audience chamber in the Hôtel de Savalette, rue Saint-Honoré, was the scene of a piece such as the comic authors could have laid claim to. A respectable Parisian from the Marais, the son of an alderman of the corporation of Paris, came to seek my advice as to whether he should leave the capital and go place himself under surveillance at Passy. I told him that his nobility was not that feudal kind which had lost everything in the Revolution and therefore fell under the suspicion of the legislator. But the bourgeois from the Marais insisted that he was covered by the law. I insisted in turn that he remain in Paris with his family, repeating that his nobility being absolutely modern, he was not in the least threatened. Then the son of the Paris alderman began to lose his temper in front of quite a few people. He raised his voice and said that he was as noble as any nobleman in France; that the office of alderman gave recognized, hereditary nobility. I tried to calm him by pretending to recognize the legitimacy of his rather unseasonable aristocratic pride and I offered to requisition him as a noble man of letters authorized to remain in Paris. 'No, sir', he returned, 'I am not a man of letters. I am the son of an alderman of the corporation of Paris; I am obliged by laws to leave and leave I shall.' He withdrew in high dudgeon.

B. Barère de Vieuzac, *Mémoires*, ed.
H. Carnot and D. d'Angers (2 vols.,
1842–4), vol. II, pp. 175–80

176 Robespierre's lists

Robespierre constructed a list of 116 'patriots with more or less talent' to cope with the vast increase in his patronage which came with the fall of the Hébertists. He also made this smaller list of men destined for high office.

Herman: Enlightened, honest, capable of the highest offices.

Dumas: Energetic and honest, capable of the most important functions.

Payan, the elder, *idem.*

Payan, the younger, *idem*, national agent of the Commune of Paris.

Moenne, *idem*, the national agent's deputy.

Julien, *fils*, *idem.*

Buchot, *idem.*

Campion, pure patriot, good for administration.

Gatteau, *idem.*

Thullier, *idem.*

Saint-Just's brother-in-law, energetic patriot, pure, enlightened.

Papiers inédits, vol. II, p. 11

177   Robespierrist appointments: the replacement of the president of the tribunal and the *agent national* of Saint-Briez (Moselle): evidence given by one of Herman's officials during Herman's trial in 1795

Herman, who knew that the majority of the popular societies were composed of Robespierre's creatures, made use of these societies to place or displace, in the administrative bodies, all those who could further or thwart his aims. He wrote to the [popular] society of Briez which, at his request, proceeded to the election of two citizens. [However they elected two men who had held office during the Prussian occupation (in contravention of the law of 7 September). When the official raised the matter with Herman] he replied coldly that this warning carried no weight and that the details given by an individual could not be compared to the motives which had determined the choice of a popular society composed of a great number of individuals and that the matter must be allowed to rest.

Buchez and Roux, *Histoire parlementaire*, vol. XXXV, pp. 50–1

178   Robespierre's values: extract from a speech of 5 February 1794

Reading this speech, it is easy to imagine the mortifications which Robespierre and, with less rancour, other members of the bourgeoisie had experienced at the hands of high society under the *ancien régime*. The importance of this feeling as a cause of the Revolution cannot be over-estimated. The essential difference between the two regimes is captured, if caricatured.

In our country, we want to replace egoism with morality, honour with honesty, the tyranny of fashion with the rule of reason, contempt for misfortune with contempt for vice, insolence with self-respect, vanity with greatness of soul, love of money with love of *gloire*, good company with good people, intrigue with merit, wit with genius, show with truth, the tediousness of dissipation with uncloyed happiness, the pettiness of *les grands* with the greatness of man, an amiable, frivolous and wretched people with one that is magnanimous, strong and happy, that is to say all the vices and stupidities of the monarchy with all the virtues and miracles of the republic (applause).

AP, vol. LXXXlV, p. 331

179 The mindset of the Robespierrist official: Herman's circular to the employees of the *commission civil*

Above all we must throw out the old clothes, leave behind that mannered *politesse* which contrasts so strongly with the bearing of a free man and which still recalls the time when there were masters and slaves. All the ministerial forms have already disappeared; you must forget even the semblance of them. Simple, natural manners must take the place of that studied countenance in which the whole worth of a *chef de bureau* or under-secretary often resides. Decorum and an unaffected gravity must be the only external signs of a man occupied with the public good; the bearing of a man in the state of nature must be upright!

A simple style, clear yet concise, stripped of all servile expressions, of all obsequious formulae in dealing with superiors; in dealing with juniors all pride, all pedantry, anything which suggests any superiority save only that of reason, of the general order established by the law must replace ministerial jargon and clutter.

E. Campardon, *Le tribunal révolutionnaire de Paris* (2 vols., 1972), vol. II, pp. 346–7

180 Decree on the Supreme Being, 18 floréal year II (7 May 1794)

1 The French people recognizes the existence of the Supreme Being and the immortality of the soul.

2 It recognizes that the proper worship of the Supreme Being consists in fulfilling the duties of a man.

3 It places in the forefront of these duties: to abominate bad faith and tyranny, to punish tyrants and traitors, to succour the needy, to respect the weak, to defend the oppressed, to do to others all the good that is in our power and to be unjust to no one.

4 Festivals will be instituted to turn men's thoughts to the Divinity and to a consideration of their own dignity.

5 They will take their names from the glorious events of our Revolution, from the virtues dearest to man and most useful to him and from the greatest benefits of nature.

6 Every year the French republic will celebrate the festivals of 14 July 1789, 10 August 1792, 21 January 1793 and 31 May 1793.

7 On successive *décades* festivals will be held in honour of the following:
The Supreme Being and Nature – Mankind – The French People – The
Benefactors of Humanity – The Martyrs of Liberty – Liberty and
Equality – The Republic – World Freedom – Love for the Fatherland –
Hatred of Tyrants and Traitors – Truth – Justice – Modesty – Fame and
Immortality – Friendship – Frugality – Courage – Good Faith –
Heroism – Disinterestedness – Stoicism – Love – Marital Fidelity –
Paternal Love – Maternal Love – Filial Piety – Childhood – Youth –
Manhood – Old Age – Misfortune – Agriculture – Industry – Our
Forebears – Posterity – Happiness.

8 The Committees of Public Safety and Public Instruction are entrusted
with drawing up a plan for the organization of these festivals.

9 The National Convention invites all those with a talent worthy of
serving the cause of humanity to have the honour of contributing to the
institution of these [festivals] by writing hymns and patriotic songs and
by doing everything capable of contributing to their grace and function.

10 The Committee of Public Safety will single out the works it considers
best calculated to fulfil these objectives and will reward their authors.

15 On 2 prairial next a festival in honour of the Supreme Being will be
celebrated.

Buchez and Roux, *Histoire parlementaire*, vol. XXXII, pp. 379–81

181   Robespierre's directives at the *bureau de police*

10 prairial

Report: Rumour-mongers in the district of Tarbes are saying that all the old
people and children will be guillotined because of a shortage of bread.

Robespierre's directive: Decree that the administrators of the district of
Tarbes will arrest the rumour-mongers and send them under close guard to
the Conciergerie [prison] in Paris. They will report without delay on the
implementation of this measure.

15 prairial

Report: The society of Jacobins of Vienne *le patriote*, department of the
Aire, has petitioned the National Convention to pass a decree including
priests in the law of 27 germinal.

Robespierre's directive: This initiative proves that this society is run by
intriguers; the petition must be shown to Payan [a local man] so that he can
give us information on this point.

23 prairial

Report: A clerk of the former Parlement has said, 'the present order of things cannot last'.

Robespierre's directive: Find the address of the delinquent and have him arrested.

27 prairial

Report: A representative-on-mission asks whether nobles must leave maritime departments or just ports?

Robespierre's directive: Both. The necessary steps must be taken to ascertain the domiciles chosen by the *ci-devants*.

28 prairial

Report: Vilde, a prisoner in the Bicêtre warns that for three and a half months there has been a plot to assassinate Robespierre, Collot d'Herbois and all the members of the Committee of Public Safety.

Robespierre's directive: Have him interrogated by Herman.

AN, F7 4437

182 Letter of the Committee of Public Safety to their colleague Saint-Just, on mission with the Army of the North, 6 prairial year II (25 May 1794)

Liberty is exposed to new dangers. The factions revive and are more alarming than ever. The crowds demanding butter are larger and more turbulent than ever though they have the least grounds for complaint; the outbreak of a prison revolt was expected yesterday and there are the same intrigues as were present in Hébert's time. All this is coupled with repeated attempts on the lives of the members of the Committee of Public Safety [there were attempts on the lives of Robespierre and Collot]. The remnants of the factions – or rather the ever-living factions – redouble their audacity and perfidy. We fear an aristocratic rising which would be fatal to liberty. The greatest danger is in Paris. The Committee needs to unite the ideas and energy of all its members. See whether the Army of the North which, thanks in no small part to you, is on the road to victory can spare you for a few days. Until you return we will replace you with a patriotic representative.

Robespierre, Prieur, Carnot, Billaud-Varenne, Barère

Correspondance de Maximilien et
Augustin Robespierre, ed. G. Michon
(1926), no. CDX

183   Payan to Roman-Fonrosa, judge in the Orange Commission, 20 messidor year II (8 July 1794)

My dear friend, as a long-serving former member of the Revolutionary Tribunal I think it proper to offer you some advice about the conduct of judges and jurors. In the first place it must be said that commissions charged with punishing conspirators bear absolutely no comparison with the tribunals of the *ancien régime* or even with those of the new. There must not be any forms; the judge's conscience is there to replace them. It does not matter whether an accused has been interrogated in such or such a manner . . . In a word these commissions are *revolutionary* commissions, that is to say tribunals which should go straight to the facts and strike conspirators without mercy: they should also be *political* tribunals; they should remember that everyone who has not been for the Revolution has been by that very fact against it because he has not done anything for the *patrie*. . . . People are ceaselessly telling the judges: take care to protect the innocent; and I say to them, in the name of the *patrie*: tremble to save the guilty.

Papiers inédits, vol. II, pp. 370–1

184   The law of 22 prairial (10 June 1794)

4 The Revolutionary Tribunal is instituted to punish the enemies of the people.

5 The enemies of the people are those who seek to destroy public liberty, either by force or by guile.

6 hose who seek to restore the monarchy or degrade or dissolve the National Convention and the *gouvernement révolutionnaire* of which it is the centre are reputed to be enemies of the people. Those who have betrayed the republic whilst commanding fortress towns and armies or in any other military capacity . . .

Those who have sought to disrupt the provisioning of Paris or to cause a dearth in the republic.

Those who have aided the projects of the enemies of France, either by facilitating the escape and impunity of conspirators and aristocrats, or by persecuting and calumniating patriots, or corrupting deputies, or by abusing the principles of the Revolution, of the laws of government measures by false and perfidious applications. . . . Those who seek to spread discouragement in order to favour the enterprises of the tyrants leagued against the republic. Those who seek to mislead opinion . . . and deprave morals and corrupt public opinion . . . whether by counter-revolutionary or insidious writings or by any other scheme.

7 The penalty for all crimes coming within the jurisdiction of the Revolutionary Tribunal is death.

8 The proof necessary to condemn the enemies of the people can be any evidence whether material, moral, verbal or written which can persuade a just and reasonable man. . . .

9 Every citizen has the right to arrest and bring conspirators and counter-revolutionaries before the magistrates. He is obliged to denounce them as soon as recognized.

12 The accused will be interrogated at the hearing and in public; the formality of the secret preliminary interrogation is suppressed as superfluous; . . .

13 If there is material or moral proof independent of that provided by witnesses, the latter will not be called unless this formality is judged desirable either to reveal accomplices or for other major considerations of public interest.

16 The law provides, for the defence of calumniated patriots, patriotic juries; for conspirators, none.

18 . . . [If it is decided not to procede with a trial] no accused may be released until the decision . . . has been communicated to the Committees of Public Safety and General Security which will review it.

20 The National Convention repeals all the provisions of previous laws which conflict with the present decree and does not intend that the laws relating to the organization of ordinary tribunals should apply to crimes of Counter-Revolution and to the activity of the Revolutionary Tribunal.

> J. M. Thompson (ed.), *French Revolution Documents, 1789–94* (1948), pp. 284–7

185 From Robespierre's speech in the debate on the law of 22 prairial

The speech was in answer to calls for an adjournment on Couthon's measure which abolished defence counsel and (implicitly) parliamentary immunity.

I demand that the draft law be discussed clause by clause in this sitting. I put my case in a nutshell. First this law is neither more obscure nor more complicated than those which the Committee has already submitted to you for the safety of the fatherland. I observe furthermore that for a long time the National Convention has been accustomed to discuss and decree on the spot, because for a long time it has been free from servitude to factions, because for a long time the vast majority of deputies has had a pronounced inclination for the public weal. . . . I demand that, without stopping to consider the proposed adjournment, the Convention discuss the projected law submitted to it, if need be until nine o'clock tonight.

Robespierre, *Oeuvres*, vol. X, p. 486

186 From the debate in the Convention on the law of 22 prairial, 24 prairial (12 June)

Carrier, one of the secretaries, gave a second reading of the decree passed in the session of 22 prairial, on the organization of the Revolutionary Tribunal.

Charles Delacroix: I notice among the crimes for which one can be sent before the Revolutionary Tribunal that of having sought to *deprave morals*. I hope that at my age I will not be thought to have a vested interest. Nevertheless I would like this crime to be defined more explicitly; because surely there was no intention of treating as enemies of the people those who let slip in their conversation or writing or pieces for the theatre a word which might make modesty blush. I move that the Committee of Public Safety be asked to give this type of crime a less vague and more distinctive definition.

This proposal was adopted.

Mallarmé: Revolutionary laws must be clear and unambiguous. I do not think that article XVI has the necessary clarity and precision. I'd like to know what is meant by the words, 'the law provides calumniated patriots with patriotic jurors'.

Duhem: Asking for definitions weakens the best of laws. We all know what a patriotic juror is: he is a man committed to the Revolution, a true friend of liberty, a warm defender of patriots when they are oppressed and slandered.

Charlier: The article is clear. What is the intention of the law? To eliminate the chatter of barristers and to give to calumniated patriots, for their defence, the conscience of a patriotic juror. I move that there be no further explanations.

N . . .: Superfluous words should be eliminated from laws: as the jurors on the Revolutionary Tribunal are patriotic by definition, I move that the word 'patriot' added to that of 'juror' be removed. . . .

Couthon: The Committee of Public Safety cannot remain silent in the face of all the reflections about the Revolutionary Tribunal which have just been made today and those which were made yesterday. It has been positively asserted in this place that the Committee wanted by sleight of hand to give itself, the Committee of General Security, representatives-on-mission and the public prosecutor [Fouquier-Tinville] the right of sending parliamentary deputies before the Revolutionary Tribunal without a prior decree by the Convention; that is to say it has been alleged that the Committee, by sleight of hand, wanted to repeal existing laws, constitutional laws, and violate the most sacred principles.

Is it not the most atrocious calumny against the Committee?

Buchez and Roux, *Histoire parlemen-taire*, vol. XXXII, pp. 205–7

187 The prison 'conspiracies'

On 28 prairial year II (16 June 1794), 37 people were condemned to death by the Revolutionary Tribunal, convicted:

of being declared enemies of the people in forming, proposing or joining a plot, of which the object was . . . to force the gates of the said prison, and then to stab with poignards the representatives of the people, members of the CSP and CSG, to tear out their hearts, to broil and eat them, and to put the most patriotic representatives to death in a barrel lined with nails.

Moniteur, 22 June 1794, cited in Croker, *French Revolution*, p. 490 (Croker's translation)

188 Payan to Robespierre, 9 messidor year II (27 June 1794)

You could not choose more favourable circumstances to strike all the conspirators. People know that all our victories are the fruit of your [i.e. the Committee of Public Safety's] work. . . . [Go on to] win great victories on the home front. Write a report which strikes all the conspirators at once; decree salutary measures concerning journalists [i.e. more rigid press censorship]; let the public functionaries since they are responsible for public morality be directed by you that they may serve to centralize and make uniform public opinion, that is to say moral government. For you have only centralized physical, material government.

Papiers inédits, vol. II, p. 365

189 The Robespierrists plan to indict Fouché: Achard to Gravier, 10 thermidor (28 July)

These days do we need more evidence than that of crime to punish a scoundrel? And can that we have sent be called insufficient? Do they not represent crime personified? . . . They comprise 19 articles. Once again, what more is necessary? . . .

I would have preferred it if M. Fouché had been asked why he had formed an *armée révolutionnaire* in the departments of Allier and Nièvre, what was his aim, what were his intentions?

Papiers inédits, vol. II, pp. 225–6

190 Fouché's counter-conspiracy: two letters written just before 9 thermidor

Josephe Fouché, 1759–1820, was successively head of the Oratorian college at Nantes, *conventionnel*, de-Christianizer and arch-terrorist. He was expelled by Robespierre from the Jacobins, and later was minister of police under the Directory, Napoleon and Louis XVIII; withal a good family man.

(a) To his sister (undated)

I want to reassure you on two points. First our little girl is a lot better and second I have nothing to fear from the calumnies of Maximilien Robespierre. The Jacobin Society invited me to come and justify myself before it; I certainly did not go, as Robespierre rules there as master. This society has become his forum. Shortly you will learn the issue of this event which I hope will turn to the profit of the republic. Adieu, good health and much love.

(b) To his brother-in-law, 5 thermidor (23 July 1794)

Brother and friend,

Rest assured, patriotism will triumph over tyranny and all those vile and despicable passions which conspire to hound it down. Just a few more days and the rogues and knaves will be unmasked and the enterprise of the honest men will be triumphant. Even today, perhaps, we shall see the traitors unmasked. Adieu, I embrace you with all my heart. The condition of our little girl is still giving us anxiety. Much love to our mother and all our old friends.

AHRF (1962), pp. 366–8

191 Police report on Tallien, Bourdon de l'Oise and Thuriot, 19 messidor year II (7 July 1794)

Citizen Tallien entered the National Convention on the 17th inst. at 1.45 and left before the end of the sitting at 2.30 and crossed the place du Carrousel and the former Hôtel Longueville with a citizen who accosted him in the main court of the Palais National; he stopped several times with this citizen, always talking with him and looking round from side to side and even stopping short to look right round; he entered 237 rue Saint-

Thomas du Louvre alone at three o'clock, where two deputies from Guadeloupe live; stayed there until 6.15 . . . went to the Théâtre de la République, left at 8.30, walked up and down the main avenue of the Jardin Egalité, left by a passage under the balconies which happened to be thronged with citizens at the time when we were following him, which made it impossible for us to catch up with him again.

Bourdon de l'Oise left the Convention after the sitting, walked in the Jardin National until 3 o'clock with five citizens unknown to us, from there went to dine at no. 58 rue Honoré . . . these citizens left at 5.30 but Citizen B. . . de l'O. . . had not yet left at 6 (day before yesterday, 17th inst.).

AHRF (1959), pp. 271–2

192   The wooing of the right: report dictated by the Commune's police officer Faro to Payan, 5 thermidor year II

[Amar and Voulland of the Committee of General Security] proceeded to the Madelonettes [prison] on 5 thermidor where they asked that their dear colleagues be brought to them; they arrived escorted by an official. [Amar and Voulland] asked them in the most pressing and affectionate terms to denounce the officials who had degraded the National Assembly in their persons by transferring them [to the Madelonettes]. They asked them the following questions: 'Are your letters intercepted? Are you refused life's comforts, such as coffee, cordials, chocolate or fruit? Is your status misprised? Has the governor refused to record your status of deputy on the register? Speak, speak, dear colleagues. The Committee of General Security has sent us to you to bring you consolation and to hear your complaints in order to punish those who have degraded the National Assembly in your persons.' Thus invited, the prisoners made numerous complaints, they were treated just like ordinary prisoners. . . . Then one of the two members of the Committee of General Security went as far as shedding tears. Drying his eyes, he proclaimed that it was a terrible crime . . . they gave orders to the governor to show them the respect due to representatives of the people . . . and ordered him (in the presence of the prisoners) to look out a comfortable house with a garden . . . for the deputies. [The spokesman for the prisoners replied:] 'This act of the Committee of General Security restores us. Thank the Committee for us and say that we will always be the friends of liberty and the National Convention.' Complaints were repeated about the state of the beds. . . .

[Payan noted:] in the evening Amar admitted to three police officers . . . that he could not help weeping at the fate of his colleagues; that he had been wrong to rage at the police; but that they did not have to execute the orders he had given on that occasion, but could treat the imprisoned deputies just as before, like the other prisoners. Prisoners in the Madelon-ettes have witnessed *Amar weep!*

Papiers inédits, vol. II, pp. 367–70

193 Rehearsals for The Barra and Viala festival: Fleuriot-Lescot, mayor of Paris, to the clerk to the Commune, 8 thermidor year II (26 July 1794)

You will find enclosed the minute of the General Council of the Commune's *arrêté* of yesterday charging me and [Payan] with asking the Committee of Public Safety for authorization for the convocation of the sectional assemblies for today. The authorization of the Committee being at the bottom of this minute, you will lose no time in sending the letter of convocation to the sections, indicating the precise purpose of this convocation. In the course of the day you will send me a copy of the *arrêté*, including the Committee's authorization.

The same to the same, later that day

It is now past six o'clock and already several sections have come to ask me for the [festival] programme and David's report on account of which they have been convoked. Whether Citizen David or the Commission for Public Instruction have sent this material or whether they have not reached you, either way tell me why you have not informed me. There is not a moment to lose.

E. Chavaray, 'La fête de Barra et Viala', *La Révolution française* (1881), pp. 420–8, 425

194 The conclusion to Robespierre's speech to the Convention, 8 thermidor year II (26 July 1794)

I conclude that, there exists a conspiracy against public liberty; that it draws its strength from a criminal coalition which is plotting in the very heart of the Convention; that this coalition has accomplices in the Committee of General Security and in the bureaux of this committee which they control; that the enemies of the republic have set this committee against the Committee of Public Safety, thus constituting two governments; that members of the Committee of Public Safety itself have joined the plot; that the resulting coalition seeks to ruin the patriots and the country. What is the remedy for this evil? Punish the traitors, purge the bureaux of the Committee of General Security, purge this Committee itself, and subordinate it to the Committee of Public Safety; purge the Committee of

Public Safety itself, to recreate the unity of government under the supreme authority of the National Convention. . . .

Robespierre, *Oeuvres*, vol. X, p. 576

195 The response of functionaries from the Quinze-Vingts section in the faubourg Saint-Antoine to the Commune's appeal for help on 9 thermidor

The Quinze-Vingts section was in the heart of the faubourg Saint-Antoine, hitherto the motor of revolutionary *journées*.

The citizens of the faubourg Antoine have not yet lost that energy which characterizes republicans, but in the present circumstances, *under a gouvernement révolutionnaire*, they need to be guided in their actions, lest they fall into the traps constantly being set for them by the enemies of the republic.

Buchez and Roux, *Histoire parlementaire*, vol. XXXIV, p. 58 (my italics)

196 At the Commune: the testimony of H. G. Dulac, employee of the Committee of Public Safety

[Couthon said]: 'We must at once write to the armies.' Robespierre said: 'In whose name?' Couthon replied: 'Why, in the name of the Convention; is it not always where we are? The rest are only a handful of factious persons who will be scattered and punished by the armed forces at our disposal.' Robespierre seemed to reflect a little; he stooped and whispered in his brother's ear, then he said: 'It is my opinion that we should write in the name of the French people.'

A. Mathiez, *The Fall of Robespierre* (1927), p. 215

197 From the chapter 'Of voting' in Rousseau's *Du contrat social*

The citizen consents to all the laws, even to those which are passed despite him . . . when someone proposes a law in the assembly of the people, what is being asked of them is not exactly whether they approve the proposition or reject it, but whether or not it is in conformity with the general will, which is theirs: every man in casting his vote gives his opinion on the above question and from a combination of the votes is extracted the declaration of the general will. *So when the opinion contrary to my own carries the day, that proves only that I was wrong, and that what I took to be the general will was not.* If my particular opinion had carried the day, I would have acted against my true wishes; and then I would not have been free.

Rousseau, *Du contrat social*,
pp. 93–4, Editor's italics

198   An account of the fall of Robespierre by the *conventionnel* Dyzez, 11 thermidor year II (29 July 1794)

To Laffitte, executive officer of the district administration at Saint-Sever:

Robespierre has gone to join Camille Desmoulins. He was guillotined yesterday with Saint-Just, Le Bas, and Couthon, who will not be going to our department, you can tell Besselère.

The speeches Couthon made at the Jacobin Club against certain members of the Convention had already antagonized people. For a month Robespierre had not attended the meetings of the Committee of Public Safety and this antagonized people more. Finally the speech he delivered against the two committees on the 8th [thermidor] brought dissatisfaction to the most extreme degree. The evening session at the Jacobin Club was the culmination. In it, Collot d'Herbois was mocked and Robespierre alone triumphed.

On the 9th, an attack on him was led by Tallien, whose head was almost touching the guillotine. Robespierre asked for the floor in order to reply; he called us all assassins because the floor was given to another first, for he was to have it next. His brother joined with him. The assembly, already very irritated, enacted the decree for his arrest. Here is what went wrong: the committees of Public Safety and General Security, charged with carrying it out, delivered the accused persons to men who, having been unable to get the Luxembourg opened, took the prisoners to the Commune. All the friends and favourites of Robespierre were there. They embraced each other, sounded the tocsin; the people gathered; 30 cannon bristled in the avenues off the place de Grève. All this was going on, and in the evening, at seven o'clock, when we went to the Convention, nobody knew anything about it. We had been saying trivial things from the rostrum for almost an hour, when suddenly we were told that the Committee on General Security had been forcibly entered and that [Hanriot] the chief of the National Guard and 17 of his adjutants, who had been held there under arrest, were freed. If Hanriot had then moved against us, only two steps away, we would have been lost. If Robespierre, instead of having fun drawing up orders at the Hôtel de Ville, had marched at the head of the eight or ten thousand men who filled the place de Grève, and if with Couthon's help he had aroused the people by his speeches, we would have been lost; but destiny decided otherwise. We finally had the sense to take some measures instead of declaiming to one another that we had to die at our post.

Robespierre was abandoned, and he is no more!

It is too bad, for the republic, that this event can be counted among the great events. The death of one man in a free state ought to make no commotion. We shall now have to wait several days to know what course events will take. I very much wish it were clear that we knew how to take advantage of liberty and that passions would cool.

Salut et Fraternité.

Richard T. Bienvenu (ed.), *The Ninth of Thermidor: The Fall of Robespierre* (1968), pp. 234–5. Copyright Oxford University Press, reprinted by permission

|6|

The Thermidorian reaction

Robespierre's colleagues in the Committee of Public Safety did not intend his fall to be the signal for a political reaction but this occurred because it was no longer possible to sustain a terrorist regime after the great French victory at Fleurus on 25 June and the subsequent occupation of Brussels. *Gouvernement révolutionnaire* was progressively dismantled: price controls were abandoned, the law of general police repealed (**199**) and the very use of the word *révolutionnaire* proscribed (**200**). The Committee of Public Safety survived as long as the Convention, which ended its session on 26 October 1795, but Larévellière-Lépeaux's description of its last weeks (**204**) shows *gouvernement révolutionnaire* in a state of complete decadence.

Levasseur in document **201** depicts the shifting political configurations which operated the reaction but, as he says, the Thermidorians merely registered a shift in the public mood: 'They studied public opinion in order to conform to it, and all their acts were the result of outside influence.' Moreover, the tone of politics during most of this period was set neither by the Men of Thermidor (the conspirators who had brought down Robespierre), nor (a slightly different thing) by the Thermidorians who assumed power, but by the Girondin survivors – the 'seventy-three' who were rehabilitated on 8 December, and those of the 'twenty-two' who had escaped the guillotine, such as Louvet and Isnard, on 8 March following. They resumed their seats on the right where they carried more authority than ex-terrorists such as Tallien.

The Girondins had the last word and, of them, more truly than of the restored Bourbons, it may be said that they forgot nothing and forgave nothing: leading Montagnard deputies were guillotined or deported, *sans-culotte* leaders in the sections were disarmed and persecuted in various ways; economic regulation was abandoned and inflation took a devastating toll; but, above all, Girondin influence is to be seen in the constitution of the year III (**202** and **203**), the last to be drafted by the Convention and the only one to be implemented. Many of its provisions directly reflected the experiences and sufferings of the Girondins. Thus public access to parliamentary debates was limited (articles 64 and 66), provision was made to change the place of residence of the legislature (articles 102–9) and the department was strengthened and the district abolished, as Thibaudeau observes, 'almost for the sole reason given by Boissy that the departmental authorities had always been for the maintenance of the established order and the district authorities against'.

By setting to work on drafting a constitution as soon as they had recovered power, the Girondins showed their concern to restore the rule of law. But free elections might well have returned a royalist majority and the constitution might have been used to vote away the constitution – as Saint-Just had said of the constitution of 1793, '*on l'immolerait par elle-même*'. Accordingly, in the last weeks of its life, the Convention, which was rapidly acquiring all the characteristics of a rump, passed the notorious law of two-thirds which forced the electorate to return two-thirds of the members of the Convention to the new legislature. This decree fatally marred the inception of the new constitution and set an example that the Directory followed on 18 fructidor of the year V when it annulled the elections because of their royalist complexion.

199 Repeal of the law of 27 germinal, 18 frimaire year III (8 December 1794)

Bourdon (de l'Oise): I am here in the name of the Committees of Legislation, Public Safety and General Security to propose that you repeal the law of 27 germinal on the general police of the republic. (Loud applause.) Everyone knows that the men against whom this law was directed have been treated with inconceivable barbarity; because without having been judged to be suspects by the *comités révolutionnaires* of Paris – whom, assuredly, no one will accuse of being soft – they were obliged to leave Paris.

The aim of the man who dictated this law is easy to imagine and notes written in his hand leave no doubt that he intended to raise his tyranny on the bodies of those who were formerly called the first two classes and the intermediary class. In sending all the former nobles away from Paris, he was depriving the citizens of that city who worked for them of their livelihood. Also, he was designating the men he wanted to destroy and increasing the indigent class, that is to say the army of the 40 sous.[1] Your committees, mindful of the motives which inspire you, thought that it was appropriate that on the day when you were recalling your colleagues [the 73 who had protested at the expulsion of the 22 prominent Girondins] you should repeal the law of 27 germinal in order to demonstrate to the people that you do not want to be just only towards your colleagues but towards all citizens. (Loud applause.)

---

1 On 5 September 1793 the Convention had voted to pay needy *sans-culottes* 40 sous for each meeting of their section that they attended.

One of my colleagues has told me that representatives of the people have issued decrees pursuant to this law; I ask that they be annulled.

Garner (de Saintes): It is in your hearts to fill the measure of justice that has been proposed to you. I observed some days ago that on the morrow of the law of 27 germinal the Committee of Public Safety had ordered all former nobles living in the maritime towns of the Vendée to remove themselves to a distance of 20 leagues; they are farmers for the most part who have never been suspect to anyone. I ask that this decree also be repealed.

Montmayau: It is not enough to repeal the law of 27 germinal, we must also establish equality. This law was contrary to equality because it conferred patents of nobility – I am referring to the passes taken by those who were obliged to leave Paris: I demand that they be abolished as well.

Bourdon (de l'Oise): This amendment was proposed yesterday at the joint meeting of the three committees and it was withdrawn as unnecessary. We no longer recognize nobility in France (applause) and it would be a mark of weakness to imagine that a miserable police pass could ever rival the sovereign will of the French people. I ask for the order of the day on account of the law which abolishes all distinctions (applause).

The order of the day was voted.
The other proposals were decreed. . . .

Réimpression de l'Ancien Moniteur (31 vols., 1863–70), vol. XXII, pp. 699–700

200 The abolition of the word *révolutionnaire*, decree of 24 prairial year III (12 June 1795)

On the report of the Committee of General Security, the National Convention decrees that no constituted authority will be called *révolutionnaire* and that those called *comités révolutionnaires* will henceforth simply be called 'surveillance committees' throughout the republic.

Mautouchet, *Gouvernement révolutionnaire*, p. 372

201 Thermidorian politics: extract from the memoirs of Levasseur

Antoine Louis Levasseur, 1746–1820, a lawyer, was a deputy to the Legislative Assembly and the National Convention, where he voted for the death of the king. After 9 thermidor he was a member of the Committee of General Security.

We have arrived at the moment when the Revolution, having reached its apogee, is going to turn back. It was time no doubt for the revolutionary regime to cease, but for the principles of the Revolution to lose nothing thereby, it had to be stopped by its own children ... a Danton or a Robespierre. ... It was not so. To consummate the resolution of 9 thermidor, its authors addressed themselves to all the parties, even to the men who, after 31 May [1793], had become the enemies of the republic: their fatal support made of 9 thermidor a veritable reaction. ...

We saw a coalition, composed of the most disparate elements, overturn Robespierre's party. It was impossible to foresee what would be the result of a victory won by such a coalition. Let us cast a glance at the various parties which composed the improvised alliance of 8 thermidor, and let us see what were the relations which were established after Robespierre's fall, in order to understand better the great struggle which remains to us to describe, and the odious reactions which bloodied it. ...

What must be noticed above all is that the Thermidorians had placed themselves at the head of the warmest partisans of 31 May [1793]; that they had joined powerfully in the impulse to the anarchical movement which had carried us so far; that nearly all of them had taken an active part in the government of the Terror; that most of them had been on missions in the departments, and there had given themselves over to reprehensible acts which they later wanted to cast on their adversaries. Thus Bordeaux was still terrified by the memory of Tallien's power, thus Marseilles and Toulon were reeking of the blood spilled by Barras and Fréron ...

The Committee of Public Safety had joined with the Dantonists to effect 9 thermidor, and in the first days which followed, Billaud, Collot and their friends seemed to move in accord with the Thermidorians; we shall soon see what causes divided them; around them were grouped those old proconsuls who, recalled by Robespierre because of their excesses, had joined the conspirators of 9 thermidor for fear of seeing the anarchical movement stop; around them were grouped likewise the remnants of the Hébertist party, who thought they would find more support among them than among the friends of Danton. Yet, I repeat, the party of the Committee of Public Safety long marched in accord with the Thermidorians, and if they divided later, it was only after circumstances that neither group had been able to foresee. Close to these men, already so little in agreement between them, began to appear the members of the old right wing, who, annihilated by the revolution of 31 May, had seen their salvation in the disagreements of the Mountain, and its resulting enfeeblement. These deputies were joined by old Mountaineers, like Thibaudeau, Chambacérès, Siéyès, who had at first rallied to us in the hope of seeing an energetic impulse given to the government of the republic, and who had since become weary of the republican energy from seeing the excesses which had disfigured it.

There still existed, at that time, another party which had not been the last to wish for the fall of the decemvirs' tyranny, and which by its vigour had powerfully served to limit the result of 9 thermidor. This party was the true and constant Mountaineers. Lecointre of Versailles, Ruamps, Duhem had been the first to come out against Robespierre, and had contributed with all their might to strike down his sinister dictatorship; but it was to the advantage of liberty that they had wanted to turn the catastrophe of 9 thermidor. They were not slow to perceive that they had been mistaken. As for me, who, like my colleagues, had been sorry to see the power delegated by us to the Committee of Public Safety degenerate into dictatorship, on learning at Namur, where I was then on mission, of the fall of the triumvirs, my first emotion was joy, but on learning which men had become influential in the Convention, my joy was quickly changed into grief. The deputies who had taken control were, for the most part, men without principles, ambitious mercenaries; with what sadness, good God, did I see my country's destiny entrusted to such hands!

I have used the term 'parties' for the various nuances of opinion which divided the Convention after 9 thermidor; but these various opinions were still far from forming what we call parties; they concealed within them seeds of discord which had not sprouted. ... Each of the nuances of opinion that I have made known had a decided aim that it wanted to have triumph at any price: the Committee of Public Safety wanted to keep power and continue without Robespierre the system that Robespierre had made triumphant. The Thermidorians wanted to get power; the Girondins wanted to recall their proscribed colleagues, and substitute for the constitution of '93 the constitution contemplated by Guadet and Vergniaud and their ilk. The moderate faction of the Mountain desired, at any price, order, calm, and peace. Finally, the pure Mountaineers, satisfied to have done justice to the dictatorship, desired to lose nothing of the revolutionary energy and, while restoring the forms of order and justice too long forgotten, to keep nevertheless the redoubtable stance towards our enemies that had already made us victorious so many times. ... The Thermidorians had no fixed opinions, no settled doctrines. They studied public opinion in order to conform to it, and all their acts were the result of outside influence. Thus, when it was clear that moderation was the general desire, they paraded moderation; Fréron even preached clemency with the same impetuosity of character that he had used to maintain severity. ... With such men a reaction was imminent. Yet their former political relations and the part they had taken in the bloody acts of the Terror stopped them for some time on the counter-revolutionary descent which sooner or later was to sweep them along. But when the opinion of the middle classes was strongly manifested, when above all the advances of the old Girondins proved to them that in politics everything is forgiven to success, they put themselves at the head of the reaction; their speeches, their journals, their acts were no longer anything but a long series of accusations against their former acts and their former speeches. They condemned themselves in the person of their former friends. They dared even more, they organized battalions of young men who, on the pretext of avenging the memory of victims of the Terror, committed in their turn unpardonable excesses. Enrolled under the name of Fréron's gilded youth, dressed with a refined elegance that caused the people to call them *muscadins* [fops], these young men spread about in the streets and public squares, dominating by physical force, insulting the patriots, and finally making their atrocious vengeance the successor to the vengeance of the *sans-culottes* with pikes and wooden shoes, whom they had in some sort replaced.

In addition, with the era of the reaction began the era of corruption; to the fierce loyalty of the Mountaineers succeeded the Thermidorian frivolity which was only too reminiscent of the monarchical French character and the shameful customs which have forever blighted the regency period. The Mountaineers had professed simplicity in clothing, frugality, austere probity; the reactionaries on the contrary paraded a desire for dressiness, for a brazen luxury, and for pleasure-seeking, altogether opposed to the republican genius. Everywhere we saw sumptuous repasts, balls, private festivals reappear, and there the enemies of the Revolution hastened to go; intrigue reappeared everywhere and with it women's influence on public affairs; beauty again became a corrupting power, and Madame Tallien was, so to speak, associated in government on the new Committee of Public Safety. Little by little the former aristocracy, which had claimed to be ruined by the requisitions and the revolutionary taxes, advertised aloud its splendour and opulence; the Thermidorians and the Girondins accepted admission in the salons of the Saint-Germain suburb, and lost there that republican ruggedness which had once rendered them incorruptible: good style became fashionable, and more than one man sacrificed his conscience to the desire to see linked to his name the epithet 'well-bred'. It is deplorable no doubt to have to take account of such puerile facts; it is certain, however, that they had the greatest influence on the last acts of the Revolution; I blush to recall that lamentable influence, but truth forces me to make it known.

I must also recall a truly shameful circumstance of the saturnalia which succeeded the reign of the inflexible republicans. Amid those balls which seemed to have become the principal occupation of people once admirable for their virtues, there was one above all which was the rage, and which future generations will not be able to believe. They established in the Saint-Germain suburb a dancing society which called itself the Victims' Ball. To be admitted to it, one had to prove membership in a family of which some member had perished on the scaffold. Such were the men who accused us of immorality! . . .

Bienvenu, *The Ninth of Thermidor*, pp. 332–6. Copyright Oxford University Press, reprinted by permission

202 The drafting of the constitution of the year III, from the memoirs of Thibaudeau, a member of the constitutional *commission des onze*

There was a monarchical party in the *commission des onze*. It consisted of Lesage d'Eure-et-Loire, Boissy d'Anglas and Lanjuinais. I omit old Durand-Maillane whose opinion was discounted. But for all that they were not supporters of the Bourbons – though Boissy d'Anglas was the object of some suspicions which I did not myself share. Subsequent events clarified these suspicions. The other members of the commission were republicans in good faith.

The commission decided unanimously to set aside the constitution of 1793. Accordingly it was taken rather as a starting point than as a basis for discussion. Many jurisconsults – some self-styled – brought along their ideas and projects. Roederer was distinguished from the rest and admitted to our meetings. Discussions were amicable and deliberations calm. We tried to find a middle way between a monarchical and a demagogic system. . . . I shall merely recall some of the principal provisions – modified, moreover, by the Convention in several respects – which show our opinions and intentions.

Declaration of Rights

Lesage d'Eure-et-Loire and Creuzé-Latouche did not want one because it would give rise to misinterpretations and be a source of dissension and anarchical agitation. These opinions did not carry the day. It was thought to remedy these disadvantages by a sort of commentary or antidote with the title 'Declaration of Duties'.

To avoid re-opening debate in the primary assemblies on the form of government, the republic, we adopted this formula: the French republic is one and indivisible instead of the following one which had been proposed: the French people constitute themselves as a republic.

Size of the country

The question was raised whether the legislature would have the right to annex or cede territory. The point was of capital importance. Some wanted to give this power only to a Convention, others only to the people themselves. We called to mind all the crimes with which the thirst for conquest had sullied the name of Rome and the death-blows which it had dealt to her liberty. We seemed to fear that one day the same cause would produce the same effects in France. The majority of the commission wanted to prevent this scourge. But at the same time, Belgium had already been incorporated into France: we could not and would not abandon it. On the contrary we wanted to consecrate this union by means of the constitution. We coveted the left bank of the Rhine and the theory of natural frontiers had many advocates in the Convention. We therefore left this important question undecided and took things as they were without giving further thought to the future. We maintained the unit of the department and replaced the district with large municipalities and municipal administrations almost for the sole reason given by Boissy that the departmental authorities had always been for the maintenance of the established order and the district authorities against. He cited 20 June 1792 and 31 May 1793. He added that the district authorities had been agents of the Terror. Although the fact was true, the conclusion drawn from it was nonetheless unsound.

Exercise of political rights

Some, such as Lesage and Lanjuinais wanted to impose as a condition payment of taxation [this was in fact the recommendation of the commission and was embodied in the constitution]; Baudin, that of being able to read and write; the rest, to allow equality its widest application. This opinion prevailed.

Legislature

The Constituent Assembly had, by rejecting the creation of two chambers, introduced an innovation which went against the principles of the greatest constitutional theorists as consecrated by the example of England and the still more recent one of the United States of America. This experiment had been unfortunate because there was no denying that it had helped precipitate the fall of the monarchy. The commission did not claim to be wiser than the founders of the American republic: the Convention had been enlightened by its own experience; the bicameral system was accordingly adopted almost unanimously. Only Berlier was not of this opinion. We called them the Senate and the Chamber of Representatives. As the word 'senate' had an aristocratic sound, the Convention called one of the chambers the Council of Five Hundred (from the number of its members) and the other the Council of Ancients (after its age qualification). All property and taxatory qualifications were rejected; there was no other distinction than that of age which was regarded as a sufficient guarantee of maturity and wisdom because there was no motive of supremacy or aristocracy behind making this division of the legislature. Baudin said that the Chamber of Representatives would be the imagination and the Senate the reason of the nation. He only wanted 40 members to represent this reason. It was objected that this number would have neither sufficient dignity nor weight. It was decided that the two chambers would be made up of 750 members, despite Lesage and Lanjuinais who found this number too large. This was precisely the number of the members of the Convention.

The executive power

Baudin and Daunou wanted two chief magistrates or biennial consuls, one of whom would govern during the first year and the other during the second. Lesage, Lanjuinais and Durand-Maillane wanted one annual president; the rest a council of at least three members. In the end we opted for five. Everyone went for such and such a number in proportion to his hopes or fears of anything which might bring back the monarchy. The way in which the executive power should be chosen received very serious attention. There were really only two options: direct (or indirect) election by the people or else by the legislative. The latter won the day. Louvet feared that otherwise the primary assemblies or their delegates for the election might one day choose a Bourbon. The majority was swayed by the fear that the executive would be too powerful if it derived its authority from popular election. We then turned to giving the executive safeguards. Lesage proposed that it be inviolable. This notion was incompatible with the republican nature of the government. It was not supported. But responsibility was hedged about with limitations, or at least that was the intention. On another head, the executive power was removed from any part in legislation and the nomination of the departmental authorities was attributed to the people. Several members of the commission found this illogical but the people had exercised this right and we did not dare deprive them of it. We carefully considered whether meetings of the departmental council should be public and, whilst rejecting this, decided that a copy of the register of their resolutions should be open to every citizen.

Residence of the legislature

To ensure its independence, it was proposed to place it outside Paris. I was of this opinion. Experience had rightly led to a fear of the influence of the capital. To this it was objected that the disturbances which had shaken it belonged to a time of revolution and that a constitutional government would be able to prevent them; that it would destroy Paris, that her population would decline, that the arts would suffer in consequence, that to abandon the city would be weakness, that the *chouans*[2] would seize it,

2 The royalist rebels of the west. Alternatively, the passage could be translated: 'royalism would take hold'.

etc. I did not consider these arguments very convincing. I replied that under a constitutional regime the police would have even less power than under the *gouvernement révolutionnaire* to prevent the commotions of a great population which it was always easy to stir up; that apart from the disturbances inherent in republics, for a long time yet France would be exposed to the dog-fights between the factions which the Revolution had created and agitated by the manoeuvres of royalists and demagogues; that the latter would have dangerous auxiliaries in the *faubourgs* and the former in the salons where the aristocracy corrupted republican morality with its principles, its luxury and every kind of seduction; that the capital would not lose much by being deprived of the presence of an unostentatious government; that it had certainly prospered under the government of the kings, who did not reside there; that were we merely to establish the legislature at Versailles and leave the executive power in Paris, that would suffice to prevent the National Assembly from being interrupted, invaded and effectively dissolved as had happened several times to the National Convention; finally that even if this arrangement were to put an end to the ever-increasing growth of the capital and even to diminish it, I should regard this merely as a fortunate outcome for the rest of France. The question remained undecided. It was agreed not to discuss the matter further. The Council of Ancients was merely given the right to change the venue of the legislature as it saw fit.

Boissy, the reporter of the commission, presented the draft constitution to the Convention on 5 messidor.

Thibaudeau, *Mémoires*, vol. I, pp. 179–86

203　Larévellière-Lépaux on the constitution of the year III

Louis-Marie de Larévellière-Lépaux, 1753–1824, was a lawyer and a deputy to the Estates-General and National Convention. He defended the Girondins after 31 May, was outlawed, went into hiding and returned to the Convention on 8 December 1794, becoming a member of the Committee of Public Safety the following year and later a Director and protector of the sect of theophilanthropy.

Many thinkers, Frenchmen and foreigners, have regarded the constitution of the year III as theoretically the best in existence. Its short duration was principally due to the circumstances that attended its birth ... and prevented it from being perfected. Before it could achieve a certain degree of stability, which time alone can confer on political institutions, it was assailed with the utmost violence by factions at home and intrigues abroad. Europe in arms was leagued against it and all the means of governing in the midst of this fearful tempest still had to be created. To this, admittedly, must be added vices which would have had to be corrected. The executive power was too weak and it had no legal means of defending itself. Thus the legislative body could, and did, demolish the constitution piecemeal and subjugate or even annihilate the Executive Directory without the latter's having any legal powers of resistance. To defend the constitution and to defend themselves, the Directors had to employ force, as on 18 fructidor, and in the process the constitution was itself violated and lost the greater part of its own force. Otherwise they were obliged to submit to unconstitutional and illegal decrees, as on 30 prairial of the year VII, when they tolerated the expulsion of their colleague Treilhard. Then the executive power was subjected to the despotic wishes of the legislative body and soon destroyed.

The members of the Executive Directory could not be present at legislative committees and that was well; what, in my opinion, was less so was that the ministers could not be present either because they alone were capable of informing the committees about the true state of affairs. Often, out of ignorance, deputies could, with the best of intentions, propose and carry measures which were not in the public interest. To prevent such great drawbacks, Daunou and Lanjuinais proposed to give the Executive Directory a veto. But, as I have already said, people were still too impassioned; this salutary measure was opposed and I have to reproach myself with having been one of its opponents.

Mémoires de Larévellière-Lépaux, re-ed. R. David d'Angers (3 vols., 1895), vol. I, pp. 237–8

204 Larévellière-Lépaux's account of the last weeks of the Committee of Public Safety

When the work of the *commission des onze* had been completed, we – that is Daunou and myself – were appointed to the Committee of Public Safety. The trident was placed in his hands; I was given the task of ending the civil strife that was devastating the western departments. This was at the end of the year III. At this period the Convention was no longer the formidable assembly it had been. ... Now it was nothing but a drifting crowd, a shapeless mass formed of the disjointed remnants of all the parties which had in turn risen and fallen in its midst. The state of the Convention faithfully reflected that of France. The Committee of Public Safety, the real heart of the state, the only centre around which one could rally, which alone could integrate and impart motion to the whole, had itself fallen into a state of complete disintegration. Although I had already been warned of this deplorable state of affairs, when I beheld it in the Committee itself I imagined that I was descending into the tomb and burying myself under the ruins of France. I experienced the cruellest anguish which can be felt by a sincere lover of his country when he sees it rushing to the abyss.

Each member of the Committee devoted his time then exclusively to his own affairs and those of his friends and supporters. The only part he played in administration was to appoint someone, or arrange for someone else to be paid money which, rightly or wrongly, he was claiming, etc. Each member was specifically assigned a governmental department. He ran it as he pleased; only his correspondence, to give it an official character, had to be signed by two other members. But, as I have already said, it was not with administration that they concerned themselves. In addition, the lack of co-ordination in the Committee was paralleled by the independent, isolated activity of the administrative commissions which functioned as they would or as they could. I say as they could, because to obtain two signatures in order to give them orders or reply to them was a very difficult matter for those members of the Committee who would nevertheless have liked to continue working amidst this chaos. Often one had to wait several days for these two signatures. These men who spent their time entirely in petty intrigues were too burdened with affairs to give their signatures and when we pressed them, Daunou and I, observing that a name is soon written, they objected that they did not want to sign anything without having read it, which was fair enough. But to pretend that they hadn't time! . . . We shall presently see what use they made of this precious commodity. Here is a typical day in the Committee of Public Safety at the time of my entry. It was the same to the end which happily was not far distant.

Cambacérès was its chairman. He arrived about 10 in the morning. Then he would walk up and down the council chamber, constantly summoning Pierre, the head of the Committee's secretariat, to ask him either nothing or the same thing several times in order to hear the delicious sound of these words 'citizen-president', which singularly flattered his vanity, ringing in his ears as often as possible. When one thinks of all the puerile vanities which have covered this highly intelligent and talented man with ridicule I will not be accused of exaggeration here [Cambacérès was subsequently duc de Parme and chancellor under the Empire]. His first preoccupation was to have a good *pot-au-feu* set up and excellent bread and wine put on the table, three things that were scarcely to be found anywhere else in Paris but here. 'My principle', he would tell us, 'is that men given up to toil both in the Assembly and the Committee ought to be provided with good restoratives, otherwise they would succumb under the weight of their labours' – a principle that was eagerly put to good use. The various members of the Committee appeared in turn between noon and two o'clock. On entering the council chamber they would say: 'Anything new, President?' 'Why, no', was the most usual reply. Thereupon the new arrival would inspect the *pot-au-feu*, administer himself some broth, take the joint of beef from the pot and serve himself a good slice which he would eat with good white bread and wash down with excellent burgundy; then he would put the hissing joint back in the pot until the succession of arrivals had reduced the latecomers to justify the proverb *tarde venientibus ossa*. Having thus satisfied his stomach he would go down to his own department to busy himself with private affairs and secret interests. Thus was concluded the work of the morning and of the day.

However, the evening, which lends itself to reflection, would reawaken anxiety for the morrow. About 9 or 10 o'clock, people re-assembled in the council chamber and everyone forthwith tried to get through decisions favourable to himself and his friends. As for general affairs, if the citizen-president brought something up people immediately exclaimed: 'Oh! President, human endurance is limited. It is impossible to sustain one's concentration for such long periods. Settle the matter yourself; you have our confidence.' And despite our most strenuous insistence, Daunou and I found it impossible to engage a discussion on the most important matters. Nevertheless two essential matters held our attention for a few minutes each evening because our heads would depend on them in the morning. These two matters were food supplies and money. 'Ah! now, President', they would always say with great anxiety, 'the finances, how are they?' . . . 'Oh! the *assignats* continue to tumble alarmingly', replied the citizen-president, 'and we won't be able to print enough during the night to cover essential payments tomorrow. By God! if this lasts any longer we risk being strung up.' Then profound terror was painted on every face. 'Oh! my God! how awful, President!' exclaimed several suppliant voices, 'go along then to Hourier-Eloi's office (he was the member of the Committee of Public Safety in charge of finance) and tell him that we beseech him at least to keep us going for 15 or 18 days. Then the Executive Directory will be in place to make what shift it can.' During the ten minutes or so Cambacérès was away, we abandoned ourselves to the most sombre reflections. On his return he promised that Eloi would do what he could and we took some comfort from this reply. 'But food supplies!' they resumed, 'do we have anything for tomorrow?' 'Oh! . . . I know nothing about that but I'll send someone to look for our colleague Roux who will give us the latest news on that front.'

Roux (de la Marne) was an ex-*procureur* of a Benedictine monastery, a fat, short, rotund man with big red cheeks. He had sufficient talents to run the affairs of a religious community successfully and to maintain good cheer in abundance. But he was surely far from being equipped to run France's food supplies at this period. Nevertheless, he had the highest conception of his own skill. In other respects he was a very nice chap but he gave himself a great air of importance and was encumbered solely by the weight of his own glory. For the rest, he was, I repeat, a good, straightforward lad and endowed with one incontestable merit which was especially valuable at this time: the ability to speak for an indefinite period of time. What happened was that when two or three thousand women from the *faubourgs* – swelled by an enormous collection of every kind of malcontent and incited by the heads of factions – came to the Committee of Public

Safety to demand bread, threatening to strangle all the members of the Committee (often repeated threats), we sent them to Roux, representative of the people with responsibility for food supplies. Roux's department and his own office were in the eaves of the Tuileries. They were reached by means of an extremely long, steep and narrow staircase. When the head of the column reached the highest steps, Roux left his office, appeared on the landing of his staircase, halted the crowd, requested silence and, whether he obtained it or not, from the height of this pulpit he began a sermon whose length might be three, four or six hours – and longer if need be depending on the petitioners' perseverance in standing there. Interruptions, shouts, threats, all were powerless to arrest the flood of this torrent which overflowed with an eloquence seasoned with all the ceaselessly repeated clichés of this period. In the end, stunned, worn out with fatigue, their bellies full of empty promises instead of bread, these wretched women gradually filed away, the men dispersed, and when all this multitude had been reduced to a small number, Roux dismissed the rest of these good wives with the exhortation to take back to their families peace and hope and above all to report to them in full the blessed and ceaseless efforts of their representatives to restore plenty to the good citizens and to thwart the tricks of the enemy. One day in germinal he harangued a vast crowd from eight or nine in the morning to five or six in the evening and in this way he saved the Convention several times from very serious insurrections.

Such, then, was the representative Roux. Invited, as I said, to come down to our council chamber, he would enter all out of breath and always very pleased with himself and his measures. 'All right, Roux, my friend', Cambacérès would say without more ado, 'our colleagues are worried about the state of food supplies. Where do we stand with those for Paris tomorrow?' 'Still the same abundance, Citizen President', Roux replied with an air of jubilation and triumph which scarcely prepared us for the rest of his reply. 'Still the two ounces of bread per man, at least in most sections!' 'Oh! devil take you!' replied Cambacérès with his Gascon accent, 'you'll have our heads off with your abundance!' For all that Roux returned to his office no less satisfied than if he had had all the grain of Africa and Sicily at his disposal in Paris. For their part the group in the Committee fell into profound consternation for a few moments. But soon a luminous thought lifted this dark cloud. It was promptly dispelled by the following exchange: 'President, have you anything ready for us at the buffet? After exhausting days like these we really must restore our strength.' 'But of course. There's a fine loin of veal, a large turbot, a big pastry and something else of the kind.' Then farewell cares, farewell fear for the morrow! The most lively high spirits succeeded dejection and fear and they gaily saved the country whilst stuffing their guts with succulent dishes and gulping down champagne; and the good cheer was seasoned with good jokes.

The reader will recall the frequent reference of matters by the Assembly to the combined committees of Public Safety, Legislation[3] and General Security. On such occasions these latter committees would be announced at about 11 o'clock or midnight; both halves of the door were opened to receive them and the Committee, gathered round the buffet, would be apprised; but it was difficult to drag even a few members away. The reporter of the Committee specifically responsible for the matter which had necessitated the joint session would give the gist in a couple of words. 'I have examined the papers', he would add, 'those are my conclusions.' 'That's fine', was the unanimous reply. 'Now let's move over.' This influx of revellers revived flagging appetites and gave new life to thirsts which were ready to give out. It was new sustenance for the merry talk which went on until three or four in the morning. Daunou and I and perhaps a few others of our colleagues never had to reproach ourselves with taking part in these sacrilegious feasts, neither those in the morning nor those at night. . . .

Just before daybreak they would leave the buffet and get into their carriages to be driven home. As for myself, I lurked in some corner waiting for the opportunity of getting some signatures I needed as they were leaving; these were sometimes easier to obtain because of the good mood induced by the meal. But I would send my coachman home early (several carriages had been put at the disposal of the Committee of Public Safety) and I proceeded through the night alone to my small apartment in the rue Copeau. My wife, dying with anxiety, was constantly on the lookout and she would only begin to breath again when she heard the ferrule of my little cane tapping on the pavement.

I swear that I am not exaggerating and that I am giving the truth, completely unadulterated. However, although this picture of the Committee of Public Safety at that time should be kept for historical accuracy and for its insights into the human heart, I must make the observation, in justification of its members, that they should not be judged too severely. The ferocity of the terrorist Committee of Public Safety and its *gouvernement révolutionnaire* was bound to lead gradually to total laxity in the one that succeeded it. Most of its members were honest, well-meaning men and we should not lay the blame for this state of affairs on their hearts or minds. This apathy, this lack of co-ordination, this letting things go their way, was the necessary result of three years of provisional government, disturbed by the most horrifying convulsions which could shake a nation and by a series of reactions which had necessarily disorganized everything. Raging fever is always succeeded by utter exhaustion.

Mémoires de Larévellière-Lépaux,
vol. I, pp. 245–55

---

3 In the Thermidorian period, the powers of the Committee of Legislation were expanded to counter-balance those of the other two committees.

Further Reading

General

Blanning, T. C. W. *The French Revolution: Class War or Culture Clash*, second edition (Basingstoke, 1998)
Bosher, J. F. *French Public Finances, 1770–1795* (Cambridge, 1970)
Cobban, A. *A History of Modern France*, vol. 1: *1715–1795*, revised edition (Harmondsworth, 1990)
Croker, J. W. *Essays on the Early Period of the French Revolution* (London, 1856)
de Tocqueville, A. *The Ancien Régime and the French Revolution* (London, 1976)
Forrest, A. *The Revolution in Provincial France: Aquitaine, 1789–99* (Oxford, 1996)
Furet, F. *Interpreting the French Revolution* (Cambridge, 1981)
Goodwin, A. *The French Revolution*, revised edition (London, 1963)
Hampson, N. *A Social History of the French Revolution* (London, 1963)
Hardman, J. *Louis XVI* (London and New Haven, 1993)
Roberts, J. M. *The French Revolution*, second edition (London, 1997)
Sutherland, D. *France 1789–1815* (London, 1985)

Part I

Barnave, A. P. J. M. *Introduction to the French Revolution*, trans. E. Chill as *Power, Property and History* (New York, 1971)
Doyle. W. 'The Parlements of France and the Breakdown of the Old Regime, 1770–88', *French Historical Studies* 6 (1970), pp. 415–59
Doyle. W. *The Origins of the French Revolution* (Oxford, 1980)
Egret, J. *The French Pre-Revolution*, trans. W. D. Camp (Chicago, 1977)
Godechot, J. *The Taking of the Bastille* (London, 1970)

Hardman, J. *French Politics 1774–1789: From the Accession of Louis XVI to the Fall of the Bastille* (London and New York, 1995)
Lefebvre, G. *The Coming of the French Revolution* (Princeton, 1957)

Part II

Arnaud-Boutteloupe, J. *Le rôle politique de Marie-Antoinette* (Paris, 1924)
Hampson, N. *Prelude to Terror: The Constituent Assembly and the Failure of Consensus, 1789–91* (Oxford, 1988)
Mitchel, C. J. *The French Legislative Assembly of 1791* (New York, 1988)
Necker, J. *On the French Revolution* (London, 1797)
Thompson, E. *Popular Sovereignty and the French Constituent Assembly, 1785–91* (Manchester, 1952)
Vovelle, M. *The Fall of the French Monarchy, 1787–92* (Cambridge, 1989)

Part III

Baczko, B. *Ending the Terror: The French Revolution after Robespierre* (Oxford, 1994)
Brunel, F. *Thermidor: La chute de Robespierre* (Paris, 1989)
Gough, H. *The Terror in the French Revolution* (London, 1997)
Hampson, N. *The Life and Opinions of Maximilien Robespierre* (London, 1974)
Hardman, J. *Robespierre.* (London and New York, 1999)
Lucas, C. *The Structure of the Terror* (Oxford, 1973)
Lyons, M. *The Directory* (Cambridge, 1975)
Palmer, R. R. *The Year of the Terror: Twelve who Ruled France, 1793–1794* (Oxford, 1989)
Patrick, A. *The Men of the First French Republic* (Baltimore, 1972)
Rudé, G. *The Crowd in the French Revolution* (Oxford, 1959)
Soboul, A. *The Parisian Sans-Culottes in the French Revolution* (Oxford, 1964)
Sydenham, M. J. *The Girondins* (London, 1961)

Index

Achard, Jean Jacques, national agent of Lyon, 155, 167–8, 232–3
d'Agoult, Captain, 51, 52, 56–8
Aiguillon, Armand duc d', deputy, 108
d'Aligre, Etienne François, first president of Parlement, 3, 18–21, 26
Amar, Jean Baptiste André, 234–5
André, Antoine d', deputy, 108
Angiviller, Charles Claude de la Billarderie, comte d', 27, 48–9
Angran d'Allerai, Denis François, 26, 39–40
Artois, Charles Philippe, comte d' (later Charles X), 20, 39, 88, 97, 99
Assembly of Notables
    (1787), xvii, 25–48, 81
    (1788) 65, 66, 70
assignats, 134, 181–2, 215, 220, 251
Autichamp, marquis d', 105
Avertissement, l', 27, 40–42, 43, 69, 87, 93

Bailly, Jean Sylvain, deputy, Mayor of Paris, 89, 93, 95, 107–108, 198
Barbaroux, Charles Jean Marie, deputy, 159–60
Barentin, Charles de Paule de, keeper of the seals, 72–3, 88–90, 95–6, 98, 99, 100, 104, 106, 195
Barère, Bertrand, 177, 202, 208, 215, 223–4, 228
Barnave, Antoine Joseph Marie Pierre, deputy, 122

Barra and Viala, festival, 217, 235
Barras, Paul, vicomte de, deputy, 242
Baudin, Pierre Charles Louis, deputy, 246, 247
Belle-Isle, Charles Louis Auguste Foucquet, maréchal-duc de, 12–13.
Bernard, Jacques Claude, *sectionnaire*, 196
Bernis, François Joachim de Pierre, Cardinal de, 14
Bertin, Henri Léonard Jean Baptiste, minister, 19–20
Bertrand de Molleville, Antoine François, naval minister, 87, 92–3, 139–40
Besenval, Pierre Victoire, baron de, 90, 105–107
Billaud-Varenne, Jacques Nicolas, member of CSP, 151, 168, 189, 199, 201, 202, 228, 242
Biron, Antoine de Gontaut, duc de, 51–2, 56, 59, 61
Biron, Armand Louis de Gontaut, general, son of preceding, 163–4
Bo, Jean Baptiste Jérôme, deputy, 194
Boissy D'Anglas, François Antoine, 240, 245, 246, 248
Bouchotte, Jean Baptiste Noel, war minister, 199, 200, 212
Bouillé, François, marquis de, general, 14
Bourbon, Louis Henri Joseph, duc de, 69–71

Bourdon de l'Oise, François Louis,
  deputy, 199, 203, 217, 218, 234,
  240–41
Boze, Joseph, painter, 143–5
Breteuil, Louis Charles le Tonnelier,
  baron de, minister, 21, 22–4, 27,
  44, 51–2, 56–61
  second ministry, 90
  Louis XVI's plenipotentiary, 123,
  124, 126, 140
Brienne, Etienne Charles de Loménie
  de, principal minister, 27, 39,
  44–53, 62–3, 75, 81, 89, 196
  and Estates-General, 64, 66–71
Brissot, Jean Pierre, deputy, 141, 151,
  152, 153, 156–7, 198
Broglie, Victor François, maréchal-duc
  de, 90, 104–107
Brunswick, Karl Wilhelm Ferdinand,
  duke of, general, 157
Buchot, Philibert, commissioner for
  foreign affairs, 224
Buzot, François Nicolas Leonard,
  deputy, 159

cahiers de doléances, xvii, 75–84, 103,
  110
Calonne, Charles Alexandre de,
  controller general, 14, 18–49, 65,
  75, 81, 109, 215
Cambacérès, Jean Joseph Régis,
  deputy, 242, 250–53
Cambon, Pierre Joseph, deputy, 163–4
Campion, Robespierrist, 224
Carnot, Lazare Nicholas Marguerite,
  member of CSP, 214, 228
Carrier, Jean Baptiste, deputy, 231
Castillon, Le Blanc de, *parlementaire*,
  26, 39
Castries, Charles Gabrielle de la Croix,
  maréchal de, minister for marine,
  8, 14–15, 27, 28, 40–42, 47
Cazalès, Jacques Antoine Marie de,
  deputy, 127
Chalier, Marie Joseph, 'martyr', 217
Chapeaux-Palasne, Julien François,
  deputy, 92
Charles IV, King of Spain, 122
Charlier, Louis Joseph, 231
Châtelet, Louis Marc Florent, duc de,
  203
Chaumette, Pierre Gaspard, 199
Chérin, court genealogist, 184, 196

Choiseul, Etienne François, duc de,
  122, 123, 126–7
Clavière, Etienne, finance minister, 156
Clergy, 11, 71, 81, 96, 101, 112, 120
  Civil Constitution of, 109, 110–11,
  115–16, 124
  laws against refractory, 124, 140
Coigny, chevalier de, 97–8
Collot d'Herbois, Jean Marie, member
  of CSP, 154–5, 168–9, 189, 199,
  200, 201, 202, 216, 228, 237,
  242
Committee of Public Safety (CSP),
  185–8, 189, 190–94, 200–203,
  213–14, 228, 235–6, 248–53
Commune, 151, 156–7, 236–7
Condé, Louis Joseph, duc de, 69–71,
  97
Condorcet, Marie Jean Nicolas de
  Caritat, marquis de, deputy, 172,
  177
Constitution
  Fundamental Laws, 51, 55–6
  general, xvii, 1–4, 76–7, 99–100,
    114
  implementation deferred, 183, 186
  Jacobin, 172–82
  of the year III, 239–40, 245–9
Conti, Louis François, duc de, 69–71,
  97
Cordelier Club, 178–9, 210–12
Coster, Joseph François, Necker's
  premier commis, 93
Couthon, Georges Auguste, member of
  CSP, 155, 189, 207, 217, 230,
  231–32, 236, 237
Creuzet-Latouche, Jacques Antoine,
  deputy, 245
Crosne, Louis Thiroux de, lieutenant-
  general of police, 51, 56, 60–61,
  105
Custine, Adam Philippe, general, 163

Danton, Georges Jacques, minister,
  member of 'first' CSP, 152–3,
  154, 157, 158, 162, 169,
  199–212, 217, 242
Daunou, Pierre Claude François,
  deputy, 247, 249, 250, 251, 253
Dauphin
  first, 89
  second, 98, 144
David, Jacques Louis, painter, deputy,
  235

deficit, 10–11, 28, 42–3, 45
Dejoly, Etienne Louis, keeper of the
    seals, 145–7
Delacroix, Charles, deputy, 231
Delacroix, Jean François, deputy, 199,
    203
Desmoulins, Lucie Simplice Camille
    Benoît, 169, 183, 199–212, 237
Dubois, Georges, Cardinal, prime
    minister, 13
Duhem, Pierre Joseph, deputy, 231,
    243
Dumas, René François, president of
    Revolutionary Tribunal, 224
Dumouriez, Charles François, general,
    foreign minister, 142
Duplay, Maurice, juror, 155, 168, 214
Dupont de Nemours, Pierre Samuel, 7,
    10–12
Duport, Adrien, deputy, 122
Durand-Maillane, Pierre Toussaint,
    deputy, 245, 247
Duret, Cordelier, 173
Dyzez, Jean, deputy, 237–8

émigrés, 124, 138–9, 140, 180, 193
Enghien, Louis Antoine, duc d', 69–71
Eprémesnil, Jean Jacques Duval d',
    parlementaire, deputy, 51, 52,
    55–8, 94, 97–8, 108
Espagnac, Marc René d'Amarzit, *abbé*
    d', speculator, 49
Estaing, Charles Henri, comte d', 93
Estates-General, 50, 54, 55, 62,
    64–103

Fabre d'Eglantine, Philippe François
    Nazaire, deputy, 162, 199, 204
Faro, policeman, 234–5
Fersen, Axel count von, 125
feudal rights, 82, 83, 101, 102,
    abolished, 109, 111, 113
Flesselles, Jacques de, 181
Fleuriot-Lescot, Jean Baptiste Edmond,
    Mayor of Paris, 213, 217, 235
Fouché, Joseph, deputy, 217, 232–3
Foulon, Joseph François, junior
    minister, 108
Francis I, Holy Roman Emperor,
    141–2
Fréron, Louis Marie Stanislas, 242,
    243–4

Fréteau de Saint-Just, Emmanuel Marie
    Michel Philippe, *parlementaire*,
    53, 108

Garat, Joseph Dominique, minister,
    158–9, 167, 172, 199–200,
    201–202
Gatteau, Pierre Germain, 224
Gensonné, Armand, deputy, 143–5
George III, King of England, 123, 182
Goislard de Monsabert, Anne Louis,
    parlementaire, 51, 52, 58
Guadet, Marguerite Elie, deputy,
    143–5, 157, 159–60, 243
Guines, Adrien Louis de Bonnières, duc
    de, 84

Hanriot, François, commander of
    National Guard, 153, 161–2, 214,
    237
Harvelai, Joseph Micault d', keeper of
    royal treasury, 22
Hébert, Jacques René, 162, 169, 201,
    208, 209, 210–11, 228
Hector, naval officer, 16
Henri IV, 71
Henry VIII, King of England, 76
Hérault de Séchelles, Marie Jean,
    member of CSP, 177, 211
Herman, Martial Joseph Armand,
    commissioner for civil
    administration, 213, 224, 225,
    226, 228
Hourier-Eloi, Charles Antoine, deputy,
    251

intendants, 8, 27
Isnard, Maxim, deputy, 154, 162, 239

Jacobin Club(s), 92, 110, 123, 131–2,
    135–6, 137, 168–9, 210, 213,
    217, 233
Javogues, Claude, deputy, 189
Joly de Fleury, Jean François, finance
    minister, 11, 23, 24, 43
Joseph II, Holy Roman Emperor, 53,
    54
Jullien *fils*, Marc Antoine, agent of
    CSP, 224

La Fayette, Marie Jean Paul Motier,
    marquis de, deputy, commander
    of National Guard, 4, 94, 144

La Luzerne, César Henri de, minister of marine, 9–10, 16–17

Lameth, Alexandre de, deputy, xvi, 114, 122

Lamoignon, Chrétien François de, keeper of the seals, 27, 50–52, 59–60, 64–6, 68, 89, 99

Lanjuinais, Jean Denis, deputy, 245, 246, 247, 249

Lanthenas, François Xavier, 156

Larevéllière-Lépeaux, Louis Marie, 248–53

La Rochefoucauld, Dominique Cardinal de, 98

La Rochefoucauld, Louis Alexandre, duc de, deputy, 108, 121

La Rochefoucauld-Liancourt, François, duc de, deputy, 91, 121

La Tour du Pin-Gouvernet, Jean Frédéric de Paulin, comte de, deputy, 127

Laurent de Villedeuil, Pierre Charles, minister, 72, 84, 99

Lebas, Philippe, deputy, 218, 237

Le Chapelier, Isaac René Guy, 109–110, 116–17

Leclerc, Jean, Cordelier, 179, 182

Lecointre, Laurent, deputy, 243

Lefèvre d'Amécourt, Adrien, 18–23

Legendre, Louis, deputy, 204

Lenoir, Jean Claude, *conseiller d'état*, 10

Leopold II, Holy Roman Emperor, 124

Lesage, Denis Toussaint, 245, 246, 247

lettres de cachet, 65, 74, 77, 78, 102

Levasseur, Antoine Louis, deputy, 242–5

Lindet, Jean Baptiste Robert, member of CSP, 184–5, 207, 214

Louis XIV, 40, 181

Louis XV, 7, 9, 10, 18, 129

Louis XVI, Parts I and II *passim*
  flight to Varennes, 126–7
  on Jacobin Clubs, 123, 131–2, 135–6
  and legislation, 91, 119, 122, 130
  promises Estates-General, 59
  on provincial assemblies, 44
  on taxation, 45–7, 73
  and the third estate, 76, 81, 87–9, 92–3, 94
  trial of, 153, 155, 160–61, 215
  views on the constitution, 2–3, 128–40

and war, 141, 145

Louvet, Jean Baptiste, deputy, 152, 159–60, 239, 247

Luckner, Nicholas, baron de, general, 142

Machault, Jean Baptiste de, controller-general, 81

Malesherbes, Chrétien Guillaume de Lamoignon de, minister, 8, 15

Mallarmé, François René Auguste, deputy, 271

Malouet, Pierre Victorie, deputy, 89

Marat, Jean Paul, deputy, 151, 162, 166, 182

Marie-Antoinette, 8, 10, 28, 51–5, 62, 73, 129, 146–7
  betrays French war plans, 125, 142–3
  divergences of policy with Louis XVI, 93–4, 97–8, 123, 125, 127–8

Maupeou, René Charles Augustin de, Chancellor, xv, 10

Maurepas, Jean Frédéric Phélypeaux, comte de, minister, 53, 128

Maximum, law of, 192, 196–8, 209, 215, 220

Mirabeau, Honoré Gabriel Riquetti, comte de, deputy, 32, 68–9, 106–107, 109, 112–13, 122

Miromesnil, Armand Thomas Hue de, keeper of the seals, 3, 9, 19, 21–7, 36–8, 42–4, 49

Moënne, communard, 224

Momoro, Antoine François, printer, 211

Montesquieu, Charles de Secondat, baron de, 26, 155

Montmorin, Armand Marc, comte de, ambassador, foreign secretary, 9, 15–16, 44, 68–9, 72, 88, 99

Morellet, André, *abbé*, Academician, 184, 195–6

Napoleon, 109, 113, 169

National Guard, 90, 107, 110, 129–30, 136–7, 138, 144, 165, 193, 214

Necker, Jacques, finance minister, 10–11, 13, 23, 24, 43, 49, 52, 53
  second ministry, 64–108

Nicolas, Léopold, printer, 155, 168

Nivernais, Louis Mancini-Mazarini,
    duc de, 72
nobility, xvi, 2–3, 8–9, 71, 76, 79–80,
    89, 112
    abolished, 89, 112, 113
    proscribed, 215, 221–4
    proscription repealed, 240–41

Orléans, (Egalité), Louis Philippe
    Joseph, duc d', deputy, prince of
    the blood, 50, 53, 65, 93, 94, 97,
    159, 184, 198
Ormesson, Henri François-de-Paule
    Lefevre d', controller general, 7,
    10–12, 24, 48

Pache, Jean Nicolas, minister, Major of
    Paris, 211
Parlement, the, and *parlements*, 18–69,
    94, 97–8, 128, 135
    criticized, 76, 77, 79, 92, 108
    abolished, 109, 112, 113–14, 120
Payan, Claude François, *agent national*
    of Commune, 184, 198, 213, 216,
    217, 224, 227, 228, 232, 234–5
Payan, Joseph, commissioner for public
    instruction, 198, 224, 235
Pétion, Jérôme, deputy, Mayor of
    Paris, 154, 159–60, 164–7, 205
Philippeaux, Pierre, deputy, 199, 200,
    206–207, 208
Pitt, William, English prime minister,
    182
Pius VI, 62–3, 111
Plenary Court, 59–60
Poligac, Yolande duchesse de, and
    circle, 87, 93–4, 97–8
Prieur (de la Côte d'Or), Claude
    Antoine, member of CSP, 189,
    214, 228
princes of the blood, 12, 38, 65, 69–71
Protestants, 54
Provence, Louis Stanislas Xavier, comte
    de, later Louis XVIII, 20, 65, 99
provincial assemblies and estates, 8,
    12–13, 29–31, 37, 39, 42, 45–6,
    67, 78, 102
Puisaye, Joseph Geneviève, comte de,
    165
Puységur, Pierre Louis de Chastenet,
    comte de, war minister, 72, 104,
    105, 106

Richelieu, Armand Jean du Plessis,
    Cardinal de, 13, 109, 112

Richelieu, Louis François du Plessis,
    duc de, 12
Robespierre, Maximilien François
    Marie Isadore Joseph, member of
    CSP, xvi, 75, 76, 83–4, 94, 108,
    110, 120–21, 122, 123, 141, 147,
    151–5
    after death, 242, 243
    in Convention, 158, 159, 160–62,
    163
    in government, 167–9, 182, 184,
    185, 198, 200, 202, 204, 207,
    209, 212
    last months, 213–38
Roederer, Pierre Louis, 145–7, 245
Roland, Jean Marie, minister of
    interior, 151, 155, 156–7, 198
Roland, Mme, Marie Jeanne Philippon,
    136–7, 151, 152, 156–8
Rollin, schoolmaster, 208
Roman-Fonrosa, Pierre Michel
    François, judge, 229
Ronsin, Charles Philippe, general,
    206–207, 208, 211
Rossignol, Jean, general, 207, 208
Rousseau, Jean Jacques, 110, 151, 153,
    159, 218, 236–7
Roux, Jacques, cordelier, 172–3,
    177–82, 199
Roux (de la Marne), Louis Félix,
    deputy, 251–2
Roux-Fazillac, Pierre, deputy, 190–91

Sabattier de Cabre, Jean Antoine, *abbé*,
    parlementaire, 53
Saint-Germain, Charles Louis, comte
    de, minister for war, 79
Saint-Just, Louis Antoine, member of
    CSP, 2, 3, 153, 183, 184, 202,
    210, 214–23, 237, 240
Saint-Priest, François Emmanuel
    Guignard, comte de, minister, 88,
    89, 90, 91, 98–100, 107–108
Salle, Jean Baptiste, deputy, 159
sans-culottes, xvi, 161, 163, 164,
    172–3, 178, 201, 214, 218
Sartine, Antoine de, minister, 181
séance royale
    of 1787, 50–51, 53–4, 64
    of 1789, 88–9, 96–104, 127–8, 130
Ségur ordonnance, 79
Siéyès, Emmanuel Joseph, deputy, 3,
    242

Talleyrand, Charles Maurice de, 111
Tallien, Jean Lambert, deputy, 218,
    231, 233–4, 237, 242
Taudeau, *abbé, parlementaire*, 21
taxation
    ancien régime, 7–8, 11–12, 29–32,
        65, 71, 73, 77, 78, 79, 81–3,
        101–102, 103
    land tax, 25–7, 37–41
    Revolutionary taxes, 111–12, 18,
        119, 133–4
Thibaudeau, Antoine Claire, deputy,
    155, 169–71, 183, 245–8
Thuriot, Jean Alexis, deputy, 217–18
Turgot, Anne Robert Jacques,
    controller-general, xv, 7–8, 10,
    12–13, 110, 195

Varlet, Jean François, cordelier, 178–9

Vendée (rising), 191, 206–207
Vergennes, Charles Gravier, comte de,
    foreign secretary, 9, 15–16, 43, 49
Vergniaud, Pierre Victurnien, deputy,
    124, 125, 143–6, 155, 243
Véri, Joseph Alphonse *abbé* de, xv, 8,
    12–13, 26
Vialard, Jacques, *sectionnaire*, 195–6
Vidaud de la Tour, Jean Jacques,
    conseiller d'état, 100
Vincent, François Nicolas, 200,
    203–204, 208, 211
Voulland, Jean Henri, deputy, 234

War, of American Independence, 7, 9,
    10–11, 15–16, 82
Wimphen, Louis Félix, baron de,
    165–6

Printed in the United Kingdom
by Lightning Source UK Ltd.
131202UK00001B/88-93/A